ROBIN WILLIAMS
AMERICAN MASTER

THE MOVIES AND ART OF
A LOST GENIUS

ROBIN
WILLIAMS
AMERICAN MASTER

THE MOVIES AND ART OF A LOST GENIUS

STEPHEN
SPIGNESI

POST Hill
PRESS

A POST HILL PRESS BOOK
ISBN: 978-1-64293-529-5
ISBN (eBook): 978-1-64293-530-1

Robin Williams, American Master:
The Movies and Art of a Lost Genius
© 2020 by Stephen Spignesi
All Rights Reserved

Cover art by Cody Corcoran
Interior design and layout by Sarah Heneghan, sarah-heneghan.com

Post Hill Press
New York • Nashville
posthillpress.com

Published in the United States of America

1 2 3 4 5 6 7 8 9 10

This is for Robin's family…

His children Zak, Cody, and Zelda
His wives Valerie, Marsha, and Susan
His brothers McLaurin and Robert
His grandson McLaurin

CONTENTS

SPOILERS ABOUND,
YE WHO ENTER HERE...

Dear Reader,

Robin Williams, American Master contains detailed, all-revealing synopses of all of Robin's movies. If you haven't seen a particular film yet and do not want it to be spoiled, then skip that chapter until after you've seen the flick.

INTRODUCTION

Legalized Insanity

You're only given a little spark of madness. You mustn't lose that madness.

—**Robin Williams**

Performing and acting? One is hang gliding, the other oil drilling. With live comedy, the total freedom you have, to go from the Ottoman Empire to Madonna, is incredible. With acting, you have certain constraints. What do I like more? Sure, I like performing full out.

—**Robin Williams, in *The New York Times*, May 28, 1989**

The title of this introduction comes from Robin's oft-repeated use of the phrase "legalized insanity" to describe what he does for a living.

We can most appreciate genius in all its forms through an artist's body of work over his or her lifetime.

Here is a brief biography of Robin (with a few pithy comments by Mr. Williams himself from his October 1982 interview with *Playboy*).

Robin Williams was born in Chicago, Illinois, on Monday, July 21, 1952. He went to elementary school in Lake Forest, Illinois, and a private day school in Birmingham, Michigan. When his father retired from Ford, the family moved to Tiburon, California, north of San Francisco. Robin graduated from Redwood High School in Marin Country in 1969.

> All my friends were Jewish, which is why I know so much Yiddish. I went to fourteen bar mitzvahs in less than a year, and it was great. My friends made me an honorary Jew and used to tell people I went to services at Temple Beth Dublin.

Robin briefly attended Claremont College and College of Marin while trying out his licks in comedy clubs around Los Angeles and San Francisco.

> I played a lot of tiny clubs, like the Holy City Zoo in San Francisco—I met Valerie there—and the Salamander in Berkeley.

This period served as a time of learning and comedy experimentation for Robin:

> In the beginning, you find yourself doing a lot of drug humor, and when you can't be funny, you can get some laughs by saying motherfucker a lot. One of the initial reviews I got tore me up, because it said I was a "scatological pubescent," and that was true. It hit me right on the nose. In the beginning, you're also imitating everybody you've ever seen—for me, it was touches of Winters and Pryor. But all of a sudden, you get to a point where you go, "Ah, I can be me. I can develop my own stuff."

Robin eventually moved to New York:

> I got there in September of '73; one of the first things I learned was the Brooklyn alphabet: fuckin' A, fuckin' B, fuckin' C . . . I was the walking epitome of furshirr meets yo' ass. . . . My first

week there, I was in a bus going uptown to see an apartment when an old man two seats in front of me suddenly collapsed and died. He slumped over against a woman sitting next to him, and she said, "Get off me!" and moved away. Somebody told the driver what had happened, so he stopped the bus and ordered everybody off, but I wanted to stay and help. The driver told me, "He's dead, motherfucker, now get off! You can't do shit for him, so take your raggedy California ass and get outta my bus!" I knew that living in New York was certainly going to be different.

Robin studied at the Juilliard School for three years. At Juilliard, John Houseman was one of Robin's instructors and Chris Reeve one of his classmates:

> Me and Chris Reeve had come in together as advanced students—Chris had gone to Cornell—and we had to catch up to the other students who'd been at Juilliard for a year. Chris lived about five blocks away, and we used to go up to the roof of his apartment building and drink cheap wine and talk about present and lost loves. Except for my friendship with brother Reeve, that first year was rough, especially at Christmastime. . . . When I came back to Juilliard . . . [the following] fall, Chris had left to do a soap opera.

After Juilliard, Robin auditioned for *Happy Days* in 1977 and his "Mork from Ork" character was spun off and given his own show—*Mork & Mindy*—on September 14, 1978, and the rest is history.

As to Robin's personal life, he married Valerie Velardi on June 4, 1978, and they had one son, Zachary. They divorced ten years later, and on April 30, 1989, Robin wed Marsha Garces, with whom he had two children, Zelda and Cody. They divorced in 2010. On October 22, 2011, Robin wed his third wife, Susan Schneider. They were married at the time of his death in 2014.

Robin Williams truly loved his work. He was more productive and more successful than many other actors who had been in the business twice as many years. His death diminished the world.

We'll give the final word(s) to Robin:

- When in doubt, go for the dick joke.
- People say satire is dead. It's not dead; it's alive and living in the White House.
- I went to rehab in wine country, just to keep my options open.
- Men wearing pants so tight that you can tell what religion they are.
- Taking Viagra after open heart surgery is like a Civil War re-enactment with live ammo. Not good.
- If it's the Psychic Network, why do they need a phone number?
- The definition of pornography is quite simple. Erotic is using a feather, pornography is using the entire chicken.
- If on your tax form it says $50,000 for snacks: Mayday. You've got yourself a cocaine problem.

Stephen Spignesi
New Haven, CT
January 1, 1997 & January 1, 2020

FOREWORD

Boss

A TV Series starring Kelsey Grammer and Why It's Relevant to Robin Williams's Story

The first episode of this 2011–2012 TV series was directed by Gus Van Sant and revealed that the mayor of Chicago, Tom Kane (played by Kelsey Grammer), was suffering from dementia with Lewy bodies, also known as Lewy Body Dementia (LBD).

Lewy Body Dementia was the disease that killed Robin Williams. No one, however—including his wife Susan—knew he had it until three months after his death, when the diagnosis was confirmed during Robin's autopsy. According to the Mayo Cynic, symptoms of LBD include visual hallucinations, changes in alertness and attention, and Parkinson's disease-like signs and symptoms such as rigid muscles, slow movement, and tremors.

What does LBD do to a person? Robin's wife Susan described it succinctly in an essay she wrote for the medical journal *Neurology*:

> Robin was losing his mind and he was aware of it. Can you imagine the pain he felt as he experienced himself disintegrating? And not from something he would ever know the name of, or understand? Neither he, nor anyone could stop it—no amount of intelligence or love could hold it back.

In *Boss*, Tom Kane knew what he had and chose to cover it up. He obtained the medications used to ameliorate some of the symptoms clandestinely, and even though we, the audience, saw the hallucinations he experienced, he pretended everything was fine.

Robin Williams never knew what he had.

He was treated for Parkinsonian symptoms, but the medications did nothing for the visual hallucinations, delusional thinking, paranoia, and other LBD symptoms.

Would it have made a difference if Robin knew what he had? We don't know and it's futile to speculate.

Can I Do It 'Til I Need Glasses?

(1977)

Q: *What role or movie of yours would you most like to forget?*

Robin Williams: *A movie I did years ago called* Can I Do It 'Til I Need Glasses?

—From a live interview on America Online
on Monday, August 5, 1996

As the epigraph above reveals, this 1977 film bears the notoriety of being the only project Robin Williams wishes he had never done.

So how bad is it? And what exactly does Robin Williams do in *Can I Do It 'Til I Need Glasses?* that he was so ashamed of?

Not much, really.

Can I Do It 'Til I Need Glasses? is a vaudevillian-style revue of skits that are nothing more than the acting out (with sets and props) of raunchy sex jokes that have been around forever. You know the type: A woman in a robe comes out of the bathroom with a ragged old bra in her hands and asks her husband if she can have ten dollars so she can go buy a new one. The husband then sarcastically asks, "What do you need a new bra for? You haven't got anything to put in it," to which the wife replies, "You wear a jockstrap, don't you?"

Ba-dum-bump.

Can I Do It 'Til I Need Glasses? has loads of female nudity, including a few full frontal nude shots that were probably quite scandalous back in the seventies. (The sensibility of filmgoers today is quite different, of course, and the nudity in *Can I Do It?*—pubic regions notwithstanding—would actually be viewed as rather tame by today's standards.)

Can I Do It? was a sequel to the film, *If You Don't Stop It… You'll Go Blind!!!*, which also consisted of a series of juvenile, risqué sex skits (and which some of the characters in *Can I Do It?* go see at the theater). The title, *Can I Do It 'Til I Need Glasses?*, is the punchline to an old joke about masturbation: A father bursts in on his son flogging his baloney and warns him that if he keeps that up he'll go blind. The son stops mid-stroke and asks his father if he can just do it until he needs glasses.

The first skit Robin appears in takes place in a courtroom, about thirty-five minutes into the film. He is a Los Angeles prosecutor in a divorce case who is charged with questioning a woman named Lucretia Frisby "whose lurid sexual escapades have shocked the nation." After Mrs. Frisby is sworn in, Robin steps up, wearing slicked-down hair, tiny round glasses, and a black bowtie and asks his first and only question:

> **Prosecutor**: Is it true, Mrs. Frisby, that last summer you had sexual intercourse with a red-headed midget during a thunderstorm, while riding nude in the sidecar of a Kawasaki motorcycle, performing an unnatural act on a Polish plumbing contractor, going sixty miles an hour up and down the steps of

the Washington Monument, on the night of July fourteenth? Is that true, Mrs. Frisby? Is that true?

Mrs. Frisby: Could you repeat that date again, please?

Robin then turns and looks right into the camera with a bemused look of exasperation on his face. And that ends this first skit, which runs a total of less than one-and-a-half minutes.

Robin's second appearance in *Can I Do It?* is in a thirty-second skit that takes place in the hallway of an office building. Robin plays a hick in the big city with a toothache who needs a dentist desperately. The suspendered country boy waits, with his jaw wrapped in a red bandana, outside a doctor's office (which has a giant tooth hanging over its door). When Dr. Fisher finally arrives, Robin says, "Oh, thank goodness you're here, doc. I'm new in this town and this tooth is killing me!" "Your tooth?" the doctor replies. "I'm afraid you've made a mistake, young man. I'm not a dentist, I'm a gynecologist." The hick is surprised and says, "A gynecologist? Whatcha got that big tooth outside your office for?", to which the impatient doctor testily responds, "Schmuck, what'd you expect me to hang up there?"

A couple of sources consulted for information about this film claim that Robin was not in the original film and that his two brief appearances were added to the film when *Mork & Mindy* became a huge hit. This may be true, since Robin's name appears nowhere in the opening or closing credits and the only way he is acknowledged is at the very end of the credits when they flash his picture with the words, "And of course…Robin Williams."

Robin probably regretted his two brief appearances in *Can I Do It?* because this movie was technically his feature film debut, and, after suffering through it for over an hour, one can easily understand why he wouldn't want that fact on his resume. It is a unique milestone in his career, though, and if you're a real Robin

Williams fan, the film is worth a rental just to see what all the hubbub is about.

(FYI: This movie has collectible status, so the prices to buy are high. At this writing (Spring 2020), eBay has it new from $55.00 to $225.00. Amazon has used copies ranging from $134.95 to $198.99.)

Popeye
(1980)

I ain't no doctor, but I know I'm losin' my patience.

—Popeye

Popeye is a strange yet immensely enjoyable movie. Robin Williams chose it as his major motion picture acting debut, which was a bold decision considering the inevitable risks in trying to use human actors to bring three-dimensional life to a cartoon character.

Sometimes it works: *Batman* (1989), *Superman* (1978), *Dick Tracy* (1990), *The Flintstones* (1994), and *The Crow* (1994) come immediately to mind. Sometimes it doesn't: *The Addams Family* (1992), *Annie* (1982), *Dennis the Menace* (1993), *Howard the Duck* (1986), and *Brenda Starr* (1992) are examples of how this kind of adaptation can often fail.

In 1979, Robin was flying high as the irrepressible alien Mork from Ork in the successful TV series *Mork & Mindy*, and it seemed a given that he would easily be able to make the move to theatrical films.

He chose a project that would appear to be a surefire winner: *Popeye* was based on a beloved character who had been a ubiquitous presence in both the comic strips and animated cartoons for decades; the script was by the renowned writer and playwright Jules Feiffer (*Carnal Knowledge*, 1971), and the film's director was the respected and successful Robert Altman, whose previous films had included *M*A*S*H* (1970), *Nashville* (1975), and *A Wedding* (1978).

There is a lot to like about *Popeye*. First of all, it is *extremely* funny. Some of the more memorable gags include Robin's flawless rendering of the way Popeye speaks—"You got a room for renk?"—as well as his meticulous recreation of Popeye's physical movements, including a dance-like double step when he walks. Also notable is his amazing facial work, particularly the way he keeps his right eye squinted shut all the time (how *did* he do that, anyway?) and his rubbery expressions. (In a January 1992 *Playboy* interview Robin said of his Popeye face, "I felt like a guy robbing a bank with a condom on his head.")

Other funny bits in the film include Olive Oyl's mother Mrs. Oyl insisting on addressing Popeye as "Mr. Eye"; the town of Sweethaven having a fifty cent "up-to-no-good" tax; and the scene in which Popeye talks to a picture of his father, which we soon see is really the words "Me Poppa" in a picture frame. (Later, this joke is echoed when we see Poopdeck Pappy, Popeye's father, talking to a picture of his long-lost son that, yes, consists of the words "Me Son" in a picture frame.)

The sets in *Popeye*—which was filmed on the island of Malta, a place Robin described to *Playboy* as like "San Quentin on Valium"—are amazing: Sweethaven is a wharf town you'd never see on any real coastline and yet the place works. The interiors combine crazy assortments of furniture and *stuff* that the players work like props. Harry Nilsson's songs at first seem so minimalist in melody that they come across almost as "nonsongs," but after hearing a few bars of them (especially Olive's "He's Large" and Popeye's "I Yam What I Yam"), they exert a kind of hypnotic effect that contributes to the overall surrealistic feel of the film.

This unreal quality so present in the movie requires some adjustments to a viewer's normal viewing expectations. Cartoon violence is depicted realistically (a huge floor lamp is picked up and wrapped around a guy's neck) and Popeye's ubiquitous pipe spins like a dervish when he gets excited—just like in the cartoon. And in the lagoon scene towards the end of the film, Popeye submerges himself and watches Bluto from beneath the water—using his pipe as a more than adequate periscope.

Popeye does not put a camp spin on the character or his world. The cast and crew simply present his world and we are immediately swept up in its unique oddness. Overall, *Popeye* succeeds primarily because of this singular commitment to "playing it straight." Granted, it's a peculiar film, but Robin Williams does a good job of creating a flesh-and-blood character out of something that had previously been only paper and ink.

Some interesting cast details from this film: *Popeye* is one of the first screen appearances of *NYPD Blue*'s Dennis Franz (he plays a rowdy tough who gets beaten up by Popeye); the mayor of Sweethaven is played by Richard Libertini, who later worked with Robin in *Awakenings;* contortionist Bill Irwin, who later had a recurring role in the TV series *Northern Exposure* as the carnival performer who wouldn't talk, appears as a Sweethaven resident whose body is squashed by Bluto; and Cindy, the Drudge, is played by none other than Robin's then-wife, Valerie Velardi.

Robin needed to spend an hour and a half each day having his makeup applied *before* being put in the latex forearms. These arms were so tight they would cut off the circulation to his real arms, necessitating periods of downtime to remove the arms and let all the muscles in Robin's own shoulders and arms relax back to normal.

WHAT ROBIN HAD TO SAY

"*Popeye* was a nice fairy tale with a loving spirit to it, and I think most people—especially movie critics—were expecting a combination of *Superman* and a Busby Berkeley musical….in the end, I think that what Altman got was a very gentle fable with music and a lot of heart." (from *Playboy*, October 1982)

WHAT THE CRITICS HAD TO SAY

Roger Ebert: "*Popeye*…is lots of fun. It suggests that it is possible to take the broad strokes of a comic strip and turn them into sophisticated entertainment. What's needed is the right attitude toward the material. If Altman and his people had been the slightest bit condescending toward 'Popeye,' the movie might have crash-landed. But it's clear that this movie has an affection for 'Popeye,' and so much regard for the sailor man that it even bothers to reveal the real truth about his opinion of spinach." (from his review on Compuserve)

Leonard Maltin: "A game cast does its best with Jules Feiffer's unfunny script, Altman's cluttered staging, and some alleged songs by Harry Nilsson. Tune in an old Max Fleischer cartoon instead; you'll be much better off." (from his *Movie and Video Guide*)

Videohound's Golden Movie Retriever: "Williams accomplishes the near-impossible feat of physically resembling the title character, and the whole movie does accomplish the maker's stated goal of 'looking like a comic strip,' but it isn't anywhere near as funny as it should be." (from the 1997 edition)

Tom Wiener: "Williams is good, but Altman can't seem to find the handle on the material." (from his *The Book of Video Lists*)

Barbara Walters: "*Popeye* [is] the kind of movie that ruins great careers and marks talented people as box-office poison." (from a 1989 *Barbara Walters Special* on ABC)

The World According to Garp

(1982)

It really has been an adventure.

—T.S. Garp

*On the day we started shooting Garp, I improvised a line and
[director George Roy] Hill called a wrap for the set. I thought,
OK, you've made your point. I won't do that again.*

—**Robin Williams, in the October 1982
issue of** ***Playboy***

Perhaps we should consider *The World According to Garp* as
Robin Williams's real film debut, *Popeye* notwithstanding?

In defense of this suggestion is the fact that *Popeye* was such
a strange film, it can justifiably be looked at as more of a movie/
pop culture experience, existing outside the normal parameters
of dramatic or comedic filmmaking. After all, Robin was playing
a cartoon character, an endeavor that brought with it a history
of behaviors and background details requiring that Robin "color

inside the lines," so to speak. Popeye is Popeye. There's not a lot of leeway in interpreting the character.

The World According to Garp, on the other hand, was Robin's first serious role as an actor playing a real person in the real world. Granted, Garp's universe is also somewhat strange, peopled as it is with transsexual football players, self-mutilating feminists, and a "pre-disastered" home (Robin convinces his wife to buy a house because, as he tells her, the odds of another plane crashing into it are astronomical); but Robin Williams gets to play T.S. Garp straight—there is hardly a hint of his manic stand-up-comedic persona (except for one brief scene in which he plays "Warrior" with his kids and Roberta the tight-end transsexual). And Robin truly astonishes with the brilliant shading and nuances he brings to the role.

The World According to Garp begins with the story of a nurse named Jenny Fields, Garp's mother. Jenny conceives Garp by having sex with a brain-dead patient in the military hospital where she was stationed during World War II (one of the side effects of Technical Sergeant Garp's brain injury was a permanent erection, which the child-craving Jenny put to good use one night after the lights were out).

Jenny names her son T.S. Garp after his father and raises him unconventionally, treating him at a very early age like an adult with whom she can be completely forthcoming and honest about all manner of subjects including, of course, sex.

After an odd childhood at the Everett Steering Boarding School (Jenny was the resident nurse at the school), Jenny moves herself and Garp to New York where she becomes intrigued by Garp's fascination with the hookers that line the streets. She befriends one young girl, talks to her about her life, and "buys" her for her son. Jenny's relationship with the girl inspires Jenny to write an autobiographical feminist tract called *Sexual Suspect*, which becomes one of the biggest bestsellers of all time and transforms Jenny into a cult figure, loved by some and hated by many.

Garp, meantime, has been working to find his own authorial voice and his first novel, *Procrastination*, is published to less-than-stellar sales. This milestone, however, persuades Helen Holm, the love of Garp's life, to marry him (she swore she would only marry a real writer), and they have their first child, Duncan.

As Jenny's fame (and its attendant danger to her) grows, Jenny retreats from the city and converts her family beach house into a retreat for battered women, rape victims, and Ellen Jamesians. (Ellen James was an eleven-year-old girl who was abducted and raped by older men who cut out her tongue so she wouldn't talk. "Ellen Jamesians" were men-hating women who had their own tongues surgically removed in tribute to Ellen.)

Garp's life becomes a succession of days of domesticity and writing. Helen leaves the house each day to go teach at "gradual school" and Garp stays home and does the laundry, cooks, takes care of the kids, and writes.

Tragedy is a constant in Garp's life, however, and true happiness seems to deliberately evade him. Terrible events dog him, including an airplane crashing into his house (flown by *Garp* director George Roy Hill in a cameo appearance), an assassination attempt on his mother, an adulterous affair between his wife and one of her gradual students, and an affair between him and an eighteen-year-old babysitter. But the worst thing to happen to him is an auto accident that breaks his jaw, puts his wife in a neck brace, blinds one eye of his son Duncan, and, most tragically, takes the life of his youngest son, Walt.

The pivotal event that caused this terrible series of tragedies was Garp's car crashing into the car of his wife's lover, Michael Milton, as Helen was performing "farewell" fellatio on him in the front seat. The force of the crash causes Helen to bite down and amputate Michael's penis. The reason Garp hit the car with such force was because he had turned off the engine and the lights and was coasting into the driveway at a high rate of speed. He liked to do this because he said it felt like flying.

Flying is an important theme running throughout *The World According to Garp* and it is significant that the movie begins and ends with Garp "flying": first, in and out of his mother's arms, and later in a helicopter after a crazed Ellen Jamesian shoots him three times in the chest.

The World According to Garp ends sadly with two dreadful events: The first is the assassination of Garp's mother; the second, the assassination attempt on Garp himself. Jenny is shot by an anti-feminist zealot; Garp is shot by an anti-male radical.

Interestingly, *The World According to Garp* provided Robin with his first opportunity to dress in drag (the classic *Mrs. Doubtfire* wouldn't come for another decade.) In order for Garp to attend the women-only, feminist memorial service for his mother, Roberta the transsexual (John Lithgow) dresses Garp as a woman so he can attend the ceremony. Garp's former next-door neighbor, the sexually-repressed Ellen Jamesian Poo, spots him and screams "Arp!" (that's all she could get out without a tongue). Poo later sneaks into Garp's wrestling class and shoots him point-blank.

The World According to Garp is a layered, metaphorically complex morality tale that works on many levels and which provides Robin Williams with a role that is as rich and textured as some of his important later roles, in such films as *Awakenings* and *Dead Poets Society*. It is both a serious drama and a sardonic black comedy at the same time.

Wouldn't it have been interesting if *Garp* had been Robin's first feature film role, followed by *Popeye* and then the others? Would *Popeye* have been savaged by the critics the way it was if it followed Robin's superb performance in *The World According to Garp*?

BIZARRE EPILOGUE

It is truly a strange world when a Robin Williams movie can figure into, of all things, the O. J. Simpson civil trial. In November of 1996, Kato Kaelin was called to testify in the civil trial against O. J. brought by the families of murder victims Nicole Brown Simpson and Ronald Goldman. During Kaelin's testimony, he revealed that the day before the slayings, he and O. J. had watched the Robin Williams movie, *The World According to Garp*. When the movie got to the scene in which Garp's wife's Helen performs oral sex on one of her graduate students in the front seat of his car (and subsequently bites off his erection), Kaelin said that O. J. talked about how the scene reminded him of the time he spied on his wife Nicole performing oral sex on one of her boyfriends in April of 1992. O. J. surreptitiously watched the two have sex through a window of Nicole's condo. This incident prompted a huge fight between Nicole and O. J. in October of 1993 that resulted in the infamous 911 call that brought several police officers to Nicole's home.

WHAT ROBIN HAD TO SAY

"[*The World According to Garp*] was like an oil drilling. I had to dig down and find things deep inside myself and then bring them up. Heavy griefs and joys, births and deaths—*Garp* is an all-encompassing look at a man's life." (From *Playboy*, October 1982).

WHAT THE CRITICS HAD TO SAY

Roger Ebert: "While I watched *Garp*, I enjoyed it. I thought the acting was unconventional and absorbing (especially by Williams, by Glenn Close as his mother, and by John Lithgow as a transsexual). I thought the visualization of the events, by director George Roy Hill, was fresh and consistently interesting. But when the movie was over, my immediate response was not at all what it should have been. All I could find to ask myself was: What the hell was that all about?" (from his review on Compuserve)

Leonard Maltin: "[*The World According to Garp* is an] absorbing, sure-footed odyssey through vignettes of social observation, absurdist humor, satire, and melodrama; beautifully acted by all, especially Close (in her feature debut) as Garp's mother and Lithgow as a transsexual." (from his *Movie and Video Guide*)

The Survivors

(1983)

You know, I never had a friend like you.

—**Donald Quinelle**

Robin Williams's 1983 film, *The Survivors*, came with a fairly impressive "pedigree." In its favor was the following:

1. *The Survivors* was an original script and the feature film debut for Emmy Award-winning writer Michael Leeson, who had written a great deal of TV (including episodes of *The Partridge Family, The Odd Couple, Happy Days, The Mary Tyler Moore Show, Rhoda, Taxi,* and *The Cosby Show*), and who would later script 1989's biting and hilarious divorce comedy/drama, *The War of the Roses* (starring Kathleen Turner, Michael Douglas, and Danny DeVito).

2. *The Survivors* was directed by Michael Ritchie, who had previously helmed such memorable flicks as *The Candidate* (1972), *Smile* (1975), *The Bad News Bears* (1976), and *Semi-Tough* (1977).

3. And perhaps most significantly, *The Survivors* starred three major talents in the film industry: veteran actor Walter Matthau, a genius at creating meticulously-crafted characters

often through nothing more than the raise of an eyebrow or a flawlessly-timed glance; the 1980s country music superstar Jerry Reed, who proved that he was even a better actor than a singer/songwriter; and, of course, Robin Williams, who had just come off a phenomenally successful run on *Mork & Mindy* as well as two truly unique films, *Popeye* and *The World According to Garp*.

So, with all this high-priced talent and Hollywood history in its favor, does *The Survivors* work?

Well, yes, it does…sort of.

The Survivors was extremely topical when it was released in 1983. As recently as November of 1982, the United States had been in the midst of a raging recession, unemployment was the highest it had been (10.8 percent) since 1940, and paranoia gripped our land like an iron hand. *The Survivors* mined this fertile socioeconomic territory by telling the story of three disparate characters, all of whom found themselves in dire financial difficulty, and whose paths crossed in an unlikely turn of events that, frankly, could probably only really happen in a movie script.

Donald Quinelle (Robin Williams) is a mid-level manager who is confident that he is on the fast track to corporate success. He's a "three-piece suit" kind of guy who drives the same station wagon to work that all his colleagues at the same level also drive. One morning he is summoned to company President Mr. Stoddard's office and he rushes there eagerly: He thinks he's in line for some big promotion or some other well-deserved accolade from the big man himself. He is greeted, instead, by an empty office… and a parrot. The parrot, whom Mr. Stoddard spent months personally training, looks at Donald and tells him, "You have been a valuable asset to this company, so this is not easy for me to say. You're fired."

At first Donald thinks it's a joke, but when Mr. Stoddard's secretary pulls a gun on him and calls him an "ungrateful turd," he knows it's for real.

Donald leaves the building shell-shocked and, thus, isn't really paying attention when he stops at Sonny's Service Station to fill up his car's gas tank. (His former company generously allowed him to use the company car through the end of the month.) Donald distractedly misses his car's gas spout with the nozzle and, instead, pumps at least ten gallons of gasoline all over the ground. He gets in the car and drives off, and then, through his rear window, we see the entire gas station explode into a raging inferno, thanks to a carelessly thrown cigarette dropped by none other than the gas station's owner, Sonny Paluso (Walter Matthau).

This catastrophe puts Sonny out of business and ends up being the pivotal event that throws him and Donald together.

Donald and Sonny both end up at the unemployment office where Sonny gets maced by an Indian civil servant when he refuses to accept that he cannot collect unemployment because he was a business owner; and where Donald spends hours in line trying to make sense of the ramblings of a well-dressed man who speaks nothing but Spanish.

After their experiences with the unemployment system, the two of them both end up at the Pit Stop Diner, where Donald sits at the counter weeping, while Sonny continuously wipes his inflamed, maced eye.

The third member of the motley triumvirate that makes up *The Survivors*, professional hitman Jack Locke (Jerry Reed), chooses this moment to hold up the diner, and he does so wearing a ski mask and speaking in an ethnic dialect.

Donald and Sonny have been pushed just a tad too far today, however, and being held up is apparently the final insult. Sonny grabs Jack's gun, and it goes off. Donald gets shot in the arm, and

Jack's mask comes off in Sonny's hand. Jack flees the diner and Donald ends up in the hospital where he is forced to endure a TV editorial blasting him for his foolish heroics and calling him and Sonny "hotshots with dumb luck."

The robbery was a defining moment for Donald, however, and he decides to go on TV and issue a rebuttal to the editorial during which he mentions Sonny Paluso by name. Jack happens to be watching Donald as he blathers on and on about the Constitution while also offering a few ludicrous observations ("the root cause of crime is criminals"). Jack, hunting for both Donald and Sonny (eliminate the witnesses is, after all, the first rule of good crimesmanship), is able to track down Sonny after learning his last name.

Jack shows up at Sonny's house to kill him; Donald arrives to apologize for saying Sonny's name on TV. They hit Jack in the head with a trophy, and they take him to the police station where he is arrested.

On the way home Donald makes Sonny stop at a gun store where he buys enough artillery to arm his own private army. Donald also signs up for a survivalist retreat where he will learn how to defend himself against the marauding "vermin" that will be everywhere when society ultimately collapses.

This is where *The Survivors* falters. The remainder of the movie is a convoluted (and unlikely) chain of events in which Jack gets out on bail and forces Sonny to take him to the survivalist camp. He wants to kill Donald because Donald knows that he was the one who "disappeared" Jimmy Hoffa in 1975 (even though Jack admits that he made that story up because no one else was taking credit, so he figured, what the hell).

The scenes at the camp are slow-paced and forced. Robin's character devolves from a poor sap dumped on by a cruel economy into a cartoon soldier who seems to have lost all grounding in reality and has transformed himself into a militaristic buffoon.

Walter Matthau is, as always, superb. And to be fair, Robin does have some funny moments and he does what he can with the character. But the scenario is so far-fetched and poorly paced that we cannot suspend our disbelief and simply enjoy the "wacky" antics of *The Survivors* as we were able to with something like the comedy *Stripes*, a movie with an equally bizarre and unlikely series of events, but one which nonetheless allowed us to enjoy its characters and storylines anyway.

There are some interesting elements in *The Survivors*, including a few Robin Williams one-liners, such as "He has a face like somebody in the road company of *Deliverance*"; "Does this make you realize that men have nipples too?"; "A professional killer with colitis? They must hear you coming!"; and "Oh, God, I love the smell of malamute in the morning!" (It's likely that those lines were not part of the original script but were, instead, improvised during shooting by the inimitable Mr. Williams.) Roseanne's TV husband John Goodman, in one of his earliest screen roles, plays one of the fanatical survivalists.

The Survivors has what you could call a happy ending, although it is an anemic conclusion to what can only be described as an average script. The ending? Donald takes off his clothes in the snow because he's freaked out by his depressing "lot in life," Walter Matthau reassures him and calms him down, and the three of them, now friends, drive off down a snowy road after they successfully escape the bloodthirsty survivalists.

AN INTERESTING BIT OF CINEMATIC SYNCHRONICITY

There is a scene in *The Survivors* (quoted in the epigraph to this chapter) that will resonate with Robin Williams's fans who also saw *Aladdin*. In *The Survivors*, Robin's character tells Walter Matthau's character, "You know, I never had a friend like you," which is very similar to what Robin's character Genie tells Aladdin ("You ain't never had a friend like me!') in the movie *Aladdin*, which came out almost ten years later.

WHAT THE CRITICS HAD TO SAY

Mick Martin and Marsha Porter: "Generally a black comedy, this movie features a variety of comedic styles, and they all work. (from their *Video Movie Guide*)

Leonard Maltin: "[*Survivors* is] combination black comedy and social satire. Likable stars do their best with [a] scattershot script." (from his *Movie and Video Guide*)

Roger Ebert: "The story gets so confused that the movie can't even account for why its characters happen to be in the same place at the same time; in desperation, it gives us a scene where Williams actually calls Reed and tells him where he can be found. Uh-huh." (from his *Movie Home Companion*)

Moscow on the Hudson

(1984)

America is magnificent.

—**Vladimir Ivanoff**

I have a defector. We're between Estée Lauder and Pierre Cardin.
—**Bloomingdale Security Guard**
Lionel Witherspoon

Moscow on the Hudson tells the story of a Russian saxophonist named Vladimir Ivanoff who plays in the Russian circus and who defects to the US during a visit to New York City.

Robin Williams plays Vladimir Ivanoff flawlessly. He easily communicates the meek and timid demeanor so common to immigrants and makes us feel what it must be like for someone from a foreign country to suddenly have to make sense of our often-chaotic culture and labyrinthine bureaucratic agencies.

The movie begins in Russia where we see how people lived before the collapse of the Soviet Union's communist government. There is a macabre fascination for many of us in these early scenes set in Russia and some telling moments stand out.

For instance, citizens walking through the streets of Moscow would automatically get into a line they saw forming, no matter what the line was for. These lines often snaked around entire city blocks and they usually meant that some merchant had gotten a shipment of some kind of commodity. It could be toilet paper or shoes. It didn't matter. The Russians would get into the line.

In one of these scenes, Robin's character finds that the line he is in is for shoes. When he gets to the front of the line, he learns that they do not have either of the pairs he wants in his size. No matter. He buys two pairs that are several sizes smaller because he knows he can trade them for something else he can actually use.

In another scene, as Robin and his circus clown friend Boris are driving through Moscow, they see a truck parked under a bridge and immediately know that the driver has black market gasoline for sale. They make a U-turn and stop. The most revealing moment in this scene then occurs when they open their trunk and take out two large containers for the gasoline. In Russia, one has to always be prepared to take advantage of any opportunity that might come one's way. This element of Soviet life is hammered home again when another car pulls up to the truck and its driver likewise removes two gasoline containers from his trunk.

Vladimir is resigned to this type of life in Russia, though, and is not interested in hearing Boris's talk of defection.

Boris plans on defecting to the United States when the Russian circus visits New York. The KGB knows of his plans and is prepared to do everything to stop him. Vladimir advises his friend to abandon his plans, but Boris is committed to the idea.

During their stay in New York, however, Boris chickens out and, uncharacteristically, Vladimir makes a spur-of-the-moment decision and defects to a security guard at Bloomingdale's. He hides under the skirt of an Italian immigrant sales clerk named

Lucia (Maria Conchita Alonso) and eventually goes home with Lionel (Cleavant Derricks), the black guard to whom he defected.

Vladimir, with the help of a Cuban lawyer (in *Moscow on the Hudson*, everyone in America is, ironically, from somewhere else), secures political asylum and embarks on a career path that includes selling hot dogs, bussing tables, driving a cab, and, ultimately, driving a limo. He develops a relationship with Lucia and eventually gets his own apartment. He writes to his family back in Russia but doesn't know if they even receive his letters.

After a time, Vladimir becomes a little disillusioned by the freedoms in America. Instead of seeing opportunity, he now sees the crime and the poverty. He becomes jaded after getting mugged. Robin plays this shift in his character's perceptions with passion and makes it completely believable. Vlad ultimately recognizes his overreaction as too extreme, however, and the movie ends with him regaining his love for his new homeland and coming to a new understanding of the social dynamic of America.

Robin effectively shows us that Vladimir was only seeing the glories of America and that, with time, he came to a more balanced understanding of what it's like to live in the United States.

In *Moscow on the Hudson*, Robin Williams plays Vladimir with skill and confidence. Even his Russian and Russian-American accent are completely believable (he also learned to play the saxophone for the movie and, according to a comment by his teacher, reached a level of proficiency equal to that of someone studying for two full years).

Coming so quickly after *The World According to Garp*, this film was a very strong addition to Robin's dramatic filmography and showed that here was one of our better young dramatic actors.

Other than the little-seen *Seize the Day* in 1986, though, it would be a good five years before Robin tackled another dramatic role that was worthy of his talents—that of the English teacher John Keating in 1989's *Dead Poets Society*.

WHAT THE CRITICS HAD TO SAY

Roger Ebert: "Robin Williams…disappears so completely into his quirky, lovable, complicated character that he's quite plausible as a Russian….[*Moscow on the Hudson* is] a rarity, a patriotic film that has a liberal, rather than a conservative, heart. It made me feel good to be an American, and good that Vladimir Ivanoff was going to be one, too." (from his *Movie Home Companion*)

Leonard Maltin: "Fine original comedy-drama….Full of endearing performances, perceptive and bittersweet moments—but a few too many false endings. Williams is superb in the lead." (from his *Movie and Video Guide*)

A friend of mine who worked as an executive chef in a well-known local restaurant told me a story that came to mind while watching *Moscow on the Hudson* for this book.

As part of a sort of "culinary exchange program," a group of Russian restaurant chefs visited the United States to observe how American chefs operated and possibly pick up a few pointers they could bring back home. My friend was one of the host chefs and his assignment was to take the Russians around to American grocery stores and markets and let them observe him shopping for his restaurant.

According to my friend, taking a group of Russians to an American supermarket was one of the most amazing and enlightening experiences of his life.

At that time in Russia, people literally waited hours in line to buy three oranges. Or two rolls of toilet paper. Or one loaf of bread. This was just the normal way things were done in their homeland.

Thus, to the Russians visiting the United States, the produce department of the typical American supermarket was an Elysian vision. Mountains of oranges and apples. Bins overflowing with heads of fresh lettuce and ripe tomatoes. And, according to my friend, what was most astonishing to his guests was the produce department's peppers sections. The Russians could not believe that Americans could buy so many different types of peppers! Red peppers, green peppers, yellow peppers, chili peppers...all the peppers one could possibly dream of.

And we won't even get into what the Russians thought when they saw entire aisles solely devoted to potato chips and pet foods. This scene is depicted in *Moscow on the Hudson* when Vladimir is likewise overcome by the coffee aisle in an American grocery store.

The Best of Times

(1986)

Let's play some football!

—**Jack Dundee**

The biggest problem with *The Best of Times* is that the story is utterly unbelievable.

The fundamental premise of the film is that Robin Williams's character, Jack Dundee, has been so emotionally traumatized by blowing a critical catch in a pivotal high school football game that it has affected his entire life and left him crippled in the self-esteem department (as evidence of his neurosis, we learn that Jack's doorbell plays his high school anthem).

The writer of *The Best of Times*, Ron Shelton, would go on to better things, including *Bull Durham* (1988), *White Men Can't Jump* (1992), and *Tin Cup* (1996); but here, because he starts with a premise that the audience really can't buy into, the remainder of the movie collapses like a house with a cardboard foundation.

Jack Dundee is a bank manager in a bank owned by his obnoxious blowhard father-in-law, "The Colonel" (Donald Moffat), a staunch supporter of the Bakersfield football team that beat Jack's team in that all-important final high school game. Jack visits a "massage parlor" once a week on the outskirts of town, but not to have sex. Instead, he pays sixty dollars just to talk about the big game, a game that has been over for a dozen years, yet still haunts the obsessive and tormented Jack.

Reno Hightower (Kurt Russell) was the all-star quarterback who threw Jack that critically important pass and he, too, has apparently been scarred by the debacle of Jack dropping the ball. He has also never left the gritty, rundown town of Taft and now owns and operates a van-painting shop. His marriage to Gigi (Pamela Reed) is a disaster and his knees are a mess.

During one of Jack's therapeutic massage parlor sessions, his masseuse (Margaret Whitton), also a Taft High alumna, gets so sick of hearing Jack whine about the dropped pass, she impulsively blurts out that he should just play the game over again and get on with his life.

Rather than dismissing this suggestion as ludicrous and unrealistic (the way people in real life would), Jack warms to the notion and decides to propose to The Colonel and Reno Hightower the idea of replaying the game.

The Colonel, seeing yet another opportunity to humiliate his loathed son-in-law, readily accepts. Reno, on the other hand, takes a bit more persuading. Jack reminds Reno that he's behind on his mortgage payments and that he has been covering for him at the bank. Jack calls in this debt and Reno reluctantly agrees to the game, telling Jack, "You're a low-life, blackmailing, chicken-shit squid."

Once the game is scheduled, the Taft team, all of whom are now overweight, out-of-shape, and in their late thirties, must train and prepare for this seemingly futile attempt at redemption.

The Bakersfield team, on the other hand, has coaches, uniforms, and equipment, and they are fit and more than ready to play. Although Taft has none of the above, the town rallies around the team anyway and spruces up for the big game.

In the midst of all this football stuff, there are several romantic subplots involving Jack and Reno and their wives, with all of these scenes *really* slowing the film.

The last third or so of the movie consists of the game and, of course, as you would predict, Jack is called in at the last minute and does catch the winning touchdown pass. Hurray, do the wave, sis-boom-bah.

Robin Williams's work in *The Best of Times* comes off as confused and erratic. He has a few moments when the kick-ass Robin surfaces (he does a little riff about "Mr. Weasel" and throws a mini-tantrum in the massage parlor that had possibilities), but overall he is not given a sharply-defined character to play and his performance suffers.

The Best of Times is one of the films that Robin considers to be part of his trilogy of failure (the other two he has mentioned as regrettable career choices were *The Survivors* and *Club Paradise*). He's got a point. *The Best of Times* is slow-paced, rambling, and boring.

Even a serious Robin Williams fan could skip *The Best of Times* and not miss a thing. Too bad. Good and talented people were involved with the project. Director Roger Spottiswoode would go on to direct the TV movies *The Last Innocent Man* (1987) and the powerful AIDS drama, *And the Band Played On* (1993); we've already talked about writer Ron Shelton; and the caliber of the cast is obvious.

But in the end, regrettably, the whole was less than the sum of its parts.

WHAT THE CRITICS HAD TO SAY

Leonard Maltin: "Some quirky, offbeat touches highlight Ron Shelton's script and the wives (Reed, Palance) are a treat but the seemingly surefire film becomes too strident (and too exaggerated) to really score." (from his *Movie and Video Guide*)

Mick Martin and Marsha Porter: "This comedy starts off well, then continues to lose momentum right up to the Rocky-style ending. That said, it is an amiable enough little movie which benefits from likable performances by its lead players." (from their *Video Movie Guide*)

Videohound's Golden Movie Retriever: "With this cast, it should have been better." (from the 1997 edition)

Seize the Day

(1986)

Oh, God, let me out of my thoughts! Let me out of these troubles!
Let me do something better with my life!

—Tommy Wilhelm

Don't watch *Seize the Day* expecting a Robin Williams laughfest:
A fun time, it is not. But is it a worthwhile viewing experience?
Absolutely.

Seize the Day is a "Learning in Focus" film produced for PBS
based on the short novel of the same name by the renowned
Jewish-American writer, Saul Bellow. (Bellow has a cameo in the
movie, making an appearance as an old man wandering the halls
of the hotel where Tommy Wilhelm and his father live.)

Seize the Day tells the dark story of Tommy Wilhelm, a Jewish
man approaching forty who finds his life disintegrating around
him, helpless to stop what seems like an inevitable downslide into
tragedy and oblivion.

Tommy was born Wilky Adler, but changed his name when
he was in his twenties with the hopes of breaking into show
business and becoming a famous actor. His father, a stern,
authoritarian, mean-hearted physician, wanted Tommy to go

into medicine, but Tommy refused, believing that he was destined for stardom (and also knowing deep down that he did not have his father's aptitude for medicine).

The movie, which takes place in 1956, begins with Tommy speeding recklessly down the road, on his way to the Connecticut children's furniture factory where he has worked for ten years as a salesman. Tommy is angry beyond words: the owner of the company arbitrarily took away half of the territory Tommy had spent a decade building up and gave it to his new son-in-law (who cockily reminds Tommy that he has a college education).

Tommy bursts into the factory, confronts his boss, Mr. Rojax, about his "demotion," and then smashes his fist in rage through a plate glass window. Tommy, of course, gets fired, and the next time we see him he is explaining to his lover Olive (Glenne Headly) why he was right and his boss was dead wrong. An overwrought Tommy tells Olive that he has to drive into New York to see a few people and find a new job, and we get the sense that Tommy's life has been one misfortune after another. We also begin to suspect that many of these catastrophes may have been Tommy's own fault. He has seven hundred dollars left to his name and he is desperate to find another eighteen- to twenty-thousand-dollar-a-year job as soon as possible.

Leaving for New York, Tommy drives Olive to church (note, he's dating a Catholic) and on the way, we find out that Tommy has been separated from his wife Margaret (Katherine Borowitz) for four years and has been unable to finalize the divorce. He has been struggling with outrageous child support payments and Olive insists that he end the marriage and marry her, and that he do it *soon* (throughout Olive's lecture, there is the unspoken "or else" hanging over Tommy's head).

During the drive to New York, we see a flashback in which Tommy's antacid-eating broker reveals that Tommy has lost most of the six thousand dollars he had invested in pesticide stocks.

Tommy moves into the New York hotel where his father lives and reluctantly tells his father that he has lost his job. His father treats Tommy's cut hand and coldly lectures Tommy about how he should have gone into medicine.

Tommy starts going on job interviews, but, in a series of painful humiliations, is either ignored or offered ridiculously low salaries. One of his good "friends," Bernie (Tony Roberts)—after hearing that Tommy needs a twenty-two-thousand-dollar-a-year salary to get by—insultingly offers him 9500—and then *allows* Tommy to pick up the lunch check.

Tommy gets so desperate he begins to consider quick and reckless solutions to his problems. He hooks up with an eccentric doctor (who might not actually *be* a doctor) named Tamkin (Jerry Stiller), who convinces Tommy to put his last seven hundred dollars into lard and rye commodities, which, of course, he promptly loses.

Then Tommy's weekly hotel rent comes due and he can't pay it, and Tommy's wife calls and demands immediate payment of his (late) child support or she'll prevent him from seeing his kids. On the verge of a complete mental breakdown, Tommy swallows what's left of his pride and literally begs his father for help.

Tommy's father, however, is a heartless despot who tells Tommy that he does not want to carry anyone on his back—including his own son—and that he will not bail him out under any circumstances.

Tommy leaves his father and runs through the streets of New York, screaming for Dr. Tamkin, hoping to get some of his money back (it turns out Tamkin didn't even put in his own half of the commodities investment).

Thinking he sees Tamkin walking into a building, Tommy chases the man (who turns out not to be Tamkin) and ends up crashing into a funeral and falling in the aisle as the shocked mourners stare in disbelief at this wild man who has disrupted their ceremony.

Tommy composes himself, puts on the proffered yarmulke, and sits in a seat at the front of the synagogue. While two women gossip about which side of the family he might be from, Tommy sits there and alternately sobs, laughs, moans, and cries out loud, now completely beaten and broken, in the midst of a total mental collapse. It is obvious to us that Tommy interprets his crashing into a funeral, of all things, at this lowest point of his life as the ultimate metaphor for his future prospects. To Tommy, the universe seems to be telling him that he's already dead.

Robin Williams gives a bravura performance in *Seize the Day*. He plays Tommy Wilhelm with such an edge, we can't help but relate to the pressure the character is experiencing and vicariously see the thin, fragile thread by which his sanity hangs.

At one point in the movie, Tommy's father (Joseph Wiseman) tells Tommy that he is turning into "a mountain of tics" and that is an apt and evocative description of how Robin Williams plays Tommy.

Robin Williams gives one of the most powerful, dramatic performances of his life, and it is yet another example of what a magnificent dramatic actor he became in the decade or so since he burst onto the scene.

WHAT THE CRITICS HAD TO SAY

Leonard Maltin: "A small masterpiece, like the Saul Bellow novel on which it's based, with a faithful screenplay by Ronald Ribman." (from his *Movie and Video Guide*)

Mick Martin and Marsha Porter: "Robin Williams is watchable in this drama, but like so many comedians who attempt serious acting, he is haunted by his madcap persona." (from their *Video Movie Guide*)

Videohound's Golden Movie Retriever: "Brilliant performances by all, plus a number of equally fine actors in small roles." (from the 1997 edition)

Tom Wiener*:* "Williams is first-rate in this sleeper." (from his *The Book of Video Lists*)

Club Paradise

(1986)

Jump off with your passion, not as a whore.

—**Robin Williams, talking about
how to make career choices**

Club Paradise holds an awkward place in Robin Williams's body of film work: It is the only movie he has admitted to making only for the money.

It is easy, though, to understand Robin's initial enthusiasm for the commercial potential of *Club Paradise*. The cast was made up of some of the hottest comic actors and stars of the eighties: Eugene Levy, Rick Moranis, Andrea Martin, Brian Doyle-Murray, and Mary Gross, as well as the legendary Peter O'Toole, the sexy model-turned-actress Twiggy, and hot reggae star, Jimmy Cliff. The script was co-written by Harold Ramis, who had just come off the enormously successful 1984 hit *Ghostbusters* (which he co-wrote and starred in) and Doyle-Murray (Bill Murray's brother), who had previously co-written the 1981 Bill Murray military comedy, *Stripes*. *Club Paradise* was also to be directed by Ramis, who had previously been behind the camera for the two giant hits, *Caddyshack* (1980) and *National Lampoon's Vacation* (1983).

Yes, all the elements were in place and everyone believed *Club Paradise* would not only be a terrific movie, but that it would also mimic the box-office success of the previous comedies in which all these creative dynamos had been involved.

So what happened?

Club Paradise is about Chicago fireman Jack Moniker (Robin Williams). Jack is completely fed up with his job. He uses an on-the-job injury as an opportunity to take a disability retirement and move to a Caribbean island owned by Great Britain and live the good life in a tropical resort for the rest of his life.

As he settles in and gets to know more about the island and its people, he learns that the resort, which is owned by his reggae musician friend Ernest Reed (Jimmy Cliff), is behind in its taxes. The slimy bureaucrat who owns the majority of the rest of the island is intent on closing Club Paradise for back taxes and selling the whole island to foreign developers who will build condos and high-rise hotels.

Jack and Phillipa (played by Twiggy, a tourist who falls in love with him and stays on the island) put together a gorgeous (but intentionally misleading) brochure to lure vacationers to the resort and hopefully raise enough money to save the place.

Robin's character in *Club Paradise* is essentially a wisecracking straight man. There is none of the manic craziness common to some of his more memorable performances and much of the humor in the movie comes from the secondary characters played by Levy, Moranis, Martin, and O'Toole (playing the figurehead governor of the island).

Club Paradise could have been funnier if Robin Williams had been given better material and especially if he had been allowed to improvise some of his scenes. The supporting cast are all consummate pros and do the best with what they are given, but overall, the script seems too slow, too convoluted, and it doesn't have enough truly funny lines or scenes.

There is an unnecessary subplot about a revolution that seems to come out of nowhere and there is not enough interaction between Robin and the other comedic stars. It would seem to be the logical move that if you have Robin Williams in your movie, unless it's a drama like *Awakenings* or *Seize the Day*, you should really make as much use of him as you can and let him *be* Robin Williams. He is collared in *Club Paradise*; his performance is subdued and restrained and he has almost no memorable funny lines, except for a few scripted wisecracks.

Andrea Martin is very funny as a *hausfrau* set loose (the first thing she tries upon her arrival on the island is hang-gliding), and Rick Moranis is terrific as the pot-smoking "wild and crazy" ladies man who ends up windsurfing twenty miles out to sea in the middle of a monster storm. Eugene Levy is good, as always, and Peter O'Toole is perfect as the lazy, flat-broke governor who is quite aware of his station in life, thank you very much, and is perfectly content to wile away his days drinking umbrella drinks and cavorting with the attractive female guests on the island. Twiggy is a surprisingly natural actress, and cinematic veterans Joanna Cassidy (as Terry Hamlin) and Adolph Caesar (Prime Minister Solomon Gundy) round out the cast.

The music in *Club Paradise* is mostly reggae, and mostly by Jimmy Cliff, and is one of the few truly terrific elements in the film.

Club Paradise could have been better considering the caliber of talent involved. Is it worth a watch if you haven't seen it? Sure, if you don't go into it expecting *Ghostbusters* or *Stripes*. It's not that it's a bad film; it's just average (or slightly below average). But when you're talking about people like Robin Williams, Harold Ramis, and Peter O'Toole, "average" for them is almost unacceptable. *Club Paradise* could have been a three- or four-star movie. Instead, it's a disappointment, but still worth seeing if you're a fan of any of the talented people involved.

WHAT ROBIN HAD TO SAY

Playboy: Are there any films you've made for reasons other than artistic ones?

Robin Williams: *Club Paradise*. They said it would be a box-office smash, a great combination of people, we'll kick ass, etc. And then [explosion sound] my ass got kicked. That's when you get screwed. Jump off with your passion, not as a whore.

WHAT THE CRITICS HAD TO SAY

Leonard Maltin: "Pleasant cast in pleasant surroundings, lacking only a script and a few more laughs." (from his *Movie and Video Guide*)

Videohound's Golden Movie Retriever: "Somewhat disappointing with [Robin] Williams largely playing the straight man. Most laughs provided by [Andrea] Martin, particularly when she is assaulted by a shower, and [Rick] Moranis, who gets lost while windsurfing." (from the 1997 edition)

Good Morning, Vietnam

(1987)

Gooooood morning, Vietnam!

—Adrian Cronauer

Good Morning, Vietnam was Robin Williams's breakout film and the movie that transformed him from a working actor into a huge star.

His earlier film work (most notably *The World According to Garp, Moscow on the Hudson,* and the little-seen but unquestionably brilliant *Seize the Day*) proved that he had cinematic potential and was undoubtedly a talented actor (and, of course, a comedic genius), but *Good Morning, Vietnam* was ultimately the perfect vehicle to wholeheartedly utilize his unique blend of manic comedy and dramatic acting capabilities.

Prior to *Good Morning, Vietnam*, Robin had not made a film in which he could act *and* perform. That duality of character is exactly what he needed to fulfill his potential, and that is what he found in Adrian Cronauer's story and Mitch Markowitz's script.

Good Morning, Vietnam was directed by the talented Barry Levinson—*Diner* (1982), *The Natural* (1984), *Tin Men* (1987),

Rain Man (1988), *Avalon* (1990), *Bugsy* (1991)—who would later direct Robin in 1992's *Toys*.

In his 1993 book *Levinson on Levinson*, the director talked about how the film ended up being a combination of scripted action and dialogue blended with Robin Williams's amazing improvisations:

> I thought the idea of the DJ was interesting. The real man was not as funny as Robin. Not too funny at all. Very serious, in fact....So we ended up changing about 40 percent of the script. Working with Robin on his routines was a little like playing football when we were kids....Robin would do a take and I'd say, "I like the thing about so-and-so. I don't think that bit works, but this is good. What about that thing you talked about the other day, about the nudist monk? Let's give that a try." Then he'd go and do another take, we'd go over it again and say, "This is good, save this. Drop that. Add this. I think we're in fine shape. Let's see if you've got any other ideas." Then another idea would emerge that wasn't really developed; we'd talk about it and explore it a little more, and then start shooting again. We shot very fast, a lot of footage, and basically hammered out that whole section of the movie. We shot it in an incredibly short period of time considering the impact it has in the movie.

Robin's performance won him a Golden Globe Award for Best Actor in a Musical or Comedy and earned him a Best Actor Academy Award nomination. His transformation from the exhausted, sullen airman newly arrived in Saigon into the raucous, multi-voiced DJ when he sits in front of the microphone for the first time is an amazing thing to see and hear. Here is how Robin began this first radio scene:

Gooooood morning, Vietnam! Hey, this is not a test, this is rock and roll! Time to rock it from the Delta to the DMZ! Is that me or does that sound like an Elvis Presley movie? [Elvis Presley voice] Viva Danang. Oh, Viva Danang. Danang me, Danang me, why don't they get a rope and hang me! Hey, is it a little too early for being that loud? Hey, too late! It's o-six hundred. What does the "o" stand for? Oh, my God, it's early!

In this first bit, Williams does his interpretation of: scenes from *The Wizard Of Oz* (with himself doing all the characters); Rod Serling doing the *Twilight Zone* opening narration in which he finds himself in the demilitarized zone; visits from Gomer Pyle, President Johnson, Hanoi Hannah, and a GI named Roosevelt E. Roosevelt who tells Adrian he is stationed in Poon Tang; Lawrence Welk; Mr. Leo, a fashion consultant for the Army whose motto is "If you're going to fight, clash!"; and Bob Fribber from artillery who wanted Adrian to "play anything…just play it loud!" All rapid fire, with the sequence, from start to finish, lasting exactly three minutes and twenty seconds.

Good Morning, Vietnam tells the story of the aforementioned Cronauer, an armed forces DJ who gets reassigned from Crete to Saigon in an attempt to bolster the morale of the ever-increasing numbers of GIs being shipped to Vietnam.

In the tradition of *M*A*S*H*'s irrepressible Hawkeye Pierce, Williams's Cronauer is an irreverent, somewhat disrespectful, defiantly anti-mainstream rebel who eschews the accepted playlist of Percy Faith, Ray Conniff, and "certain ballads by Mr. Frank Sinatra," and instead plays the Beach Boys, Martha and the Vandellas, and James Brown. Not surprisingly, the GIs love him (especially his friend and aide Edward Garlick, played by Forest Whitaker in one of his earliest film roles), but, aside from General Tyler (Noble Willingham) the brass can't stand him. J.T. Walsh's character Sergeant Major Dickerson in particular (who is inexplicably—but hilariously—in Saigon because of prostate problems) works diligently (and ultimately successfully) at getting rid of Cronauer.

Good Morning, Vietnam is very entertaining and most effective when (not surprisingly) Robin's character is on the radio or interacting with his fellow military types. The film could have done with less of him teaching the Vietnamese English and playing softball with them, as well as without the subplot involving his romantic pursuit of a young woman from his class. These moments are less successful, but do not seriously detract from the overall excellence of the film or Robin's performance in it.

WHAT ROBIN HAD TO SAY

"Barry Levinson, [Paul] Mazursky, they were comics. So they understand the beast. And that's why they can work with someone like me. And know when to say no, and to put up like those kind of rubber road cones when you're learning to drive and you hear that—bang!—but you didn't break the car. And that's why [Barry Levinson] was great." (from a PBS interview with David Frost)

WHAT THE CRITICS HAD TO SAY

Roger Ebert: "*Good Morning, Vietnam* works as straight comedy, and it works as a Vietnam-era *M*A*S*H*, and even the movie's love story has its own bittersweet integrity. But they used to tell us in writing class that if we wanted to know what a story was really about, we should look for what changed between the beginning and the end. In this movie, Cronauer changes. War wipes the grin off of his face. His humor becomes a humanitarian tool, not simply a way to keep him talking and us listening." (from his *Movie Home Companion*)

Leonard Maltin: "Williams is the whole show here....His manic monologues are so uproarious that they carry the rest of the film, which has a weakly developed 'story' and often irrelevant musical interludes." (from his *Movie and Video Guide*)

Mick Martin and Marsha Porter: "Williams's improvisational monologues are the high points in a film that meanders too much, but Forest Whitaker also shines." (from their *Video Movie Guide*)

Videohound's Golden Movie Retriever: "[Robin] Williams spins great comic moments that may have been scripted but likely were not as a man with no history and for whom everything is manic radio material.... The character ad-libs, swoops, and swerves, finally accepting adult responsibility. Engaging all the way with an outstanding period soundtrack." (from the 1997 edition)

The Adventures of Baron Munchausen

(1988)

I don't have time for flatulence and orgasms! I hate that face you make me make! Please, please, no! I don't want any more bodily functions!

—The King of the Moon's
detached head

This $46 million special-effects extravaganza tells the story of the legendary Baron Munchausen, a mythic figure about whom stage plays were written and who everyone believed perished in some amazing adventure.

The movie is, without a doubt, an enchanting viewing experience, but it speaks volumes about the extraordinary and inestimable talents of Robin Williams that his brief ten minutes of screen time (in a two-hour plus movie) provided the most enjoyable moments of the film. Robin's performance—short enough to be considered a cameo—is funny, engaging, and the liveliest sequence in the film. He isn't even credited under his real name, but rather as Ray D. Tutto, which is a play on the name of Robin's character, the King of the Moon, also known as *re di tutto*, the "King of Everything."

Robin's scene takes place on the Moon. The Baron (John Neville) and his young companion Sally (Sarah Polley) have flown to the Moon in a hot-air sailing ship (the balloon is made from lady's undergarments) to seek help from the Baron's dear friend, the King of the Moon, in saving Sally's besieged hometown.

Robin's character *literally* illustrates the idea of the mind and body being two distinct and separate "entities." The King of the Moon (and his wife, the Queen, played by Valentina Cortese) have detachable heads. Their heads are actually screwed on, and the two parts of their person—head and body—are in constant conflict. The head wants to disconnect from the vile and repulsive body and only concern itself with the "higher things" of existence, while the body is only interested in the baser pursuits, primarily sex and food.

When the Baron and Sally first arrive on the Moon (a surrealistic place where the buildings travel around like pedestrians on a sidewalk), the King's head has freed himself from his body and is floating around in space. After greeting the Baron (*"Bene venuti a luna, Baroni!"*), the King informs Munchausen that he is now King of Everything, not just the Moon, and proves his point by making some chirping noises and telling them that he just invented Spring. His new title is *re di tutto*—"but you can call me Ray."

The King tells the Baron that the Moon is now just a small part of his domain and that without him, there would be nothing: *"Cogito, ergo, es,"* the King says to the Baron. Translation: "I think, therefore, you are."

This prompts young Sally to inform the Baron, "Your old friend's a lunatic." The King then tells them that Munchausen's many adventurers are a distraction to him and that he considers the Baron to be "like a mosquito in the Taj Mahal." The Baron reminds the King that, without his adventures, there would *be* no King of the Moon and this irritates old Ray. He imprisons the Baron and Sally in a room atop a giant pedestal, and then the King laments the existence of his "revolting body," which is busy chasing the body of his Queen. "It's hard to believe my body and I were ever connected," he whines to the Baron and Sally. "We are so totally incompatible. He is just dangling from the food chain and I am in the stars."

The King's body recaptures its head, screws it on tight, and immediately changes into a flesh-colored glutton. "I'm baaaaack!" he exclaims to one and all. "I got lips again and I'm gonna use 'em, baby!" he tells his Queen.

The King then proclaims, "I'm your elephant of joy!" and raises his "trunk," with the appropriate accompanying screeching sound (this would seem to be an improvised Robin Williams bit, as he'd done it previously in concert and elsewhere). He then begins disgustingly stuffing fruit into his mouth and belching and when he sees the Baron there is food and juice all over his face. Apparently, the King's body doesn't know what its head does when it's separated because the King says to the Baron, "Hey, I know you! You're the little guy who tried to make off with my Queen last time you were here! We'll have no more of that, piccolo Casanova!"

Sally and the Baron are then put into a cage, but the King's head again escapes from the body and rhapsodizes that it is now free again "to concentrate on higher things!"

The body quickly recaptures the head with a butterfly net, though, and leads it off as the head cries out, "Let me go! I've got tides to regulate! Comets to direct!"

Later, the Queen's detached head frees the Baron and Sally and informs them that the King is home in bed with her body.

The Queen's head repeatedly makes little orgasmic noises, and when the adolescent Sally asks the Baron why she's doing that, the Baron embarrassedly tells her that the King is off "tickling her feet." We then see the King in bed with the Queen's body… tickling her feet!

The King eventually discovers that her head is gone ("Where is your head? No wonder you're so quiet.") and then figures out that she's with the Baron: "You are with that little man! You told me size don't make a difference!"

The King vows to kill the Baron and sends a three-headed vulture after him. The bird dives for the Baron and Sally, but they split up, and the bird rips itself apart trying to chase both of them at the same time. The King's body dies when the center bird crashes into the ground and the head cries out, "The body is dead! Long live the head!" He decides that he doesn't need a body after all, but then he sneezes and flies off into space.

And thus ends Robin Williams's ten minutes of screen time in *The Adventures of Baron Munchausen*. The rest of the movie is no less bizarre and fantastic.

Robin's performance in this movie is terrific fun and, again, one of the most engaging and exciting sequences in the film. The movie as a whole has some sluggish spots, but it also boasts appearances by the supremely gorgeous Uma Thurman (as Venus) and cameos by Sting and Elton John's percussionist Ray Cooper.

Is *The Adventures of Baron Munchausen* worth watching if you haven't seen it? Yes, if you're a Robin Williams fan and want to see one of the odder entries in his filmography. Just be aware, though, that after his scenes (which occur about a third of the way through the movie), you can watch the rest of the movie a little less attentively and still enjoy it for its spectacular and amazing effects.

WHAT THE DIRECTOR HAD TO SAY

Terry Gilliam: "The thing with Robin is, he has the ability to go from manic to mad to tender and vulnerable. He's the most unique mind on the planet. There's nobody like him out there." (*Playboy*, January 1992)

WHAT THE CRITICS HAD TO SAY

Leonard Maltin: "Breathtaking special effects go hand in hand with Gilliam's outlandishly funny and far-out ideas; a visual feast that's worth staying with through its occasional lulls." (from his *Movie and Video Guide*)

Videohound's Golden Movie Retriever: "[A]n ambitious, imaginative, chaotic, and under-appreciated marvel....Wonderful special effects and visually stunning sets occasionally dwarf the actors and prove what Gilliam can do with a big budget." (from the 1997 edition)

Portrait of a White Marriage
(1988)

I've got more filters than a pack of Marlboros.
—**Air Conditioner Salesman**

Robin appears at eighty-two minutes into this okay comedy as an air conditioning salesman pitching his products and services to Martin Mull. He seems to ad-lib his brief bit of dialogue, which, after some banter about the woman who just left Martin Mull's room, includes:

> Air conditioners, air conditioners. We got your maintenance, your installation, and your hardware. Everything. One stop before you drop. It's all right in there. I've got more filters than a pack of Marlboros. And also fifty feet of rubber hose.

It's not unreasonable to presume that this appearance was probably done as a favor.

WHAT THE CRITICS HAD TO SAY

Alali Gabi: "I will never understand such judgments of actors who have the opportunity to choose their projects with which to associate their name and yet choose to be featured in uninteresting and worthless productions." (Translated from Romanian. From https://filmelelafotofinish.blogspot.com/, November 27, 2017)

Dead Poets Society

(1989)

We are food for worms, lads. Because believe it or not, each and every one of us in this room is one day going to stop breathing.

—John Keating

There are some who might interpret the subtext of *Dead Poets Society* as validation of a rigid and harsh disciplinarian style of upbringing and education. These advocates do have a point, but one's ultimate assessment of this absorbing period piece will depend largely on how one views life and our time on this globe: Is life a harsh and merciless battle to be won through denial, steadfast focus, and, of course, structure and discipline? Or is it a wondrous journey that should be savored and enjoyed through the embrace of spontaneity, joy, and an honest acknowledgment of the fleeting nature of the brief time we all have above ground?

In *Dead Poets Society*, Robin Williams plays John Keating, an English teacher at the New England all-boys prep school, The Welton Academy. Keating's first instructions to his students is for them to tear out an essay in their poetry text because he believes the guy who wrote it doesn't know what he's talking about (he calls it "excrement"). He then asks them to stand on his desk, one at a time, in order to get a different view of the world. Keating's code of conduct is based on the axiom *Carpe diem*: "Seize the day." He believes his young charges should challenge authority and conventional wisdom and make bold and daring moves, for such actions, he assures them, will undoubtedly yield growth and enlightenment.

When Keating was a student at Welton, he and a few like-minded classmates formed a club they called the Dead Poets Society. They would gather in a cave and read poetry aloud in an attempt to acquire some of the transcendental wisdom of such writers as Tennyson, Blake, Emerson, Thoreau, and other "free-thinkers." As an instructor, Keating rouses the adolescent passion of his students (and hopefully *all* students who watch the film) to break free from the rules and demands of school, their parents, society, etc. A group of his students accept his challenge, reincarnate the Society, and begin holding secret meetings—gatherings that are completely against the rules of the school.

As with any period piece (this one takes place in the 1950s), the sensibility of the times takes some getting used to. Today it is unfathomable to believe that a group of sixteen- and seventeen-year-olds would be considered rebellious because they read poetry aloud to each other. And yet, the story and the excellent performances take over and we are caught up in the life-and-death struggle between one student and his father, a struggle that ultimately ends in tragedy.

Robert Sean Leonard (of future *House M.D.* fame), in only his third theatrical film (the first two were forgettable: 1987's *Bluffing It* and 1988's *My Best Friend Is a Vampire*), plays Keating's student Neil Perry, the son of a man who is a cold and controlling authoritarian.

Neil wants to act; his father (Kurtwood Smith) wants him to be a doctor. Keating encourages Neil to stand up for what his heart wants and Neil subsequently defies his father by acting in the school play, against the old man's orders. Mr. Perry shows up at the play, drags his son home, and tells him he is pulling him out of Welton and sending him to a military academy because of his disobedience. Later that evening, Neil puts a bullet through his brain (with his father's gun) and his father is the first one to find him.

Back at Welton, the powers-that-be need a scapegoat...and John Keating ends up the unlucky winner. The headmaster makes the surviving members of the Dead Poets Society sign a declaration that Neil killed himself because Mr. Keating encouraged all of them to act in a self-indulgent and reckless manner. Keating gets fired and the headmaster takes over his English class.

The first day with the headmaster as teacher is the day Keating is departing for good. He stops in to his old classroom to retrieve his personal belongings and while he is in the back room, the headmaster asks one of the students to read aloud the very essay Keating had made them tear out of their books. The students cannot bear this painful irony for very long and as Keating is leaving, the members of the Society all stand on top of their desks in tribute to him and his philosophies.

Robin Williams's performance in *Dead Poets Society* is a very good dramatic achievement (he received Golden Globe and Academy Award nominations), though he cannot help veering off into the Land of Robin now and then. John Wayne doing Shakespeare? Sure, why not? A surfer dude on *American Bandstand*? Okay. Robin also adds a touch of sadness to Keating's character that is quite effective. And Australian director and Academy Award nominee Peter Weir, responsible for such thoughtful and textured films as *Picnic at Hanging Rock* (1975), *Gallipoli* (1981), *The Year of Living Dangerously* (1982), *Witness* (1985), and *The Mosquito Coast* (1986), brings a unique sensibility to the film, often eliciting from Robin a more nuanced performance than American directors have sometimes demanded of him.

All in all, *Dead Poets Society* is a notable artistic achievement for all concerned.

WHAT ROBIN HAD TO SAY

"[*Dead Poets Society*] is not a performance as much as it is a statement of philosophy." (from a PBS interview with David Frost)

"Originally, my character was supposed to have leukemia, which would have been *Dead Poets Love Story*. Then Peter Weir said, 'Let's lose that. Focus on the boys.'" (from *Playboy*, January 1992)

"I like the point of the movie, of trying to find the passionate thing in your life, finding some sort of passion." (from *The New York Times*, May 28, 1989)

WHAT THE CRITICS HAD TO SAY

Roger Ebert: "[Williams's] performance is a delicate balancing act between restraint and schtick. For much of the time, Williams does a good job of playing an intelligent, quick-witted, well-read young man. But then there are scenes in which his stage persona punctures the character—as when he does impressions of Marlon Brando and John Wayne doing Shakespeare. There is also a curious lack of depth to his character...Keating is more of a plot device than a human being." (from his *Movie Home Companion*)

Leonard Maltin: "Well made, extremely well-acted, but also dramatically obvious and melodramatically one-sided." (from his *Movie and Video Guide*)

Videohound's Golden Movie Retriever: "Williams shows he can master the serious roles as well as the comic with his portrayal of the unorthodox educator. Big box office hit occasionally scripted with a heavy hand to elevate the message." (from the 1997 edition)

Cadillac Man

(1990)

I do for you, maybe one day you do for me.

—Joey O'Brien

Cadillac Man is another unique entry in the Robin Williams film catalog: It is one of the few of the many movies he's done in which he does almost none of his manic, patented Robin Williams shtick (*Awakenings, Seize the Day,* and *Being Human* are some of the others). In fact, the car dealership's customers and Lauren Tom's Chinese restaurant waitress character are funnier than Robin.

Robin's performance is an edgy, dramatic one with some comedic overtones that do not really provide him with the opportunity to mimic or improvise, even for a moment. Sure, he has several funny lines and scenes, including a scene that cracks up co-star Lori Petty (who plays his girlfriend Lila) in which he dons a wig and imitates a foreigner asking to see a Cadillac Allante, and then tells her eagerly, "We're gonna play Mandingo again!" But throughout the film there is none of the complex, stream-of-consciousness type of material for which he is so famous. Even in the heavy drama *Dead Poets Society*, he did John Wayne doing *Hamlet* and a few other bits that were classic Robin.

Robin's *Cadillac Man* character, Joey O'Brien, is overwhelmed by his life: He has an antagonistic ex-wife Tina (Pamela Reed), who threw him out because of his womanizing and ended up with the house he paid for; an unmanageable daughter Lisa (Tristine Skyler) to whom he is a stranger; a high-maintenance, demanding, married mistress Joy (Fran Drescher), who wants to leave her husband for him but insists on a full emotional commitment from Joey (something he is incapable of); a naive, ditzy girlfriend Lila (Lori Petty), who designs bizarre clothing that she wants Joey to help her sell; and a mob loan shark (Paul Herman) Joey owes twenty grand to who begs him, "Joey, don't make me wait too long. Please, Joey."

But Joey loves to sell. *Cadillac Man* opens with Joey shamelessly trying to sell a widow a new car—at her husband's funeral. When he arrives at work, Joey learns that he needs to sell twelve cars in two days or be one of the salesmen who loses his job in a staff reduction when the dealership he works for, Turgeon Auto, moves to a new location.

As if all this personal turmoil was not enough, on Sunday, during the big sale, Larry (Tim Robbins), the husband of Donna the receptionist (Annabella Sciorra), drives his motorcycle into the dealership and takes everyone—the salespeople, the customers, and even Fran Drescher's pain-in-the-ass dog (played by Drescher's real-life dog Chester)—hostage. Larry suspects Donna of having an affair with someone at the dealership (she is—her boss Jackie Turgeon Jr.) and finally, he just can't take it anymore.

The remainder of the movie consists of the hostage standoff, which Joey orchestrates so that he, instead of the others, is the focus of Larry's obsessive attention. He does this by telling Larry that he was the one having the affair with Donna and that there was no one else at the dealership involved with her. Joey "takes the hit" for Jackie and it isn't long before he bonds with Larry and convinces him to give himself up.

The film concludes with Joey's life regaining some semblance of order: The loan shark forgives Joey's loan in gratitude for saving the life of his son (who worked at the dealership washing cars); the grateful Turgeons give him a guaranteed spot at the new place; his ex-wife Tina actually considers taking him back; and he becomes a minor celebrity. The only losers are his mistress Joy and girl-friend Lila, but throughout the ordeal it becomes rather obvious that those were both dead-end relationships anyway.

In *Cadillac Man*, Robin stretches himself yet again. After the success of *Good Morning, Vietnam*, he could have easily gone for another broad comedy. Instead, he did what could be called a dramatic trilogy, *Dead Poets Society, Awakenings,* and *Cadillac Man.*

WHAT THE CRITICS HAD TO SAY

Mick Martin and Marsha Porter: "Well acted and often hilarious." (from their *Video Movie Guide*)

Leonard Maltin: "Williams is terrific as usual [but the] wildly uneven film tests the mettle of even the staunchest Williams fans, swinging helter-skelter from comedy to melodrama, dragging and then picking up again. Infuriating at times, then occasionally redeemed by a great moment." (from his *Movie and Video Guide*)

Videohound's Golden Movie Retriever: "A lesser comedic talent might have stalled and been abandoned, but [Robin] Williams manages to drive away despite the flat script and direction.... Williams and [Tim] Robbins are often close to being funny in a hyperkinetic way, but the situations are dumb enough to rob most of the scenes of their comedy." (from the 1997 edition)

Awakenings

(1990)

There is deity within you.

—**Robin Williams, from a PBS
interview with David Frost**

One might make a case that Robin Williams's performance in
Awakenings, for all its gravity and sincerity, does not succeed and
should not be counted as one of his better roles.

Why?

Because on first viewing, Robin's Dr. Malcolm Sayer is pas-
sionless—which is all the more ironic when one considers that
the theme of the film is the reigniting of passion in the hearts and
souls of the newly-awakened catatonics.

But Robin's restrained, understated delivery is exactly why his
performance *does* work. He is playing a man whose life is devoted
to science. Dr. Sayer (modeled on Oliver Sacks, the author of the
film's source book) is, after all, a man who spent five years trying
to extract one decagram (ten grams) of myelin from four tons
of earthworms only to prove that it's impossible—something his
new boss (played by John Heard) knew as soon as he heard the
experiment described.

We need to also remember that Robin Williams was in his thirties when he made *Awakenings,* and yet his Dr. Sayer bears the weight of many more decades than three or four. Robin carries himself as a much older man and it is a tribute to his genius that we believe wholeheartedly that we are watching a man in his fifties, possibly nearing sixty. Dr. Sacks is bearded and burly; Robin is bearded but *plays* burly. He uses his physical presence to communicate illustrative information about this quiet, dedicated doctor.

The movie begins with Dr. Sayer taking a job at a chronic hospital in the Bronx, a place where they have wards nicknamed "The Garden" because all they do there is feed and water its residents. Sayer is astounded by the resignation on the part of the staff to the hopelessness of the patients, many of whom have not moved or spoken on their own for thirty years.

Sayer begins researching their histories and learns that a great many of them had encephalitis as children. He theorizes that they may all be in a stage of Parkinson's disease that has them hopelessly trapped in bodies that will not respond to their brain's commands. He tries treating one patient, Leonard Lowe (played with penetrating honesty by Robert De Niro), with the drug L-DOPA and, to his wonderment, he finds the previously catatonic man up one night writing his name. He then convinces the hospital and its supporters to fund L-DOPA therapy for all of the vegetative patients. The hospital does, and one by one they all come back to our world.

Robin Williams plays Dr. Sayer's amazement at this development with subtlety and grace, and yet he also allows us to see how overwhelmed he is by suddenly having to deal with all the myriad personalities for which he is now responsible. Again, we remember that Dr. Sayer is a man who rarely interacts with people. He is a research scientist and now—look at what his research hath wrought! In the scenes in which the newly awakened patients reacquaint themselves with the wonder of life, Robin allows some of the manic energy he is so well-known for to surface, albeit in a restrained and tentative way.

It isn't long, however, before Leonard begins developing tics and manifesting strange physical behavior and Dr. Sayer realizes that the drug is failing. The final third of the film, focusing on Leonard's rapid disintegration and eventual return to a vegetative state, belongs almost completely to Robert De Niro. But it is through Robin Williams's eyes that we see Leonard's downfall and it is with Robin Williams's emotions that we experience the heartbreak and feelings of helplessness Dr. Sayer must live with as his patient—and his friend—ends up catatonic once again.

The interaction between these two great actors is spellbinding to watch. In the January 1992 issue of *Playboy*, Robin Williams talked about working with De Niro on *Awakenings*:

> **Playboy**: That touching scene when Leonard awakens—were you off camera doing things to make him laugh?
>
> **Robin Williams**: Bob would say, "Surprise me." So I did Harvey Fierstein talking to him. "Leonard, sweetheart, lose the puppy on the pajamas. Come over here, darling, did Mom bring you that terrycloth robe? Do you want some slippers?" I could drop him doing that.

Awakenings touches on many themes, including appreciating life and not taking it for granted; the ecstasy of new love; the painful quandary of not being able to provide experimental, possibly helpful medical care because of the cost; and the problem of what to do with patients who are quite simply not going to get better, no matter how committed and optimistic their doctors may be.

Awakenings is a powerful and moving film that, coming so soon after *Dead Poets Society*, proved that Robin Williams was not only one of our best comedians, he was also one of our finest dramatic actors as well.

The film also boasts terrific performances by Julie Kavner as sympathetic nurse Costello; Penelope Ann Miller as Leonard's love interest, Paula; Ruth Nelson as Leonard's mother, Mrs. Lowe; and especially Anne Meara, as the awakened patient Miriam.

WHAT ROBIN HAD TO SAY

"[*Awakenings* is] deeply sad, but also so exhilarating, the way that all of Oliver's work is. He makes you examine these supposedly negative and horrifying things from another perspective and say, yes, there is great pain…but he also says, look at the power of the human spirit and more than just the spirit, the power of the mind. There is deity within you. That is that spark, that divine thing. And it stems from creation, that thing that is soul. *Anima* is what the Greeks call it. And that's what I was fascinated by with Oliver's writing and with *Awakenings*: That which can shine through." (from a PBS interview with David Frost)

WHAT THE CRITICS HAD TO SAY

Roger Ebert: "Dr. Sayer, played by [Robin] Williams, is at the center of almost every scene, and his personality becomes one of the touchstones of the movie. He is shut off, too, by shyness and inexperience, and even the way he holds his arms, close to his sides, shows a man wary of contact. He really was happier working with those earthworms. This is one of Robin Williams's best performances, pure and uncluttered, without the ebullient distractions he sometimes adds—the schtick where none is called for." (from his *Movie Home Companion*)

Leonard Maltin: "Powerfully affecting true-life story…Williams is superb as the doctor." (from his *Movie and Video Guide*)

Videohound's Golden Movie Retriever: "Occasionally over-sentimental, but still providing a poignant look at both the patients—who find themselves confronted with lost opportunities and faded youth—and at [Oliver] Sacks, who must watch their exquisite suffering as they slip away. De Niro's performance as the youngest of the group is heartrending, while Williams offers a subdued, moving performance as the doctor." (from the 1997 edition)

Dead Again
(1991)

Thanks to fate—the only cosmic force with a tragic sense of humor—you burn somebody in one life, they get a chance to burn you back in this one. It's the karmic credit plan: Buy now, pay forever. If you'll excuse me, it's my karmic burden to load some cat food.

—Dr. Cozy Carlisle

This stylish, smart, exciting, and intricately-plotted thriller is enjoyable from start to finish and it is easy to understand why Robin Williams agreed to participate. His part, though, consists of little more than two brief scenes that could have been played by any actor with a modicum of talent.

But, of course, Robin Williams possesses a tad more than a modicum of acting talent, and thus, his two small scenes are two extremely powerful moments, and the character he plays is one of the movie's most memorable.

Robin plays Dr. Cozy Carlisle, a disgraced and "disbarred" psychiatrist with a foul mouth who is reduced to working in a grocery store and who acts as an informant for Kenneth Branagh's character, private investigator Mike Church.

Robin's first scene takes place in a refrigerated meat locker and is less than three minutes long, but he is unforgettable in those brief few seconds. Dr. Carlisle's first words in the scene are to Church, "Fuck you, I'm on a break." He is then told that he has inherited some money from a deceased former patient of his. Church makes a crack about the patient's impotence, and Robin laces into him, giving us a glimpse into why he's so bitter:

> Hey, thumbdick! I was a damned good shrink. Sixteen-and-a-half years I worked with a lot of people through a lot of shit. Okay, I slept with a patient or two. It's not like I didn't care about them. I loved being a doctor. I used to not charge half my patients. Then the fucking state comes along. They send some bitch under cover. And I'm fucked. It ain't fair, is it?

Cozy also lectures Branagh on smoking:

Dr. Cozy Carlisle: Someone's either a smoker or a nonsmoker. There's no in-between. The trick is to find out which one you are, and be that.

Mike Church: Yeah, well, you know, I'm trying to quit.

Dr. Carlisle: Don't tell me you're trying to quit. People who say they're trying to quit are basically pussies who cannot commit. Find out which one you are, be that. That's it. If you're a non-smoker, you'll know.

Mike Church *(dismissive and with contempt)*: Thank you. Nice place you got here. *(under his breath)* Fucking fruitcake.

As Church gets more and more involved in a murder mystery spanning decades, he decides to return to Dr. Carlisle for advice and possible insight into who murdered Margaret Strauss (Emma Thompson in a dual role).

Robin's second scene also takes place in the grocery store and is also less than three minutes long. In this scene he explains reincarnation and past-life regression to Branagh and another character, Thompson, as he rearranges cans on the grocery store shelves. Disheveled and needing a shave, Robin communicates an edgy impatience with people who cannot keep up with him intellectually, as well as an obvious empathy for Thompson's emotional crisis.

Robin Williams is listed in the credits at the end of *Dead Again*, but is not named during the opening titles, nor does his name appear anywhere on the original movie poster. This could have been because Robin knew that his name would detract from the other stars and possibly influence people's perception of the film before it was even released.

If this was his thinking, he was probably right. After all, Robin Williams's name on a film implies a certain *something*—sure, it's essentially an indefinable something, but it *is* present and Robin wanted the excellence of this film and the performances in it to be the main focus for reviewers and moviegoers alike. This was a classy move, and Robin did his part in contributing to the merit of the film by turning in a sharp, potent, and unsettling performance that does justice to the terrific scenes scripted for his character, the bitter and irascible Dr. Cozy Carlisle.

Dead Again is terrific and a major achievement for Branagh, who speaks with two distinct accents in his dual role—his normal British accent for his role as composer Roman Strauss, and (most entertainingly) in a flawless American accent for his private dick character, Mike Church. Branagh's directing in *Dead Again* is also wonderful and the final sequence that resolves the mystery, answers all the unanswered questions, and ties up all the loose ends, is an engaging blend of black-and-white and color, slow motion, and inventive camera work.

Dead Again is a must-view for lovers of thrillers, superior acting, literate writing, and the film noir genre.

Paramount's promotional copy for *Dead Again* describes the film as being in the "classic tradition of *Spellbound* and *Rebecca*." In a rare instance of truth in advertising, this time, the studio's advertising department is absolutely on-target in their praise for *Dead Again*.

WHAT THE CRITICS HAD TO SAY

Videohound's Golden Movie Retriever: "Literate, lovely to look at, suspenseful, with a sense of humor to match its high style." (from the 1997 edition)

Roger Ebert: "*Dead Again* is like *Ghost* for people who grew up on movies that were not afraid of grand gestures. This is a romance with all the stops out, a story about intrigue, deception, and bloody murder—and about how the secrets of the present are unraveled through a hypnotic trance that reveals the secrets of the past." (from his *Movie Home Companion*)

The Fisher King

(1991)

Thank God I'm me.

—Jack Lucas

There's a lot going on in *The Fisher King*. In fact, some may say there's too much going on, but this does not change the fact that it is a rich, smart, and superbly acted film that has a mythic-allegorical subtext and structure that prods the viewer (almost demands, actually) to reconsider its meaning long after the movie ends.

Jack Lucas (Jeff Bridges) is a New York City radio shock jock who ends his show with the sign-off, "Thank God I'm me." His radio persona is a blend of Bob Grant, Rush Limbaugh, and Howard Stern. He thinks nothing of dismissing callers with an insulting and rude rebuff that belittles and intimidates people who are often under great emotional stress when they call his show.

Edwin is one of Jack's frequent callers and a certified "lonely guy." One day Edwin calls Jack to tell him he met a girl who he thinks might like him. Jack tears him apart, telling him that yuppie girls could never like him and that they should all be wiped off the planet. Edwin takes Jack's advice to heart and returns to the restaurant where he met the girl, only this time, he's got a shotgun with which he shoots and kills seven people before turning the gun on himself.

One of the people Edwin kills was the wife of Parry (Robin Williams), a homeless eccentric who, three years later, rescues Jack from becoming a barbecued wino. One night, as Jack is preparing to commit suicide by jumping into the New York Harbor, a bunch of street punks come along, grab the former DJ (with the cinder blocks still tied to his ankles) and cover him in gasoline. These cretins are ready to light a match and set Jack ablaze when Parry arrives and scares them off.

Parry rescues Jack and takes him to a basement where he clandestinely (and probably illegally) lives. Parry became completely unhinged after his wife's murder, and now he sees and converses with fat flying cherubs and believes that the Holy Grail is in the library of a wealthy New York businessman.

After Jack wakes up the next morning, Parry tells him that the three most important things in life are respect for all living things, a nice bowel movement, and a navy blazer. (Parry also remarks, "Hey, gravity works!"—a favorite Robin Williams line.)

Because of his own role in the death of Parry's wife, Jack becomes somewhat obsessed with Parry and returns the next day. Parry takes him to an office building where he watches a dowdy but pretty girl named Lydia (Amanda Plummer) as she eats lunch and shops. Jack learns that Parry does this every day and this adds to his fascination with this strange New York City eccentric.

As Jack is bonding with Parry, other storylines are also unfolding in *The Fisher King*, including Anne's unconditional and unrequited love for Jack (he's been living with her for the past three years); Parry's distant love for Lydia; Jack's attempt to redeem himself by "rescuing" Parry; the billionaire with the Holy Grail's accidental suicide; and Jack's slow move towards sanity and the resumption of his career.

As noted earlier, a lot goes on in this film, including scenes in which the naked Parry teaches Jack how to break clouds apart with his mind; a Chinese restaurant double-date scene that comes off as a bit pointless; an assault on Parry that leaves him in a coma; Jack's scaling of the billionaire's building to retrieve the Grail for Parry; Lydia's slow acceptance of Parry's love; Jack's rejection of Anne; Jack's ultimate redemption for his "crime"; and many others.

Does *The Fisher King* work?

Sort of. It is a very haphazard and occasionally baffling movie and it has a draggy middle section. It comes off as too long and a little self-indulgent.

But Robin Williams gives a magnificent performance, something that can be described as "controlled lunacy," and that must be looked at as the flip side of the coin to the role he played in *Awakenings*. In *The Fisher King*, he's insane and ends up in a mental institution; in *Awakenings*, he's brilliant and ends up in a hospital for catatonics where he tries to rescue them from their own minds. (Robin was nominated for an Academy Award for Best Actor for his work in *The Fisher King* and won a Golden Globe for his performance).

Something Gilliam succeeds at is effectively showing us Parry's interior metaphoric mental states transmuted into reality. He gives us an honest depiction of what it's like to be mentally ill and to hallucinate uncontrollably. The dancing scene in Grand Central Station and the many appearances of the fire-breathing Red Knight (that only he can see) are all very real to Parry, and Gilliam makes us see and vividly experience his delusions.

The Fisher King has a happy ending. And it also has the notoriety of being the first movie in which Robin Williams does a full frontal, total nude scene. Robin dances around completely naked in Central Park and gives the famous (yet reclusive) Mr. Happy about a minute of screen time.

Critics are ambivalent about *The Fisher King*. All acknowledge Robin's superior work, but, in the end, there seems to be unanimous agreement that the film could have been better. It is a milestone performance for Robin, though, and, thus, is definitely worth watching.

WHAT ROBIN HAD TO SAY

"[Director Terry Gilliam] is like John Huston, one of those people who has a vision, a way of seeing the world. Some people think it's askew, some think it's brilliant. Terry shoots stuff that has a half life. You walk out and it hits you. Whew! Shit! Fuckin' sixty-foot samurais! Red knights! Icarus! Simple things! He creates images that are shot into your skull." (from *Playboy*, January 1992)

WHAT THE CRITICS HAD TO SAY

Leonard Maltin: "Unusual and absorbing, both comic and tender, this takes the viewer on quite a journey." (from his *Movie and Video Guide*)

Roger Ebert: "A disorganized, rambling, and eccentric movie that contains some moments of truth, some moments of humor, and many moments of digression. The filmmakers are nothing if not generous: we get urban grit, show biz angst, two love affairs, the Holy Grail, the homeless, an action sequence, a dance sequence, and an apocalyptic figure on a horse who rides through Central Park with flames shooting from his head. Even with such excess, at 137 minutes the movie shows signs of having been pruned of some of its quiet spots—or did they intend to have all those scenes, back-to-back, in which people shout at each other?" (from his *Movie Home Companion*)

Mick Martin and Marsha Porter: "That madman of the movies, Terry Gilliam, has created yet another adult-oriented fairy tale that will win the hearts of those who haven't lost their sense of wonder." (from their *Video Movie Guide*)

Videohound's Golden Movie Retriever: "Your reaction to the silly ending depends entirely on how well you're bamboozled by a script that equates madness with enlightenment and the homelessness with holy fools." (from the 1997 edition)

Hook

(1991)

Seize the day!

—Wendy's butler Tootles, upon being given
back the magic marbles that
once again allow him to fly

Robin William plays Peter Pan in Steven Spielberg's *Hook* and it is one more of the man-boy roles that have become a peculiar trademark of his movie career (other examples of these types of "big/little kids" include Robin's characters in *Popeye, The World According to Garp, Toys, Jumanji,* and, especially, *Jack*).

Very few do these types of roles successfully. (Tom Hanks, in his brilliant performance in *Big,* is one who does.) Robin has perfected portraying the wide-eyed innocent who is also world-weary and cynical—all at the same time, and within the same persona.

Hook begins in the present time, and in the present life of Peter Banning, a mergers and acquisitions fanatic who seems to live with his cell phone attached to his ear. He makes promises to his kids he never keeps, and his family feels they are nothing more than an interruption of his work.

74

Peter has promised to take his family to London to visit Wendy, the woman who raised him. Even though he has not seen Wendy in ten years, he is still reluctant to take the time away from his job to make the trip.

Well, it turns out that Peter Banning is actually Peter Pan grown into an (uptight) adult and, over the years, he has completely forgotten his childhood adventures in Neverland and who Wendy really is. Ironically, Peter now has two children of his own, a boy and a girl who possess the sense of magic and wonderment that commonly permeates many moments of a happy childhood.

It isn't long after Peter and his family arrive in London that the past is awakened and Peter's troubles begin. Much to Peter and his wife Moira's horror, their two beloved children are kidnapped from their beds, and the police can find absolutely no clues to their whereabouts. The truth, however, is revealed to Peter by a tiny flying pixie named Tinkerbell (Julia Roberts) who transports him to Neverland, where he is forced to accept that he has been dropped into a childhood nightmare that he had completely buried away in his memory, that he is the "boy who never grew up"—Peter Pan.

During his forced stay in Neverland, Peter meets Captain Hook, the Lost Boys, Smee, and all the other characters from the fairy tale. Eventually, he has to reacquire his childhood state of mind so he can learn to fly again, vanquish Hook, and rescue his children, who have been brainwashed into thinking the nefarious bewigged Hook is their real father. (Jack might have been a tad convinced of this for a short while, but Maggie never believed it.)

Robin Williams is very good in *Hook* and, once again, he commits his entire being to his role. We never for a moment doubt that he is a puffy, middle-aged father who is thrust into an impossible and magical situation where the normal rules of an adult world do not apply. In Neverland, food only appears if you believe it's in your empty dish. People can fly only if they sincerely think happy thoughts. And lost boys live and sleep in trees as fairies fly around, causing mischief and watching over things.

Julia Roberts plays Tinkerbell with passion, something that had to be a little difficult, considering that she had to spend hours wearing a flying harness and emoting to a special effects blue screen. Roberts looks fantastic in her short, sexy red haircut and even shorter "fairy" dress.

Dustin Hoffman is quite convincing as Captain Hook, and he gives a performance faithful to the character in the book, although we always envisioned the good captain as tall and thin. We're so used to the brilliant Dustin Hoffman playing powerful dramatic roles—as he did in *Midnight Cowboy* (1969), *Lenny* (1974), *All the President's Men* (1976), *Marathon Man* (1976), *Rain Man* (1988), and *Outbreak* (1995)—that we sometimes forget that he is capable of much more playful performances, as in *Tootsie* (1982), *Dick Tracy* (1990), and, here, *Hook*. Hoffman's Hook wears a long, curly black wig and boldly flaunts his shiny steel hook, which he tops with a cork and covers in red velvet when he sleeps. The hook, appropriately, almost becomes a character in the film.

Regarding the sets in *Hook*: They are spectacular, yet oddly sterile. Neverland—with all its bridges, and trees, and strange structures—is reminiscent of Sweethaven, from Robin's film *Popeye*, but, in this case, the patently artificial "comic book" feel of Sweethaven doesn't work as effectively for the realm of Neverland. There are a few gorgeous special effects matte shots in *Hook* that are breathtaking, but the main sets where most of the action in the (at times, interminable) Neverland sequences look manufactured, something we really don't want for this magical land.

Hook culminates in a sword fight between Pan and Hook for the "parentage" of Peter's two children. Peter has regained his ability to fly, thanks to Tinkerbell's help and "happy" thoughts of his kids, and they all ultimately return to London with glorious memories and (especially for Peter) a new outlook on life.

Steven Spielberg is brilliant at evoking the sensibility of childhood, that magical time when almost anything seems possible, and fantasy and reality whimsically change places almost at will. But the overwhelming logistical requirements of *Hook* possibly distracted Spielberg and the others responsible for the film's faithfulness to the story. Yes, *Hook* works and is a meticulously professional achievement, but there is definitely something missing. Some of the Neverland scenes are a little boring, a genuine odd feeling while watching a Steven Spielberg film. Maybe the movie's too long? Maybe more time and effort was expended on the sets and costumes than the development of the characters? Perhaps all of the above? The conclusion, however, is that *Hook* boasts a terrific performance by Robin Williams that, unfortunately, takes place in what must be described as an average, somewhat overlong film.

ANOTHER INTERESTING BIT OF CINEMATIC SYNCHRONICITY

In *Hook*, when Peter returns to London and gives the butler Tootles back his marbles (everyone had always said Tootles had lost his marbles!), allowing him to fly again, Tootles soars out the window, and cries, "Seize the day!" This maxim holds a special significance to Robin Williams's career. First, in 1986, Robin starred in *Seize the Day*, the adaptation of the Saul Bellow novel; second, the adage "seize the day" was the code of conduct for Robin's character John Keating, in the 1989 film, *Dead Poets Society*; and now, in *Hook*, thanks to Peter Pan's efforts, the aforementioned Tootles can once again proclaim his own personal motto, "Seize the day!"

WHAT ROBIN HAD TO SAY

"Steven [Spielberg was] amazing. At first you think, here's a guy who basically deals in visuals. But no, he knows every movie that's ever been made. He's seen every movie twice. So he knows if someone did something before. And from that, he can give you an idea that goes beyond that. The weird thing that I never expected from him was this humanistic, behavioral directing. I thought he would be more into special effects. Just the opposite. The special effects he likes, they're fun—but he'll suggest pulling back, or adding a little bit more, trying things to make the story have a reality base. If it works, it'll play because the human element works, because of the inter-relationships of the characters, not because of all the effects. The effects will be like this wonderful icing. But if the cake sucks, the icing won't mean shit." (from *Playboy*, October 1992)

WHAT THE CRITICS HAD TO SAY

Roger Ebert: "The crucial failure in *Hook* is its inability to reimagine the material, to find something new, fresh or urgent to do with the Peter Pan myth. Lacking that, Spielberg should simply have remade the original story, straight, for this generation." (from his *Movie Home Companion*)

Leonard Maltin: "If this is Peter Pan for the '90s, give us the '50s instead." (from his *Movie and Video Guide*)

Videohound's Golden Movie Retriever: "The sets and special effects are spectacular; the direction less so. Big-budget fantasy lacks the charm it needs to really fly. Still, kids seem to love it." (from the 1997 edition)

Shakes the Clown

(1991)

You're a clown, aren't you?

—Mime Jerry

Clowns hate mimes. Who knew?

Shakes the Clown is a very strange, oddly compelling, but ultimately disastrous movie that was written and directed by the deliberately psychotic, often screaming comedian Bobcat Goldthwait.

The whole movie takes place in Palookaville, a bizarre all-clown town where Shakes and his colleagues practice their craft at birthday parties and then drink themselves into oblivion (especially Shakes) at the town's all-clown bar, the Twisted Balloon. There is apparently a regimented caste system in clown world. Rodeo clowns hate circus clowns. TV clowns look down on birthday party clowns. And all clowns hate mimes.

Robin Williams appears uncredited as mime instructor Jerry in two brief scenes.

In the first scene, Shakes goes undercover as Mime Chuck and attends one of Jerry's classes. It appears as though much of this scene was improvised by Robin, since Mime Jerry does a few jokes Robin has used elsewhere. Robin has repeatedly used a favorite joke about someone's pants being so tight you can tell what religion he is (a reference, of course, to the fact that Jews are always circumcised), and he uses this same gag in the mime class.

He also uses a joke about Shakes's penis being like "a roll of quarters" (a reference he has also made elsewhere), as well as asking Shakes if he's "on medication," a common riff of Robin's stand-up routines. Mime Jerry also mimes "puberty" in which he pretends he's got an erection the size of a broomstick. And we all know how much Robin loves "Mr. Happy" jokes.

Robin's second scene is at the conclusion of the movie when he appears as a guest on Shakes's new kid TV show and does the "trapped in a box" mime routine he had been trying to teach his motley crew of students during his mime class.

Robin's scenes are funny and he definitely adds to the movie, but he does not succeed in elevating this film above what it unquestionably is: a failed attempt at creating a dark, offbeat, cult comedy like *The Rocky Horror Picture Show* (1975) or *Eating Raoul* (1982).

The idea of an all-clown town is a funny idea and it could have worked, but much of Goldthwait's script is just not funny.

An oddity in the filmography of Robin Williams, *Shakes the Clown* is nonetheless worth watching just to see how Robin can take three minutes of screen time and hit a home run. (He's actually a pretty good mime, if you happen to like mimes, of course. If you're a clown, and you don't, we understand.) If you want to skip the rest of the movie, Robin appears about an hour into *Shakes* and then again at the very end.

You might also want to muddle through to the end of Shakes just because of La Wanda Page (TV's *Sanford and Son*'s Aunt Esther) who, believe it or not, has almost all the funny lines in the movie and is the only character who will consistently make you laugh.

WHAT THE CRITICS HAD TO SAY

Leonard Maltin: "Excruciating would-be-comic mishmash.... Aimless, crude, and headache-inducing, not even salvaged by Williams's brief, unbilled appearance as a mime teacher." (from his *Movie and Video Guide*)

Videohound's Golden Movie Retriever: "Meant as a satire of substance-abuse recovery programs and the supposed tragedies of a performer's life, the film is sometimes zany, but more often merely unpleasant and unamusing." (from the 1997 edition)

FernGully: The Last Rainforest

(1992)

Humans can't feel anything. They're numb from the brain down.

—**Batty Koda**

Robin Williams's character of Batty Koda in the animated film *FernGully: The Last Rainforest* is the creative ancestor of Robin's Genie character in *Aladdin*. Both films came out in 1992, and in Batty, Robin hinted at the brilliant multi-character persona he would take on in *Aladdin*.

Batty first appears about ten minutes into the film as an escapee from an animal testing laboratory where he was subjected to all manner of bizarre and painful experiments, including having electrodes implanted into his brain.

FernGully is an enchanted rainforest peopled by tree sprites, talking animals, and magical beings, both good and evil. Many, many years ago, the mystical forest spirit Magi Lune (Grace Zabriskie) succeeded in imprisoning the evil demon Hexxus (Tim Curry) in a giant tree, locked away forever, powerless and unable to do any more harm. Magi tries to teach the young tree fairy

Crysta (Samantha Mathis) about the past and about Hexxus, but she is young and carefree and thinks Magi worries needlessly.

But what the rainforest denizens don't know is that humans have begun invading FernGully, marking trees with big red Xs, and then cutting them down with huge saws and a machine known as the Leveler.

Crysta, during an ill-advised trip to where the machines are cutting trees, rescues Zak, a young human worker, from a falling tree by magically transforming him into a tiny creature the same tiny size as she. Zak and Crysta become friends and ultimately must save FernGully from destruction after Hexxus's tree is cut down and his evil, noxious, pollution-loving spirit is freed.

Robin's character Batty helps the two young people save the forest, all the while throwing out some hilarious wisecracks and pop culture references (which he absorbed while being experimented on in the lab) that remind us very much of Genie. Batty recites Shakespeare, imitates Bette Davis and John Wayne, does Luke Skywalker, and speaks in California surfer lingo.

After summoning the magic powers of nature to defeat Hexxus and the Leveler, Crysta, Magi, and the others watch as Zak plants a seed which instantly grows into a giant tree, a blossom that serves as the beginning of the rebirth of FernGully.

Robin Williams adds a lot to *FernGully*, and his character is the cleverest and funniest in the film. It's clear that some of Batty's dialogue was improvised by Robin, and he definitely makes the film more enjoyable and much less saccharine than it could have been without his irreverent wisecracking from the sidelines.

This eco-fable is well worth watching, if only to experience an abridged version of *Aladdin*'s Genie character.

WHAT THE CRITICS HAD TO SAY

Roger Ebert: "Although the movie is not a masterpiece, it's pleasant to watch for its humor and sweetness. Kids may like it." (from his *Movie Home Companion*)

Leonard Maltin: "Lively and enjoyable, if not memorable, with plenty of laughs for grownups in the free-flowing dialogue of Batty Koda, a wacked-out bat voiced by Robin Williams." (from his *Movie and Video Guide*)

Videohound's Golden Movie Retriever: "So-so script with politically pristine environmental message may grow tiresome for both adults and children, though decent animation and brilliant coloring enlivens the tale." (from the 1997 edition)

Aladdin

(1992)

You ain't never had a friend like me!

—Genie

After *Aladdin* was released in 1992, Robin Williams and the producers of the film remained deliberately coy about how much of Genie's "performance" in the film was spontaneous improvisation by Robin and how much was actually scripted by the film's writers. Noted film critic Roger Ebert, in his three-star review of the movie, said, "I would like to know which came first, the pictures or the words, because Williams sounds like he's improvising as he careens from one character to another."

Ebert is right: Genie is a manifestation of the ultimate Robin Williams riff—a freeform, stream-of-consciousness romp that is even more wonderful when Genie's eye-blink transformations are added to the experience.

Genie first appears about thirty-five minutes into the film and his first manifestation is as an old Jewish guy. Here is a rundown of fifty-one of the identifiable transformations that the ebullient and irrepressible Genie makes during the film:

1. An old Jewish Guy (first character)
2. A Las Vegas emcee and comedian
3. A Scotsman
4. A dog
5. A jive street guy
6. Arnold Schwarzenegger
7. A ventriloquist
8. Ed Sullivan
9. Groucho Marx
10. A maître d'
11. A snobby yuppie
12. A hick
13. A surfer dude
14. A song-and-dance man
15. A dragon
16. William F. Buckley
17. A Peter Lorre ghoul
18. Robert De Niro
19. A stewardess
20. Carol Channing as a stewardess
21. A Shakespearean character
22. A sheep
23. Pinocchio
24. A magician
25. Maurice Chevalier
26. A Roman centurion
27. Arsenio Hall
28. An effeminate tailor
29. A game show host

30. A drum majorette
31. Peter Allen
32. Harry, a commentator at the Thanksgiving Day Parade
33. June, another commentator at the Thanksgiving Day Parade
34. A lion cub
35. A goat
36. A buxom dancing girl
37. Rodney Dangerfield
38. Jack Nicholson
39. A professor
40. A light bulb
41. A bumblebee
42. A submarine
43. A bandleader
44. A one-man band
45. A commercial announcer
46. A script continuity person
47. Another script continuity person
48. Cheerleaders
49. A baseball pitcher
50. A pinball machine ball
51. A tourist in a Hawaiian shirt and Goofy cap (final character)

This may look like just a laundry list of characterizations, but Robin's transformations in the film are quick, clever, and funny, and they illustrate the mercurial, amazing way his mind actually works.

The more mainstream, run-of-the-mill transformations (the dog, the dragon, the light bulb, the submarine, etc.) were probably in the original script, but the remaining, over-the-top, pop culture characterizations (Arnold Schwarzenegger, Ed Sullivan, Groucho Marx, Carol Channing, William F. Buckley, Arsenio Hall, Jack Nicholson, etc.) may have been improvised by Robin and then drawn by the animators to accompany his shtick.

The character of Genie gave the creators of *Aladdin* an opportunity to have some fun with the whole Disney gestalt. Number 23, Pinocchio, was the first reference to the Disney universe; followed by number 34, the lion cub (a possible hint of 1994's *The Lion King*); number 45, the commercial announcer; and the final character, number 52, the tourist in the "Goofy" cap.

The most blatant acknowledgment of the Disney corporate identity came with number 45, the commercial announcer. After Princess Jasmine accepts Aladdin's marriage proposal, Genie says to him, "Aladdin, you've just won the heart of a princess! What are you gonna do next?", an obvious, in-your-face reference to Disney's ubiquitous Super Bowl commercials in which an announcer asks members of the winning team the same question and they respond enthusiastically, "I'm going to Disney World!" And to make the plug even more obvious, as Genie poses his question, "When You Wish Upon A Star" can be heard on the soundtrack (they did stop short, however, of actually having Aladdin announce that he was, indeed, going to Disney World).

The Aladdin fairytale is well-known: The lovely young princess Jasmine is told that she must marry within three days and that her chosen betrothed must be a prince. Jasmine, an independent young lady who wants to marry for love, flees the palace and runs into Aladdin, at this time a street urchin who survives by his wits and the quick fingers of his companion, Abu the monkey. The two hit it off, but ultimately part. Aladdin later finds the magic lamp. He uses his first wish to become a prince, thereby assuring himself of Jasmine's hand in marriage—even though he must deceive her to get it.

Into all this romantic intrigue is factored the evil vizier, Jafar, who not only wants Jasmine but also plans on taking over as sultan after betraying her father.

Jasmine and Aladdin's story ends happily, after many frightening battles with Jafar and many exciting adventures with Genie and a magic carpet.

Some people—those generally not thrilled with animated films—probably began watching *Aladdin* prepared to dislike it. People who usually didn't cotton to cartoons probably never had the desire to see *The Lion King, Beauty and the Beast, The Little Mermaid*, or any of the other classic Disney animated flicks. Some of them have likely never even seen *101 Dalmatians*!

But *Aladdin* won a lot these folks over. Many considered watching it equal to that of watching a film that had live actors in it. And to add to the enjoyment, they were watching a Robin Williams movie to boot, who made the G-rated, ninety minutes fly by.

WHAT ROBIN HAD TO SAY

In the September 1996 issue of the kids' magazine, *Disney Adventures*, Robin Williams was interviewed and had some interesting things to say about his most recent role. Here are a few of his comments about playing Genie:

> **Disney Adventures**: What's the best thing and worst thing about being Genie?
>
> **Robin Williams**: The best thing is I've got phenomenal powers. The worst part? My leeettle tiny living space.
>
> **Disney Adventures**: Who would be your ultimate master?
>
> **Robin Williams**: Hmm, who would be the kindest and the best? Well, Gandhi wouldn't ask for much—the wishes would

be kept to a minimum: peace in India, world peace. I'd say, "Oh, that's easy, boss! Come on, get serious." Mother Teresa, just because she would have me do good things. I don't think all of a sudden she would say, "I want my own fragrance!"

Disney Adventures: Since Genie has been stuck in a bottle for 10,000 years, how does he know all the pop culture icons that he morphs into and portrays?

Robin Williams: It's not like he doesn't get cable! He can travel forward and backward in time. He's traveling at the speed of life. He knows many things from other times.

Robin also revealed during the interview that the one thing he would change about Genie if he could would be to give him a little more hair.

WHAT THE CRITICS HAD TO SAY

Roger Ebert: "Robin Williams and animation were born for one another, and in *Aladdin* they finally meet. Williams's speed of comic invention has always been too fast for flesh and blood; the way he flashes in and out of characters can be dizzying. In...*Aladdin*, he's liberated at last, playing a genie who has complete freedom over his form—who can instantly be anybody or anything." (from his *Movie Home Companion*)

Videohound's Golden Movie Retriever: "Superb animation triumphs over average songs and storyline by capitalizing on [Robin] Williams's talent for ad-lib with lightning speed genie changes, lots of celebrity poofs, and even a few pokes at Disney itself." (from the 1997 edition)

Toys
(1992)

I like jokes.

—Leslie Zevo

Toys director Barry Levinson uses the ethereal and haunting Enya song "Ebudae" on the *Toys* soundtrack (the song is sung in Gaelic and is about the spiritual role of women), but instead of enhancing the cinematic moment, it comes off as inappropriate and confusing. Levinson uses the song in a scene where Robin Williams's character Leslie Zevo and his sister Alsatia (Joan Cusack) are driving in their father's funeral procession. Leslie is driving a toy car similar to the kind used in the bumper car rides at carnivals and he keeps banging into the limousine in front of him. "Ebudae" is almost hymn-like, and when used effectively, can imbue a scene with a sacred feel that is most moving. But in *Toys*, the song is wasted. And that is the overwhelming impression one gets when watching *Toys*: It squanders talent, set design, music, and, of course, money.

When an eccentric toymaker dies, he passes on his strange and colorful toy factory to his military-general brother rather than his son and daughter, even though his children are the two people who are truly kindred spirits and would continue on in the tradition of their offbeat dad. The uncle immediately implements security procedures and begins making war toys, much to the dismay of Leslie and Alsatia. The story revolves around Leslie and Alsatia's attempt (with the help of their cousin Patrick, the general's son) to regain control of the factory and to stop the manufacture of killer toys, which are really prototypes for new and deadly remote-controlled war weapons.

But *Toys* is not sure what it wants to be. Is it a comedy? A fantasy? A dark satire? In a sense, it is all three, and none of the above.

It's a comedy thanks solely to the genius of Robin Williams. When he gets a chance to be *Robin*, he comes up with some truly funny (and seemingly improvised) lines, including a crack that has significance following Robin's legal problems with Disney over the use of his voice in *Aladdin*. In a scene where Robin's character Leslie is doing market tests for a pair of gigantic toy ears, Robin says, "These ears are so big, we're going to have a legal problem with Disney." He also has a funny moment when he arrives for a meeting wearing a jacket from which smoke is pouting from the pockets. It's a "smoking jacket," of course.

Is *Toys* a fantasy? Yes, because of the sets and the whole-hearted commitment the cast and crew makes to the surrealistic fantasy world the toy factory exists in. In a 1992 interview with Roger Ebert, Robin described *Toys* as "*Willy Wonka* meets *Dr. Strangelove*." He told another interviewer the movie was like "Fisher-Price Meets Fellini," or "Disneyland Designed by Dante." Robin also said the film was like "Dada Meets Magritte." Roger Ebert described the movie as "*The 5,000 Fingers of Dr. T* Meets *L'Avventura*." And indeed, visually, *Toys* is all of that and more. But the fantastic set designs and vibrant colors are not enough to carry the film.

Is *Toys* a dark satire? Yes, because it wants to be like *Dr. Strangelove* and make a statement about war, war toys, and military budgets. But the final confrontation between the new and deadly military toys of Leslie's uncle and the innocent wind-up toys that once belonged to Leslie and Alsatia comes off as too long, too overblown, and ultimately boring.

Toys is worth viewing if only for the visual effects and set designs: They are truly of Academy Award-caliber excellence (although the film's visual design was not nominated) and amazing to watch.

But as an engaging movie with a story that intrigues and entertains, *Toys*, unfortunately, just doesn't play.

WHAT ROBIN HAD TO SAY

During an interview with Jay Leno on *The Tonight Show with Jay Leno* to promote *Jumanji*, Robin talked about being a father and setting an example for his kids. He acknowledged that sometimes it's hard to offer himself as a model: "[My] kids look at [me] and go, 'Hey, you made *Toys*.'"

WHAT THE CRITICS HAD TO SAY

Videohound's Golden Movie Retriever: "Disappointingly earnest comedy...Flat characters; generally falls short by trying too hard to send a message to viewers about the folly of war." (from the 1997 edition)

Tom Cunneff: "This is unlike any film you're ever seen, a *Dr. Strangelove* meets *Willy Wonka and the Chocolate Factory*. Although the movie often misfires, it's heartening that something this bizarre can get made in Hollywood....Although this seems like a perfect role for Williams, he is too subdued." (from a review in *People*, January 11, 1993)

Mrs. Doubtfire

(1993)

Could you make me a woman?

—Daniel to his brother Frank

Mrs. Doubtfire, like *Good Morning, Vietnam*, gives Robin Williams the opportunity to both act *and* perform, a creative context in which his greatest talents can blossom and be spotlighted.

Mrs. Doubtfire is a supreme achievement for Robin, as is his portrayal of the character Mrs. Doubtfire. He successfully creates two completely different personalities and makes them dance, both literally and figuratively.

Mrs. Doubtfire opens with an amazing scene of Robin's character, Daniel Hillard, plying his trade providing the voices for cartoon characters, in this case, a parakeet (Pudgy) and a cat that bear a striking similarity to Tweety Bird and Sylvester the Cat of Looney Tunes fame. Robin (as Daniel playing Pudgy) sings a difficult aria from *The Marriage of Figaro* and does a flawless job with the Italian pronunciation.

Daniel quits, though, when the producers refuse to allow him to veer from the script and insert an antismoking message into the cartoon. When he surprises his kids by meeting them at school, we learn that Daniel losing a job is not that uncommon an occurrence and that he is actually a textbook definition of the word "irresponsible."

So what does Daniel do? Does he contritely call his wife Miranda (Sally Field), a successful and busy interior designer, tell her what happened, and then start looking for another job? No. Instead he throws a wild birthday party in their home for his son Chris, complete with animals from a petting zoo, kids hanging from the chandeliers, and dancing on the dining room table. This is the insane scene Mom comes home to and it is the final insult; the straw that breaks Miranda's back. She tells Daniel she can't take it anymore and she wants a divorce. Daniel pleads with Miranda to go to therapy with him but she has had it with his immature and thoughtless antics and out he goes.

Daniel stays for a while with his gay brother Frank and his partner Jack, both brilliant makeup artists—a necessary plot device, of course, but one that works, thanks to the wonderful performance by Harvey Fierstein as Frank. The way Harvey plays Frank, you completely believe he wouldn't want to be anything but a makeup genius.

A court hearing grants Miranda temporary sole custody of the kids, and the judge gives Daniel ninety days to find a job and establish a stable residence in order for the ruling to be changed to joint custody.

Daniel then meets with his assigned court liaison, Mrs. Sellner, who innocently asks him what he used to do for a living. In a very funny scene, Robin does a series of characters for Mrs. Sellner, but she doesn't even crack a smile. In lightning-quick cuts, Robin as Daniel imitates a preacher, an alien, a man from India, a monster, Groucho Marx, Zeppo Marx, James Bond, a car salesman, Ronald Reagan, Walter Brennan, Humphrey Bogart, an opera singer, and even a hot dog (Robin straightens his spine, keeps his arms tightly by his sides, and reclines in the chair as though he were encased in a giant bun). Mrs. Sellner sits stone-faced through all this and then asks him if he thinks he's funny. "There was a time," a chastened Daniel responds, "when I found myself funny."

Daniel takes a job as a shipping clerk at a local TV station and rents a small apartment. One day, Miranda arrives an hour early to pick up the kids and Daniel notices she's carrying a classified ad. She is looking for a nanny, she tells him, and Daniel surreptitiously changes the phone numbers in the ad so that she won't get any calls. Daniel then calls Miranda as several different applicants for the job, each one of them a major loser.

In his calls, Daniel pretends that he's a singer with the punk band Severe Tire Damage (a real band); Ilsa Immelman, a Swedish transsexual; a hick (who apparently was keeping someone in a cell); a foreigner who can only say, "I am job"; and finally, an elderly English woman named Euphegenia Doubtfire who had previously worked for many years with the Smythe family in England. After the nightmare calls Miranda had been receiving, Mrs. Doubtfire is clearly her dream nanny.

Daniel then enlists the services of Uncle Frank and Aunt Jack, who try several female personas on him, including a Gloria Swanson type, a Cuban with black hair, a Jewish grandmother type, and a Barbra Streisand type, before finally settling on the buxom, matronly version of Mrs. Doubtfire that prompts Frank to comment, "Any closer, you'd be Mom."

Mrs. Doubtfire starts working at the house (after leaving Daniel's day job at the TV station), cooking, cleaning, and watching the kids; it isn't long before she becomes a beloved part of Miranda's household. Miranda, meanwhile, has begun dating a wealthy client of hers, Stu (Pierce Brosnan), and Daniel must stay in character as he watches this guy move in on his family.

Complications develop when Daniel must be present at a birthday dinner party for Miranda as Mrs. Doubtfire, *and* as Daniel at a dinner meeting with his boss to discuss the possibility of his doing a children's show at the TV station—both at the same restaurant at the same time.

Daniel has to do several quick changes in the women's bathroom during that fateful evening and Robin Williams does a terrific job with the physical humor required for these scenes.

Ultimately, Daniel's ruse is revealed and the court rules him unfit and says he can only see his kids in supervised situations. In the meantime, he gets the position at the TV station that he wanted, hosting a children's show as the kindly and knowledgeable Mrs. Doubtfire. One day Miranda visits the studio and tells him that the kids were happier when Mrs. Doubtfire was a part of their lives. She realizes Daniel has changed and she arranges things so that he can be with them for a few hours every day after school—unsupervised.

The performances in *Mrs. Doubtfire* are superior, from Sally Field as the beset-upon yet soft-hearted Miranda, to Harvey Fierstein's flamboyant portrayal of Frank. Pierce Brosnan plays the wealthy British entrepreneur Stu with a nice demeanor of confused dignity; and the kids are all quite believable (especially Lisa Jakub as the eldest girl Lydia—she has down pat that arrogant disdain that teenage girls can wield like a chainsaw).

Mrs. Doubtfire is one of the most important movies Robin Williams made, and it is one of the few in his body of work that effectively utilizes all of his prodigious talents in the same movie.

WHAT THE CRITICS HAD TO SAY

Roger Ebert: "Everyone knows that [Robin] Williams is a mercurial talent who loves to dart in and out of many different characters and voices. But a little of that goes a long way, and already has. There's a scene here, for example, where Williams 'does' a dozen voices for an employment counselor, and the movie stops cold for this vaudeville act, just as the Marx Brothers movies always paused for Harpo's instrumental solos. Any review of *Mrs. Doubtfire* must take into account Dustin Hoffman's transvestite comedy, *Tootsie*, which remains by far the better film: more believable, more intelligent and funnier....Williams, who is also a good actor, seems more to be playing himself playing a woman." (from his *Movie Home Companion*)

Mick Martin and Marsha Porter: "Robin Williams is a howl..." (from their *Video Movie Guide*)

Videohound's Golden Movie Retriever: "Williams schtick extraordinaire with more than a little sugary sentimentality." (from the 1997 edition)

Being Human

(1994)

This is the story of a story. Once upon a time, there was this story,
and the story said to itself, "How shall I begin?"

—Opening narration

Being Human is an important film, if not a total success, simply
because of its far-reaching insights and unique and honest narrative voice. That said, there is no denying that *Being Human* is one
strange little movie.

Being Human, which is narrated by actress Theresa Russell as
the all-knowing "Storyteller," tackles enormous themes, including
the true meaning of identity and the search for self; slavery and
the master/slave paradigm; the concept of karma; the theory of
reincarnation; the impact of fear on a person's code of conduct;
and the impact of divorce on children in a modern, industrialized
world. Any *one* of these themes would be enough to be the focus
of a film.

Being Human explores colossal themes, and this ambitious
scope is surely what must have attracted Robin Williams to the
film and convinced him to participate.

In *Being Human*, Robin plays five separate roles, all of whom are named Hector, and all of whom are reincarnations of the same soul.

The wraparound story that begins and ends the film is about a divorced, ex-con father who is seeing his two children for the first time in years.

Robin plays this incarnation with sensitivity and is very effective at communicating the heartfelt pain and guilt his character is feeling about neglecting his children during the years they were growing up. Hector is literally overwhelmed by his teenage daughter, a pretty young girl who is so poised, so confident, and so smart, that Hector spends much of his time with her awed by her presence and wondering just where the hell she came from.

Hector's son, the youngest child, has not reached that state of ironic, contemptuous disdain towards his father that his sister has achieved and still remembers back to when Hector used to hug him so hard he couldn't breathe.

The two kids and their dad reach an understanding on a moonlit beach one night and the movie ends with the soul that is Hector finally learning from his past and making an obvious breakthrough to a higher plane of consciousness.

Throughout *Being Human*, we learn that in each of Hector's incarnations he has been a slave.

The first Hector is a prehistoric man who lives in a mountain cave with his mate and their two young children. This Hector is a slave to many things. He is a slave to his environment, a harsh landscape from which he must glean enough food each day to feed his family. He is a slave to fear, because he never knows when his children may be killed by wild animals or his wife sickened by bad food or water. And he is a slave to the strangers who come one day in boats and simply take, for their own, his woman and his children. Hector, knowing he cannot fight all of these men with their bows and clubs, makes a halfhearted attempt at holding on to what is his by screaming "Mine!" at the departing boats, but it doesn't do any good. We see that Hector is either a coward or a pragmatist, and we ultimately realize the truth is that he is equal parts of both.

Hector's next incarnation is as a slave in ancient Rome. Hector's master, Lucinnius (John Turturro), has been ordered to die to settle a debt that he cannot pay. Lucinnius has reluctantly agreed to this sentence and orders Hector to kill himself and accompany him into the next world. Hector is horrified by this command but agrees to help his master kill himself and then to commit suicide immediately after. Hector, who is in love with one of the household's slave girls, recants on his promise, however, and as soon as Lucinnius is dead, takes his master's shoes and flees with his lover Thalia.

It seems that in this incarnation, Hector's soul has evolved somewhat and has found an inner source of bravery and a desire for self-preservation. As a Roman slave, Hector was bound to his master, but in the end, he is the one who achieves true freedom—not the faux freedom of death pathetically embraced by his former master, a man who obviously could not find the courage to fight for his own life.

Hector's next incarnation is as a nomad of the Middle Ages, traveling by wagon and on foot across Europe. This segment, the narrator tells us, is a love story, and the object of Hector's affection, even though he is married, is an Italian beauty named Beatrice. Hector and Beatrice break off from their fellow travelers and Hector accompanies Beatrice to her home, where it is obvious that he is welcome to remain as her lover and companion if he so desires.

Hector briefly revels in the comforts of a home and family, but ultimately leaves Beatrice and continues on with his travels, his sights set on his own home and family, still a great distance away. This Hector seems to have learned devotion and commitment and has acquired the moral strength to renounce temporary happiness for the more permanent and lasting joys of his own wife and family.

Hector's last, pre-modern reincarnation is as a shipwrecked New World voyager who is in love with Ursula, a woman who wants nothing to do with him. He and his fellow passengers are stranded on an island and must find food and water or perish. Hector's soul seems to have backslid a bit in this incarnation: He hoards food and wine from the others and tries to steal Ursula away from her lover. This segment concludes with Hector leaving for Lisbon and accepting that he will never possess Ursula.

Being Human then travels to New York in the present time and we meet up with the latest Hector. He has legal (and possibly criminal) problems with an apartment building he owns in which the floor collapsed. He frantically tries to tie things up so he can go pick up his kids for a very important weekend. He borrows his girlfriend's flower delivery car and they all ultimately end up at the beach, where *this* Hector uses the lessons of the past to heal some old wounds and reestablish his relationship with his children.

Being Human is ambitious and well-conceived, but there are too many sluggish spots and, for short-attention span viewers, not enough "in-your-face" explanation of the complex and layered themes running throughout the film.

Nevertheless, this movie must be counted as one of Robin Williams's most important films, simply because it is a daring and unexpected artistic choice from the guy who did *Good Morning, Vietnam* and *Popeye*.

Robin Williams deserves kudos for not falling into the trap of giving his fans and his audience (only) what they expect. That willingness to take creative risks is the mark of the true artist.

The 1983 film, *Local Hero*, is a wonderfully quirky, very original movie about the denizens of a small Scottish fishing town who are suddenly faced with the rather attractive problem of being offered huge amounts of money to sell their properties to an oil company seeking to build in the exact location of their town.

Local Hero was written and directed by Bill Forsyth, as was the subject of this chapter, the film *Being Human*; unfortunately, *Being Human* is not the classic *Local Hero* is, nor is there the likelihood that it will become a cult favorite in the years to come, as has *Local Hero*.

WHAT THE CRITICS HAD TO SAY

Mick Martin and Marsha Porter: "Ambitious comedy drama promises more than it delivers....One of Williams's periodic chancy ventures away from his comedic roots occasionally strikes gold, but often seems overly restrained." (from their *Video Movie Guide*)

Videohound's Golden Movie Retriever: "Writer-director Bill Forsyth's big-screen meditation on the plight of unexceptional men is neither funny (as were his earlier films) nor very dramatic." (from the 1997 edition)

Nine Months

(1995)

You want Anastasia?

—Dr. Kosevich (Robin Williams), asking
Rebecca (Julianne Moore), in active labor,
if she wants anesthesia

Robin Williams appears in *Nine Months* for all of thirteen minutes out of the film's 103 minutes, yet his moments are among the funniest scenes in the movie.

In terms of getting laughs, buffoonish Tom Arnold (as Marty) comes second, followed by his wife Gail (Joan Cusack); the two stars of the film, Hugh Grant and Julianne Moore, are not that funny in *Nine Months*.

Isn't it amazing (to borrow one of Robin's favorite words) that Robin is such a phenomenal comic genius that he can steal a movie from its leads—while appearing in about ten percent of the film's scenes—and (this is the best part) while improvising most of his dialogue with brilliant abandon?

Rebecca (Julianne Moore) and Samuel (Hugh Grant) are a loving, yuppie-type couple who have reached a point in their relationship familiar to many: She wants to get married and have kids, he wants no part of either. But Rebecca gets pregnant accidentally and even though Samuel freaks out, he is initially supportive and accompanies her to her obstetrician for her first visit.

Enter Robin Williams.

Robin plays Dr. Kosevich, a Russian doctor who previously worked mainly with animals as a medical researcher in Leningrad. (It wouldn't be a surprise if Robin had the choice of which nationality to make his character and chose Russian because he had hit such a home run when he played Vladimir Ivanoff in *Moscow on the Hudson*. Just a guess, but it makes sense.)

Rebecca and Samuel get Dr. Kosevich because the doctor they were originally referred to was away. They agree to use Kosevich without knowing anything about him.

Robin's first scene in *Nine Months* begins when Rebecca and Samuel enter his office and find him talking on the phone in Russian to his mother back in Leningrad.

"If it's not one thing, it's your mother!" he tells them when he hangs up the phone, and their first visit with the good doctor begins.

Kosevich introduces himself and tells them that in Russia, he was Chief of "Obstruction," no, he meant "Abstraction," no, "Obstetrics!", and that he has just received his license to practice medicine in the United States.

Dr. Kosevich then asks Rebecca what was the date of her last menopause. He, of course, means menstruation, and when Rebecca asks, "Period?", Kosevich replies, "End of sentence!" He tells them he has written a computer program that will give them an exact due date for their baby.

The due date is December 8th and the date of conception was March 17th. Samuel goes ballistic: He is not the father, he exclaims. He was away on the seventeenth. Rebecca insists that the doctor check the computer again and a flustered and panicking

Dr. Kosevich realizes that he had used the computer program for *simians*, instead of humans, and that her correct due date is actually December 15th, with a conception date of March 23rd. During his attempt to uncover his error, Dr. Kosevich whines and whimpers and shouts that he could not take the pressure as he bangs the computer keyboard trying to determine the right answer. This is "feces flying into the fan," he tells them, but then calms down when they accept his new dates. This is a very funny scene, and Robin plays it perfectly.

Dr. Kosevich then informs them that it is now time for the physical exam and tells Rebecca, "Let's go take a look at your Volvo." He will even warm his hands for her, he tells them.

He escorts them into the exam room and tells Rebecca, "Take off your clothes and get undressed." He then proceeds to "adjust" the stirrups table by making the top half fly up and slam down, and after it stops going crazy, he tells them "Okay, I think we've worked out all the insects!"

At this point, Rebecca and Samuel have had enough and they flee his office in terror.

The scene then shifts to the hallway where they run into Tom Arnold and Joan Cusack's characters, friends of theirs who absolutely *revel* in parenthood. Samuel and Rebecca hide the fact that they were seeing an obstetrician, but the truth is revealed when Dr. Kosevich comes running out with Rebecca's pocketbook and tells her, "You have a small pussy." He has seen cat hair on her purse and he tells them that they have to get rid of Samuel's cat because Rebecca is pregnant.

The rest of the movie focuses on Rebecca and Samuel's relationship—or temporary lack of one. Rebecca leaves him after he forgets to show up for her first ultrasound. Samuel ultimately realizes how foolish he is acting and they finally get back together.

Robin appears again at the end of the film when both Rebecca and Gail go into labor at the same time. Even though they had dumped him, Rebecca and Samuel end up with Dr. Kosevich because their doctor is once again away and the hospital is extremely crowded and busy when they arrive. The two women end up giving birth in the same delivery room, and both babies are delivered by Dr. Kosevich. (Samuel and Rebecca's son is his very first delivery—guess he wasn't Head of Obstetrics in Russia, right?)

The delivery room scenes are the funniest in the movie. Robin is marvelous. He tells Rebecca to get up on the table, "immediately if not later," and then shows her what seven centimeters dilation looks like by spreading open his mouth with his fingers.

He then asks her if she wants "Anastasia." When Samuel badgers him about whether or not he actually knows what he's doing, he screams, "Shut up, you limey prick!" and asks for Valium for himself.

Dr. Kosevich then orders five things for Rebecca: An enema, a pedicure, an epitaph, an epidermis, and an EpiLady. Rebecca is finally the one who screams, "Epidural, asshole!"

Kosevich apologizes and tells them that he wants to buy a clitoris (he means thesaurus, of course).

At this point, the anesthesiologist arrives with a gigantic needle to give Rebecca her epidural. Robin then does the funniest bit of business in the movie: He is flamboyantly explaining to Samuel the biological imperative in having women give birth when he suddenly sees the anesthesiologist's needle. "That is why women have the babies," he expounds. "Because men can't handle the paaaaaaaaaa…" at which point he passes out on the floor.

He comes to in time, though, and delivers Marty and Gail's daughter, as well as Rebecca and Samuel's son.

Robin gets off a couple of terrific one-liners after the babies' births. First, he tells Joan Cusack and Tom Arnold's characters, "You have a girl—unless I cut the wrong cord!" And then he tells Rebecca and Samuel that their son is very handsome, and that "He has very big testicles, too!," to which Samuel replies, "Yes, well, he would have!"

Nine Months is definitely worth watching if you're a Robin Williams fan. He isn't in it very much, but when Robin is as good as he is in this film (he improvised most of his lines), a little Robin goes a long, long way!

WHAT THE CRITICS HAD TO SAY

Roger Ebert: "One of those movies where the outcome is abundantly clear to everyone but the hero, who remains in the hapless position of playing dumb, because if he didn't, there wouldn't be a plot." (from his *Movie Home Companion*)

Videohound's Golden Movie Retriever: "Williams [offers] his usual manic flair as a Russian obstetrician…[*Nine Months*] doesn't go out on any limbs, but is a pleasant diversion anyway." (from the 1997 edition)

To Wong Foo, Thanks for Everything! Julie Newmar

(1995)

How Three Sisters! How Chekov!

—John Jacob Jingleheimer Schmidt upon
hearing that three drag queens are driving to
Hollywood together

Robin Williams has a funny, two-minute scene in *To Wong Foo*, appearing as a multilingual, slick-as-silk booking agent who gives Vida (Patrick Swayze), Chi-Chi (John Leguizamo), and Noxeema (Wesley Snipes) cash for their two prize airline tickets and turns them on to a car dealership where, if they mention his name, any car on the lot is fifty bucks.

Robin appears at fourteen minutes into the movie wearing a sport jacket, a gigantic medallion, and an improbable, blue, beaded hat with what looks like a satin brim.

He visits the restaurant where the three drag queens have just made a triumphant entrance and tells Vida (in Italian) she is beautiful and kisses her hand. Vida responds with "*Enchanté*," to which Robin replies, "Oh, you spoke French! How *bi*!"

He then slides into their booth next to Chi-Chi, calling her his "little piñata." After basking in their assembled drag queen glory, Robin gushes, "Look at you! I'm like a compass near north!"

The "ladies" then tell him that they're all going to Hollywood together and Robin says, "How *Three Sisters*! How Chekov! That's fabulous!"

After they all agree to drive cross-country, Robin gives them a card: "Crazy Elijah: My Cars Are My Children." Chi-Chi tells him he's a lifesaver, to which Robin replies, "All day sucker!"

Robin then snaps his fingers and leaves.

Robin's character of John Jacob Jingleheimer Schmidt could justifiably be regarded as a distant cousin of his refined and elegant Armand Goldman character in *The Birdcage*. Here, though, he plays it a little over the top, but considering the rest of the cast, his is probably the most restrained performance in the film.

The remainder of the film tells the story of the three "girls'" trip to Hollywood. They get stranded in the small town of Snydersville where their infectious gaiety (sorry), flamboyant style, and no-nonsense attitudes transform the townsfolk from drab, bored, hopeless hicks into fashionable, hip, exuberant party animals.

To Wong Foo is entertaining and a lot of fun. The three leads—Swayze, Leguizamo, and Snipes—are great.

WHAT THE CRITICS HAD TO SAY

Roger Ebert: "I cannot be quite certain, but I believe *To Wong Foo, Thanks for Everything! Julie Newmar* is the first movie about drag queens to be rated PG-13. And it earns that PG-13 rating by being so relentlessly upbeat, wholesome, and asexual that you walk out of the theater thinking of the queens as role models;

every small town should be as lucky as Snydersville, and have its values transformed by them….It's amazing how entertaining it is in places, considering how amateurish the screenplay is and how awkwardly the elements of the story are cobbled together. I feel like recommending the performances, and suggesting they be ported over to another film. The actors emerge with glory, for attempting something very hard, and succeeding remarkably well. They deserve to be in a better movie." (from his *Movie Home Companion*)

Videohound's Golden Movie Retriever: "Hot on the high heels of *The Adventures of Priscilla, Queen of the Desert* comes the sanitized for your protection Yankee version. And it's all about hanging on to your dreams, and how we're all the same inside, with politically correct gay drag queens doing the sermonizing….One-dimensional characters, flat direction, and inconsistent script undercut exceptional performances by Swayze and Leguizamo." (from the 1997 edition)

Peter Travers: "In her features (*Antonia* and *Jane*) and documentaries (*Hookers, Hustlers, Pimps and Their Johns*), [director Beeban] Kidron finds the quiet spaces that help define characters. Although these faux girls are rarely quiet, Kidron at least sees to it that they don't turn into butts for straight jokes or grotesque parodies of women." (from *Rolling Stone*, September 21, 1995)

Jumanji

(1995)

A game for those who seek to find a way to leave their world behind. You roll the dice to move your token; doubles gets another turn. The first player to reach the end wins.

—The "Jumanji" instructions

Beginning with a forest scene that visually alludes to the opening sequence of *ET: The Extraterrestrial*, Robin Williams's 1995 fantasy adventure film *Jumanji* is a thrilling story of horrible, impossible creatures sent to our earthly realm by a supernatural game with a distinctly nasty personality and a vicious sense of humor. Yet *Jumanji* is, at the same time, a touching and emotional tale of childhood and lost innocence.

Jumanji begins in Brantford, New Hampshire, in 1869 with two young boys burying the Jumanji game. They are obviously terrified of the game and glad to be rid of it.

The scene then shifts to Brantford one hundred years later. It is now 1969, and Alan Parrish, the timid young son of a successful shoe manufacturer, hears the drums sounds that the game sends out (but that only certain people can hear). He pulls the game out of the ground at a construction site near his father's factory.

When he opens the game, the pieces fly into place by themselves. He begins playing the game with Sarah (Bonnie Hunt), a girl from his school who has just brought his bike back after it was taken by her bully boyfriend. The two find that the game presents them with a riddle—the words swirling into sight (reminding viewers of the ubiquitous Magic 8 Ball toy)—after each roll of the dice.

The first riddle reads "At night they fly, you better run, these winged things are not much fun." This is immediately followed by squeaky sounds coming from the fireplace. The clock chimes and a frightened Alan accidentally drops his dice, causing the next riddle to appear: "In the jungle you must wait, until the dice read five or eight." To Sarah's horror, Alan is then sucked into the center of the game. Sarah is attacked by swarms of vicious bats and she flees the house in terror.

Jumanji then jumps ahead twenty-six years.

Judy (Kirsten Dunst) and Peter (Bradley Pierce), two sweet kids who recently lost their parents in a skiing accident, are moving into the Parrish house with their new guardian, Aunt Nora (Bebe Neuwirth). Healthy these kids are not: Judy is a compulsive liar, and Peter hasn't spoken a word since the death of their parents. The kids are soon told something unsettling by the exterminator brought in to get rid of the bats (uh oh) in the attic. He tells them that the rumor around town is that Alan Parrish was murdered by his father in this very house and his body was cut up in pieces and hidden in the walls.

Following this alarming and frightening news, it isn't long before Judy and Peter hear the ominous Jumanji drums and find the old game hidden away in the attic. When they open the game, the pieces (Sarah and Alan's from the past, remember) are still in place and cannot be budged. Peter then adds two new game pieces. Judy rolls a six and is presented with the riddle, "A tiny bite can make you itch, make you sneeze, make you twitch."

Judy and Peter are then attacked by giant mosquitoes, which Judy fights off with a tennis racket. Peter then rolls a two and is told, "This will not be an easy mission, monkeys slow the expedition." The two astonished siblings then hear noises in the kitchen being made by hordes of vicious monkeys that trash the kitchen and hurl knives at them when they investigate. Peter rolls again ("doubles gets another turn") and throws the all-important five. His riddle reads, "Its fangs are sharp. He likes your taste. Your party better move post haste." A giant lion appears and chases them, but, out of nowhere, a bearded jungle man clad in leaves and skins appears and fends off the lion.

This jungle man is none other than the long-lost Alan Parrish (played by Robin Williams) who has been "waiting" in the jungle for the past twenty-six years. Peter's roll of a five rescues Alan from his Jumanji-caused imprisonment.

Alan is ecstatic to be back, but at first does not realize that his parents are dead and that he did not return to the time that he left. He runs through the town and finds a poor, rundown shadow of the bright and friendly hamlet he left as a kid. Robin Williams is very good in these scenes and we can feel his sorrow as he realizes that everything and everyone he knew and loved is gone. His family's shoe factory is abandoned and a refuge for the homeless. He learns that his father exhausted his entire fortune trying to find him after he disappeared in 1969.

A dejected Alan returns to his old family and cleans himself up (while singing the theme from *Gilligan's Island*). Judy and Peter try to persuade him to finish the game, and he eventually agrees, but then realizes that they are all playing the game that he and Sarah started back in 1969, and in order to complete it, Sarah has to resume playing as well. The three of them go visit the emotionally scarred Sarah (now making a living as a psychic named Madame Serena) and persuade her that the only way to be free from the terror of the past is to finish the game they started those many years ago.

Sarah finally gives in and the rest of the movie recounts the adventures the four of them have to survive (not an easy task) in order to finish the game and be free of its hold.

Jumanji is one of Robin Williams's most enjoyable films and, again, the *Good Morning, Vietnam* and Genie identity are nowhere to be found, proving once again Robin's facility at creating realistic characters that are clearly separate of his stand-up persona.

WHAT ROBIN HAD TO SAY

"You basically run down the hall and things start breaking apart and…there's a Teamster with a little 'X' going 'I'm the rhino.'" (*The Tonight Show with Jay Leno*, 1995)

"There's a scene in the movie where [I] wrestle a crocodile. And there's things in the movie—part of them are computer effects and the rest are animatronics, which means they're like Muppets on steroids. I was wrestling this crocodile and I pounded it on the head and all of a sudden from inside I hear, 'Hey!' There was this guy going, 'Hey man, it's me! It's Jim! Cut the overacting man, man! It's hot in here! I just had a burrito! Don't do that!'" (*The Tonight Show with Jay Leno*, 1995)

"I hope to show it to my kids. I mean, my four-year-old enjoyed *Pulp Fiction*." (*The Tonight Show with Jay Leno*, 1995)

WHAT THE CRITICS HAD TO SAY

Roger Ebert: "The underlying structure of the film seems inspired by—or limited by—interactive video games. There is little attempt to construct a coherent story. Instead, the characters face one threat after another, as new and grotesque dangers jump at them. It's like those video games where you achieve one level after another by killing and not getting killed. The ultimate level for young viewers will be being able to sit all the way through the movie." (from his *Movie Home Companion*)

Videohound's Golden Movie Retriever: "[R]elies too much heavily on cutting-edge special effects to make up for a thin story. Many of the creatures and effects are utterly too bizarre and unsettling for younger audiences." (from the 1997 edition)

The Birdcage

(1996)

I'm the only guy in my fraternity who doesn't come from a broken home.

—**Armand's son, Val**

It looks like young men playing leapfrog.

—**Conservative Senator Keeley's wife Louise,
upon seeing Armand and Albert's China pattern**

There is precisely one scene in *The Birdcage* in which Robin Williams lets loose: Exactly once do we experience the full force of the comedic genius who can, in an instant, transform himself into everyone (and everything) from Jack Nicholson to an unsuccessful sperm cell battling an unyielding diaphragm.

Robin's character, Armand, is directing his life partner, Albert, in a rehearsal of a new song he has just written (actually a song by Stephen Sondheim) for their very successful and extremely popular drag show in Armand's south Florida club, The Birdcage.

The (not too bright) young man who is playing Albert's love interest in the scene is confused about the meaning of the song and asks if he should "feel" anything. Armand tells the dancer that

117

he can go right ahead and "feel"…Bob Fosse, Martha Graham, Twyla Tharp, Michael Kidd, and Madonna—and Armand explains his artistic suggestions by bounding all over the stage and performing mini-versions of these brilliant choreographers' dance styles, complete with flawless reconstructions of their trademark leg and arm routines. Armand concludes his direction by telling the young man to feel all of this *inside*, however. This is a hilarious scene, and the one that the producers wisely chose to use in all the TV commercials for the movie—even though it does mislead somewhat by suggesting that Robin is as wacky as this throughout the entire movie, something that he is most assuredly *not*.

The Birdcage (a remake of the very popular and successful 1978 French farce *La Cage Aux Folles*) opens with an amazing camera shot that begins out over the water, speeds onto the beach, and then glides right into Armand's drag club, The Birdcage, where the "We Are Family" production number is being performed.

The first time we see Robin Williams as Armand, he is strolling through his club, resplendent in silk and gold, kissing favored patrons and checking in on the kitchen help. The next number coming up features the club's headliner, Starina, a flamboyant female raconteur and vocalist who is played by Armand's partner, Albert (Nathan Lane). But Starina, Armand learns, refuses to perform. She is throwing a tantrum. Armand must placate her and convince her to go on, which she eventually does.

While Starina is performing, Armand meets with his twenty-year-old son, Val (Dan Futterman), who was raised by him and Albert. Val gives his father some earthshaking news: He is getting married, and his fiancée's father just so happens to be Senator Keeley (Gene Hackman), a right-wing conservative who is the co-founder of the Coalition of Moral Order—a man who believes that the Pope is too controversial and that Billy Graham and Bob Dole are too liberal.

Val wants his father to meet his future in-laws, but he does not want them to know the truth about Armand's lifestyle, and he especially does not want them to know the truth about "Auntie Albert." Val and his fiancée, Barbara (Calista Flockhart), have told her parents that Val's dad is a Cultural Attaché to Greece and that Val's mother is a housewife.

At first, Armand angrily resists his son's request to act straight and tone down the apartment, but ultimately he consents to the charade and agrees to send Albert away for a few days while the Senator and his wife (Dianne Wiest) are in town.

Upon hearing of the plan to send him away, Albert goes into histrionics and tells Armand that his heart is breaking over this terrible rejection. Armand relents and decides to try and pass Albert off as Val's "Uncle Albert."

In the meantime, Armand and Val also decide to enlist the help of Val's mother (Christine Baranski), a successful businesswoman who has not seen her son in twenty years.

The last half hour or so of the movie is the dinner party at Armand's apartment, a comedy of confusion and errors during which Albert appears in drag as Val's mother (looking very "Mrs. Doubtfire"-ish!); Val's real mother arrives; and Armand and Albert's gay Guatemalan house servant Agador (played dazzlingly by Hank Azaria) serves them some strange soup that he just "made up" after revealing to Armand that he has not prepared an entrée.

There is also a subplot in the film involving Senator Keeley's coalition co-founder Senator Jackson, who is found dead in the bed of an underage black hooker. When interviewed about the death on a "CNN"-like station, the young lady said, "Well, he looked kind of funny, but he was smiling so I didn't worry," which, of course, becomes the definitive sound bite for the scandal. This development sets the media on the trail of Keeley and his family and acts as the catalyst for the final sequence in which (1) Val and

Barbara reveal the truth to her parents; (2) the media is camped outside The Birdcage waiting for the Senator to emerge; and (3) Albert and Armand facilitate the Senator's escape by dressing him in drag and turning him into what one woman describes as "the ugliest woman I've ever seen in my life."

Robin Williams's performance in *The Birdcage* is one of the finest of his career. He plays this "middle-aged fag" (which is the way he describes himself to his son in the movie) with a dignity and *gravitas* that perfectly complements the incredibly outrageous *tour de force* performance of Nathan Lane. And aside from the scene described earlier in which he wildly imitates the choreographers (something one might not expect the usually very subdued Armand to do), there isn't a moment when his portrayal of fifty-year-old gay Armand does not ring true.

The remainder of the cast is, likewise, superb. Nathan Lane plays Albert like a swishy, flaming queen. Some have suggested that his performance validates a stereotype but, let's face it, there *are* incredibly effeminate gay drag queens in the homosexual community and Nathan acknowledges their mannerisms and predilections with his performance, but never demeans or degrades them for a moment.

It is clear that Lane—and the entire cast and crew for that matter—approached this project with respect and good humor and affection for the people they are playing, and this regard shows in every scene of the movie. We come away from *The Birdcage* liking these people—*a lot*.

It is not an exaggeration to state that *The Birdcage* is one of the funniest comedies of all time. The writing is sharp; the directing, inventive; the performances, Oscar-caliber. And it was a mainstream hit at the box office as well. A movie about gay drag queens turning into one of the most successful movies of all time. Who'd've figured?

WHAT ROBIN HAD TO SAY

On his spontaneous "explosion" of dancing during Albert's rehearsal: "It just came about. Armand's this choreographer. It came out in rehearsal one day....It wasn't difficult because Mike [Nichols] always let us try things. Nathan and I would go off and do strange and wonderful things....When you improvise something, it all comes into place...Always great to do that Martha Graham. Twyla is great because you can fling your head around. You get that lovely whiplash." (from *The New York Times*, March 31, 1996)

WHAT THE CRITICS HAD TO SAY

Roger Ebert: "The first time Mike Nichols and Elaine May, who helped define improvisational comedy in the 1950s, have worked together on a movie. What mostly sparkles from their work here is the dialogue, as when the senator's daughter, trying to cast the situation in the best possible light, explains that South Beach is 'about two minutes from Fisher Island, where Jed Bush lives.'" (from his *Movie Home Companion*)

Videohound's Golden Movie Retriever: "Somewhat overlong but well-played remake." (from the 1997 edition)

Jack
(1996)

I just want to be a regular star.

—Jack

Despite scathing critical reviews, *Jack* was the number one film its opening weekend of August 9, 1996, proving two things: that fans don't always listen to critics, and that Robin Williams could unquestionably "open" a film. Reuter's news service spelled it out the following week:

> Once again movie audiences defied the critics and flocked to see a film that received a lukewarm reception from the experts. The Francis Ford Coppola-directed Robin Williams movie *Jack* opened at the top of the box-office chart this weekend. It earned an estimated $11.3 million. A *Variety* poll of critics in major cities showed that nine liked Jack, twenty did not, and seventeen were mixed.

Some of the reviews were so negative they bordered on the ridiculous. One especially hysterical review was by the *Today Show's* Gene Shalit, who was apoplectic and personally offended by *Jack*. Shalit's overreaction and verbal histrionics (often unnecessarily hyperbolic) diminished him. Shalit hated *Jack* so much that if he employed a rating system for his reviews (which he does not), he would have given it zero stars out of four.

Granted, *Jack* has its share of problems. But the film is also heads above some of the other dreck that is released each year to better reviews than Shalit (and others) gave *Jack*.

Jack tells the story of a boy who is born with a rare disease that causes him to age physically at four times the normal rate. He is born after only ten weeks in the womb and by the time he is ten, he looks like a forty-year-old man.

For his entire first decade, Jack's overprotective mother (Francis Ford Coppola fave Diane Lane) and resigned father (Brian Kerwin) keep him at home and have him tutored by Mr. Woodruff (Bill Cosby), a kindly and intuitive man who provides the voice of reason that finally convinces them that Jack needs to go to school with other kids (some of the funny moments in these "housebound" scenes include Jack throwing a gooey eyeball at the taunting neighborhood kids and snoring while sleeping between his parents).

From here, the film moves on to Jack's first days at school, his acceptance by a group of his classmates after they realize he's tall enough to be a terrific basketball center, and his immediate infatuation with his teacher, Miss Marquez (Jennifer Lopez). Okay, there are two (exactly one too many) broken desk gags where a too-big Robin squeezes into a tiny desk, tips over, and ends up on the floor.

But it must be acknowledged that Robin Williams's talent is such that he immediately transmutes his physical appearance with his performance, completely convincing us that there is, indeed, a ten-year-old boy living inside a hairy forty-year-old body.

Ten-year-old minds working the way they work, it isn't long before one of Jack's new friends persuades him to impersonate the principal when his mother comes to visit the school because of his own misbehavior. Jack pretends he's the school principal and is convincing enough that the boy's mother, Dolores Durante (Fran Drescher) actually makes a pass at him and slips him her phone number. This is a very funny scene, especially when Jack sticks his hands under his jersey and makes fake breasts while gawking at Dolores's cleavage in the kind of juvenile way only boys that age can get away with.

There follows a few gross farting and eating scenes and a lame collapsing tree house sequence that the film could have done without, but these don't really detract from the main story, which is Jack's increasing realization that his time is limited and that he may not live to see twenty. This new awareness is effectively and poignantly illustrated in a scene where Jack and his classmates are instructed to write an essay about what they want to be when they grow up. As one little girl talks about her dreams, we see Jack multiplying twenty-eight times four and circling the result: one hundred and twelve.

Jack withdraws from school after an angina attack caused by this sudden profound understanding of his lot in life, and it is weeks before he can be convinced (with a great deal of help from Mr. Woodruff and Jack's entire class) to come back.

There are a few noticeable "Robin Williams" moments in *Jack*. One is when he does a goatee joke and says, sheeplike, "That would be baaaad!" a line he's used often in his comedy, and the other is a Dr. Kevorkian joke that is too adult for it to have genuinely come from a ten-year-old.

Also unsettling is the scene in which Jack goes to the bar where Fran Drescher hangs out and he gets drunk. The scenes in which Jack talks about impotence and divorce with Michael McKean do not work and the eventual bar fight that ends with Jack in jail derail the pace of the film and detract from its gentler tone.

There are also a couple of noticeable plot holes, one of which is, if everyone in town knows about Jack and his condition, why doesn't Dolores?

The film ends with an epilogue that takes place seven years later at Jack's high school graduation. Jack is now physically sixty-eight years old and he gives a mawkish valedictorian address that concludes with him riding off for a night of partying with his seventeen- and eighteen-year-old friends.

Jack is yet another example of Robin Williams stretching as an actor, and for the most part, he gives an effective and sadly moving performance.

WHAT ROBIN HAD TO SAY

"I could relate to Jack's desire to be with other children because I also lived in a big house on a lot of land, but way away from everybody else. I would come home and there were no brothers or sisters. It was lonely. It was stimulating in the sense that I had a lot of toys, or whatever. But there is that need for contact, the good and the bad of it." (from an interview in *The Boston Globe*, August 9, 1996)

"This is the last one. This is the ultimate one. This is the metaphor gone beyond the hyperbole into simile. I can't do it anymore after this. I'm 45. This is way beyond the Peter Pan syndrome." (from *TV Guide*, August 3, 1996)

WHAT THE CRITICS HAD TO SAY

Roger Ebert: "Williams works hard at seeming to be a kid inside a grown-up's body, and some of his inspirations work well. But he has been ill-served by a screenplay that isn't curious about what his life would *really* be like." (from his *Movie Home Companion*)

Tom Gliatto: "Williams moves through the film very lightly, never overdoing the physical comedy of a giant squeezing in among other schoolchildren, not milking the pathos of a boy who has to touch up his graying, thinning hair. Williams himself seems to have grown into an unexpectedly soulful actor." (from a review in *People*, August 12, 1996)

Richard Schickel: "One is left wondering why Williams has granted early retirement to his inner anarchist, what dark need compels a great clown to become a sad, fuzzy one in movies only Bob Dole—faking it—could love." (from a review in *TIME*, August 12, 1996)

Variety: "Something of a companion piece for Coppola to *Peggy Sue Got Married* in the mild, gentle way it deals with a fantastical 'what if' situation, this new effort has just one thing to say and says it with no sense of surprise or drama. Blandness and lack of daring characterize nearly every minute of the very long two hours, which are marked by a high degree of professionalism at the service of little content." (July 29, 1996)

Aladdin and the King of Thieves

(1996)

I was having an out-of-movie experience.

**—Genie, during his transformation into
Pumbaa, the warthog from *The Lion King***

Robin Williams did not perform the role of Genie in the second film of the *Aladdin* series, *The Return of Jafar*, because of contract problems with Disney.

He returned for this third installment, however, and, once again, scored enormously with his freewheeling, free-associating portrayal of the always-blue Genie.

The third chapter of Aladdin and Jasmine's story features the much-anticipated wedding of the two young lovers. It also tells the story of Aladdin's dangerous and exciting search for his long-lost father, a quest that leads him right into the deadly hidden den of the foreboding King of Thieves.

But it is Genie who interests us as Robin Williams fans and here is a rundown of the almost ninety character transformations Genie makes during the film (he outdid himself this time!).

1. An entire caravan entering Agrabah

2. A princess

3. A pixie

4. A tuxedoed emcee

5. A bride in a wedding gown

6. An Italian manicurist

7. A white-haired evangelist

8. An earring

9. Ethel Merman

10. A French painter

11. Fred Astaire

12. A rabbi

13. A giant exploding pig

14. Rocky (as played by Sylvester Stallone)

15. Groucho Marx

16. A street kid with his hat on backwards

17. A truck filled with flowers

18. A surfer-dude parking valet

19. A woman

20. A maître d'

21. A harem girl bursting out of a cake

22. Woody Allen

23. A pair of talking bunny slippers

24. A radio talk show host

25. A clock

26. A tailor

27. A cameraman

28. An entire choir

29. James Brown

30. A reporter for *Lifestyles of the Rich and Magical*

31. Jack Nicholson

32. The rabbit from *Alice's Adventures in Wonderland*

33. A beefeater-type guard

34. A cowboy

35. An entire army of samurai warriors

36. Forrest Gump

37. A pot-bellied construction worker

38. Rain Man (as played by Dustin Hoffman)

39. Mrs. Doubtfire (as played by…well, you know)

40. Harpo Marx

41. Zeppo Marx

42. Groucho Marx

43. An effeminate wedding planner

44. Elvis (or an Elvis impersonator, depending on your interpretation)

45. A fashion show emcee

46. Several yuppie marketing guys

47. Bing Crosby

48. Bob Hope

49. Robocop

50. An entire armed SWAT Team

51. A troupe of Scottish bagpipers

52. A cavalry

53. A team of paratroopers

54. Pocahontas

55. A waiter

56. A fortuneteller

57. Several constellations

58. A necktie

59. A fisherman riding on the back of a fish

60. Louis Armstrong

61. A football referee

62. Albert Einstein

63. The planet Saturn

64. A Jetson

65. A tree

66. A grumpy old Grandpa

67. Triplets

68. A basketball

69. Shaquille O'Neal

70. A pair of bumper cars

71. A stewardess

72. Don Vito Corleone, the Godfather (as played by Marlon Brando)

73. Pumbaa the warthog from *The Lion King*

74. A dog

75. Señor Wences

76. A prisoner

77. The Oracle

78. A Southern lawyer

79. A paratrooper with a machine gun

80. A swami

81. A hick farmer

82. A professional wrestler

83. A sportscaster

84. Ozzie Nelson

85. All of the bridesmaids at Aladdin and Jasmine's wedding

As we saw in the *Aladdin* list of characters, Robin is capable of instantly changing from one wacky incarnation to another and he proves this again in *Aladdin and the King of Thieves*—only this time he adds even more strange denizens to the Agrabah population!

ROBIN ON THE GENIE, PART 1

"I went into a room and started improvising, and these guys just kept throwing ideas at me. It just got wild. They let me play. That's why I loved it—it was like carte blanche to go nuts. Of course, there were times when I'd go tasteless, when I knew the mouse was not going to approve. 'Oh, come on, boy. Rub the lamp, the big spout. Don't be afraid.'" (from *TV Guide*, August 3, 1996)

Robin also revealed during the interview that the one thing he would change about Genie if he could would be to give him a little more hair.

ROBIN ON THE GENIE, PART 2

In the Fall 1996 issue of *Disney Magazine*, Robin talked about what was on his mind while working on the sequel to *Aladdin*: "The Genie," he reveals, "comes closest to my own stand-up performances." He described the animators who tried to keep up with him as "all traveling at the same speed of light." Tad Stones, the director and producer of *Aladdin and the King of Thieves* noted, "It's a good thing we lay the vocal tracks first; it gives us enough time to draw all the characters Robin comes up with."

When asked how he came up with his stream-of-consciousness creations, Robin joked, "I do a good take, they give me food."

"Something happens," he continued. "It's almost uncontrollable." He also admitted to censoring himself: "It can get too bizarre or too blue, and I certainly don't want to scare children or drag them through puberty in five seconds."

THE *ALADDIN AND THE KING OF THIEVES* INTERVIEW ON *THE TODAY SHOW*, 1996

In early August of 1996, Robin appeared in a taped segment with Al Roker on *The Today Show* for an interview to promote both *Jack* and the upcoming video release of *Aladdin and the King of Thieves*.

Robin is absolutely amazing in these brief five- or six-minute interviews and this appearance was no exception. He kept Al Roker laughing almost the entire time they were talking.

Roker introduced the taped interview by talking about Disney's 1994 apology to Robin for using his Genie voice without permission in *Aladdin* merchandise and his first question to Robin was about the reconciliation:

> Yeah, I'm back working for the Mouse! It just took one big stuffed plush toy…it was a Pamela Sue Anderson doll!

Al Roker then asked Robin why he liked playing the Genie:

> Just because he can be anybody. Because, you know, he can switch. *[Walter Cronkite voice]* I can be Walter Cronkite for a minute and then *[Carol Channing voice]* become Carol Channing! I didn't know that's possible! *[in his own voice]* It's just a total freedom.

They then showed a clip from the original 1992 *Aladdin* movie during which Robin commented on the Genie character:

> Because he's magical, anything's possible…there's no time reference…he's not bound by any particular thing. He can bring

in any different character from any time…be any person at any given moment.

The talk then turned to Robin's mega-hit from earlier in the year, *The Birdcage.* Roker asked Robin if he had had any idea when he was working on *The Birdcage* that the movie would be the enormous hit it became. "I just knew that it was funny," Robin replied. "And I knew that if it was that funny, people would go. That it would kick like that? I had no idea that it would do that well." Robin also said that because the movie had so many funny moments, he had hoped that people would see it more than once to "pick up what they missed the first time."

After a funny scene from *The Birdcage,* Al Roker asked Robin, "Is that the point of the exercise now, to do things that are maybe a little bit different?"

Robin explained that he tried to keep expanding his body of work by trying different aspects of acting that allowed him to "explore other human behavior." He then remarked, "And for me, that's why I want to just play characters," which led to a clip of the schoolyard scene from *Jack.*

After the clip, the talk turned yet again to Robin's penchant for taking on "man-boy" roles. Al Roker asked him if *Jack* was his last "man-child" movie, to which Robin replied, "I've done enough man-boy parts. After *Hook* and *Jumanji,* they said, 'Here's another man-boy part.' I went, 'Get real! I'm having sex with my wife! Come on, I'm not a boy! I'm forty-four! Look at me! I'm furrier than the gorilla in *Congo!*'"

This naturally led the conversation about Robin's amazing hairiness. Al Roker queried him about why his hirsute appearance was made fun of so much in *Jack.*

> I've actually gone to the zoo and had monkeys come up to the cage and go, "What am *I* doing in here?"…They've actually

tried to groom me....They thin it out occasionally for movies now just so it doesn't distract. They just take a weed-whacker... two guys from Seattle..."I'm sorry, Robin, we just can't get through that damn thunder-brush on your thighs! And I'm not going near your butt!" I've actually seen bugs get trapped in it going, "Kill me! Kill me!"

This hilarious interview came to a close with one of the funniest bits Robin has ever done. He starts off talking about the newly-released movie *Independence Day*, telling Al Roker (who had not seen it yet) that an earthling (Jeff Goldblum) was able to crash the alien mother-ship by downloading a virus into the ship's computer.

And I thought, my God, how can that work? And I realized, it's Windows 95! And there's Bill Gates going [*as Bill Gates*], "See, it even hits an alien mother ship and crashes *that* system! Hi, I'm Bill Gates, and if you enjoyed Windows 95, what about Doors 96? [*as a demon*] It allows me access to your soul! Don't be afraid! WORSHIP ME!"

Al Roker, laughing uproariously, shook Robin's hand and thanked him for the interview, and when they returned to *The Today Show* studio live, Al had one thing to say: "Wow."

Well put.

The Secret Agent

(1996)

Pull yourself together. Remorse is for the weak and weakness is the source of all evil on this Earth. There's a time coming— and it's gonna be sooner rather than later—when this will be understood by governments and individuals: that there can be no progress and no solutions until you make a rational decision to exterminate the weak.

—The Professor

Robin Williams's character the Professor presumably kills himself at the conclusion of this film adaptation of Joseph Conrad's novel *The Secret Agent*, which is yet another in a string of Robin Williams films in which suicide is either a theme or plays a role in the narrative. The qualification of "presumably" is because we don't see the explosion that kills him, but he does squeeze the detonator ball to trigger the bomb he's wearing. At that moment, the movie goes silent, and the last scene is a freeze frame of the face of the Professor.

Is this conclusion true to Joseph Conrad's source novel? This is how the novel ends:

And the incorruptible Professor walked too, averting his eyes from the odious multitude of mankind. He had no future. He disdained it. He was a force. His thoughts caressed the images of ruin and destruction. He walked frail, insignificant, shabby, miserable—and terrible in the simplicity of his idea calling madness and despair to the regeneration of the world. Nobody looked at him. He passed on unsuspected and deadly, like a pest in the street full of men.

So we don't know. Conrad left the ending ambiguous in order for the reader to come to his or her own conclusion. In the novel we don't see the Professor detonate the bomb; in the movie we see him squeeze the detonator, but we don't see the explosion and don't know if it actually went off.

Robin Williams's performance in *The Secret Agent* is one of his best, and one of the finest in the film. He is in his "smiling madman" persona throughout, and his blasé attitude about the possibility of imminent death by explosion—for others *and* himself—is truly chilling.

The Conrad novel is set in 1886 and is about anarchists and spies and double agents and terrorism. It's a compelling read, but the movie adaptation is somewhat slower-paced. The movie stars Bob Hoskins as the double agent porn merchant Verloc, Patricia Arquette as his out-of-his-league wife Winnie, and Christian Bale as Winnie's mentally-challenged brother Stevie. Winnie later admits that the only reason she married the successful merchant Verloc was to assure a safe and comfortable home for her brother.

Tragedy—due to deception and avarice—permeates Verloc and Winnie's life and they, along with Stevie, all end up dead by the end of the movie.

The Secret Agent was not well-received by critics and fans, yet it does boast some superb performances and an admirable attempt at adapting what has come to be considered by many a literary classic.

WHAT THE CRITICS HAD TO SAY

Roger Ebert: "Robin Williams is grim and effective as the Professor, who walks the city with bombs strapped to his body." (from RogerEbert.com, December 13, 1996)

Peter Stack: "This thick, leaden production starring Bob Hoskins and Patricia Arquette—and an uncredited Robin Williams—has a sophomoric air, even though it faithfully follows the book." (from the *San Francisco Chronicle*, December 20, 1996)

Frank Ochieng: "A nostalgic sleepy and literate period piece spy drama that periodically captures your attention when least expected. Not as stimulating as one could imagine but nevertheless credible." (from TheWorldJournal.com, June 7, 2003)

Hamlet

(1996)

A hit, a very palpable hit…

—Osric

Perhaps I have too contemporary a sensibility, or maybe I'm just shallow, but I found sitting through Kenneth Branagh's four-hour, full-text version of William Shakespeare's *Hamlet* something of a chore.

It's not that I don't like Shakespeare. I do. One of my most enjoyable evenings ever at the theater was seeing Fred Gwynne (remember Herman Munster?) perform in *Macbeth* at the Shakespeare Theater in Stratford, Connecticut.

And there is no dismissing the brilliance of Shakespeare's writing. It's always a thrill to recognize an incredibly well-known and oft-used line or phrase from Shakespeare and hear it in its original use and context. *Hamlet* is a veritable cornucopia of such linguistic concoctions. To wit:

- "This above all: to thine own self be true."
- "Something is rotten in the state of Denmark."
- "Murder most foul."

- "Brevity is the soul of wit."
- "Though this be madness, yet there is method in't."
- "What a piece of work is a man!"
- "The play's the thing."
- "To be, or not to be: that is the question."
- "To sleep: perchance to dream."
- "What dreams may come."
- "Get thee to a nunnery."
- "The lady doth protest too much, methinks."
- "I must be cruel only to be kind."
- "Alas, poor Yorick."
- "Sweets to the sweet."
- "Good-night, sweet prince."

No, the problem I had with Branagh's colossal production was the way Shakespeare's words were actually *spoken*.

Shakespearean language is syntactically complex and relentlessly imagistic and poetic. It commonly takes time for the words to sink in and reveal their true brilliance. Branagh and company spoke with such rapid-fire cadence (shooting for, it is presumed, a true conversational rhythm), it became a daunting task to keep up with them. Since many are not as intimately familiar with *Hamlet* as Branagh and company obviously are, their explosive diction, combined with the fact that the cast all had thick English accents, made at least half of the dialogue completely unintelligible. Branagh, in particular, as Hamlet, had the lion's share of the lines in the play and often spoke so quickly and with such a breathless delivery that at times his words sounded like a foreign language.

That said, there is no denying that Branagh's *Hamlet* is a masterpiece. It is the first film shot on glorious 70 millimeter since Ron Howard's 1992 epic, *Far and Away*, and it is the only full-text version of the play ever filmed (it also reunited Branagh with Robin Williams—they had worked together in 1991 in *Dead Again*).

The story is familiar: When the play opens, young Hamlet, Prince of Denmark, is shocked to learn that his mother Gertrude has married his father's brother, Claudius, less than a month after the king's untimely death. Hamlet's father appears to him as a ghost and tells him he was murdered by Claudius and enjoins him to avenge his death. Hamlet's inner torment over whether or not to actually kill his uncle is the emotional engine that drives the play to its tragic and bloody conclusion.

The visuals in *Hamlet* are extraordinary and Alex Thomson's cinematography makes stunning use of the full capabilities of the wider film. The scene that concludes Part 1 (most theaters showed *Hamlet* with a fifteen-minute intermission about two-and-a-half hours into the film) is particularly notable. It is the last scene in Act 4, in which Hamlet, after a brief conversation with the traitor Rosencrantz, gives a lengthy speech that begins, "How all occasions do inform against me and spur my dull revenge! What is a man, if his chief good and market of his time be but to sleep and feed?" Hamlet, dressed completely in black from head to toe (he is, after all, still in mourning for his father), delivers this soliloquy on a huge, glaringly white, snow-covered field. As the Prince's words become more impassioned and his anger more intense, the camera pulls back ever so slowly, widening the shot until, at the powerful conclusion of the speech—"O, from this time forth, my thoughts be bloody, or be nothing worth!"—Hamlet is but a black speck in the center of a giant white landscape. Truly a breathtaking moment.

But the reason *Hamlet* is included in this book is, of course, because of Robin Williams's participation in the film.

Robin plays a minor role, that of Osric, a royal courtier who serves as a referee in the fatal sword fight between Hamlet and Laertes. (Robin's *Comic Relief* cohort, Billy Crystal, also appears in *Hamlet*, likewise in a minor role. Crystal plays the gravedigger who digs up the skull of Hamlet's jester, Yorick, prompting Hamlet's famous, "Alas, poor Yorick" speech.)

Robin first appears about a half hour before the end of the film. (This is the second scene of Act 5 in the text.) He is dressed in a uniform and carries a sword. He has a beard, but no hair on his chin, and his hair is styled in spit curls that drape over his forehead. Robin does not have many lines in this scene (most of which he delivers in a watered-down English accent) and his only other task in the film is to referee the aforementioned deadly duel. Osric is ultimately stabbed in the stomach during the duel and he dies as the English army invades the castle.

Robin gives a good performance, his handful of lines notwithstanding. He does one little bit of physical comedy when he bows to Hamlet and hits a table with his sword, but overall, he plays Osric straight.

Regarding the company of actors in *Hamlet*, it's fair to speculate on whether or not the inclusion of Robin, Billy Crystal, Gérard Depardieu, and Jack Lemmon was "stunt casting" by Branagh. Admittedly, such high-profile, mostly comedic actors are a bit of an anachronistic distraction, but is that Robin and company's fault?

For many reasons, most of the cast members do not surprise us when we hear them recite Shakespeare's words. But in the case of these other albeit talented, yet somewhat "unexpected" actors, Shakespeare's language sounds strange issuing from their lips. Billy Crystal's performance, in particular, is noticeably jarring: One almost expects Billy to lapse into a bit of comedic shtick as he recites some of the odd dialogue his character speaks.

As for Robin, people laughed out loud when he first made his entrance, even though neither Osric's lines or actions were even remotely funny. People laughed at the mere *sight* of Robin Williams. This kind of knee-jerk reaction on the part of an audience to the mere sight of an actor cannot, in the end, be good for the film.

Was Robin (and the others mentioned) miscast? Perhaps. Maybe Branagh wanted to attract an audience not normally familiar with Shakespeare. As the excerpt below from the review by critic Roger Ebert notes, though, others felt the same shock upon seeing "non-Shakespearean" actors reciting Shakespeare.

If you are not a Shakespeare fan and are considering seeing *Hamlet* just to see Robin, you might want to skip the film. Robin's tiny role in the flick may not warrant a four-hour (plus intermission) commitment. If you *are* an aficionado of Shakespeare, then you will probably greatly enjoy this elaborate, yet lengthy, *complete* version of what some consider one of Shakespeare's greatest works, and what has often been regarded, as *Entertainment Weekly* critic Owen Gleiberman described it, "the pivotal text in all of English literature."

WHAT THE CRITICS HAD TO SAY

Roger Ebert: "[Branagh's] *Hamlet* is long but not slow, deep but not difficult, and it vibrates with the relief of actors who have great things to say and the right ways to say them. Robin Williams, Jack Lemmon, and Gerard Depardieu are distractions, their performances not overcoming our shock of recognition." (from his syndicated column, *On Film*)

Owen Gleiberman: "Branagh's *Hamlet* is…reminiscent of a horror film, but a very different one: It's like an Elizabethan version of *The Shining*. Shot on huge, bold, dazzlingly well-lit sets, it too is about a man led to dementia—and murder—by a ghost preying on his demons. It doesn't help that the performances of Billy Crystal and Robin Williams are corny and flat-footed." (from *Entertainment Weekly*, January 24, 1977)

Deconstructing Harry

(1997)

The most important words in the English language are not "I love you" but "It's benign."

—**Harry Block**

Robin Williams has a very small role in *Deconstructing Harry* and it is one of his strangest. He plays Mel, an actor and alter ego of the main character Harry Block (Woody Allen) who, while shooting a film, is distressed to learn that he is out of focus.

Literally.

In real life, Mel is blurry (or "soft" as the fictional director tells him). Mel replies, "I've gained some weight," to which the director clarifies that Mel is empirically soft focused, rather than just pudgy.

Robin plays his role completely straight; i.e., he's not funny. In fact, we get a glimpse of Robin the Disciplinarian in a scene in his apartment after shooting wraps for the day because he's out of focus. He is recounting the problem to his wife Grace (Julie Kavner) and his obnoxious young son is chanting, "Daddy's out of focus, Daddy's out of focus." Mel/Robin takes it for a few seconds and then explodes in what was clearly Robin's real-life "dad" voice, "Reuben! Stop it!"

144

Mel thinks a good night's sleep will solve the problem, but the next morning he's even more out of focus. He concludes he needs to see a doctor who immediately tells him, "I've never seen anything like this," and prescribes eyeglasses for his wife and kids. The scene then shifts to the "real" Mel (Harry, played, of course, by Woody Allen) talking to his psychiatrist, who tells him, "You expect the world to adjust to the distortion you've become."

Deconstructing Harry is a complex, multifaceted, psychological (and fairly funny) "deconstruction" of Harry Block, a Woody Allen doppelganger. Woody was nominated for a 1998 "Best Writing, Screenplay Written Directly for the Screen" Academy Award for his script. Matt Damon and Ben Affleck won the award for *Good Will Hunting*, which also starred Robin Williams, and for which Robin won a Best Actor in a Supporting Role Oscar.

WHAT THE CRITICS HAD TO SAY

Roger Ebert: "The film has rich comic bits; the most original involves Robin Williams as an actor who is concerned that he's losing his focus—and is (he's out of focus in every scene)." (from rogerebert.com, December 24, 1997)

Owen Gleiberman: "*Deconstructing Harry* is Woody Allen's naughty-boy confessional movie, a disquietingly candid and funny portrait of a pathological narcissist. What's most shocking about the film isn't the rudeness (or lewdness) of Harry's behavior. It's how neatly his lecherous obsessions interlock with the familiar contours of the Allen persona. This is the story of a man who, beneath it all, cannot love, and that, when you think about it, is what Woody has been telling us about himself for 20 years.... Some may view *Deconstructing Harry* as a stunt, and an ugly one at that, but I think it's Allen's most bracing movie of the '90s." (from *Entertainment Weekly*, December 19, 1997)

Fathers' Day

(1997)

You mirth machine.

—Jack Lawrence to Dale Putley

Knowing what we now know about Robin's ultimate fate, it is especially chilling to hear the following come out of the mouth of his character Dale Putley the first time we meet him in *Fathers' Day*:

> For years I've thought about killing myself. It's the only thing that kept me going.

Granted, these words were written by the film's co-writers, Lowell Ganz and Babaloo Mandel, to communicate a core aspect of one of their characters, but still…

Fathers' Day has the rep of being a middling movie, but the negative reviews and criticism are somewhat unwarranted. The personnel involved are stellar—from the director and writers to the all-star cast—and all of them do their best. (Some have argued that particular assertion though: Julia Louis-Dreyfus was unjustly nominated that year for a Golden Raspberry Award (a "Razzie") as Worst Supporting Actress in a Movie for her performance as Carrie Lawrence, Billy Crystal's on-screen wife. Her performance is fine.)

Many Robin Williams fans enjoyed the film, and it is worth a viewing, its purported assorted flaws notwithstanding. (Also, on a personal note, as a writer who has done books about *The Sopranos* and the Beatles, it was especially satisfying to see *Sopranos* alumni in the movie ("Beansie" (Paul Herman) and "Skip" (Louis Lombardi)) and to hear a John Lennon/Beatles reference ("All You Need is Love") from Robin.)

There appears to be some improvisation in the film and there is one Robin scene where this is obvious: Standing in front of a mirror and trying to decide which persona to don to meet his son, Robin becomes a "New York" street dude, a surfer dude (with the middle name of Rainbow), a hip-hop guy, a smoking jacket/pipe kind of guy, and a guru. (He also later does Elvis. Twice.)

The plot's a tad convoluted, but it ultimately works.

Collette Andrews (Nastassja Kinski) tracks down two former lovers (Robin and Billy) and tells each of them that they are the father of her missing sixteen-year-old son Scott. She does this, even though it's not true, with the hope that they'll find him. And they do. And that's essentially the story the movie tells. The movie concludes with Robin and Billy Crystal returning Scott to his parents, and Scott taking each of his "fathers" aside and telling them that he is his real father. However, the audience now knows (Collette earlier admitted she doesn't know who the real father is, but does know it's definitely not one of our two stars) that neither Billy nor Robin are his father and Scott did it because he had grown to love them both and didn't want to hurt either one of them. Billy Crystal's character recognizes the lie; Robin's may or may not.

There are some fun references in the flick. There's an O. J. Simpson reference when Billy Crystal says he feels like he's in a

STEPHEN SPIGNESI

white Bronco as Robin drives super slowly, straddling two lanes on the highway with cars lining up behind him. There's a "mime" reference in which Dale admits to being one at one point and Jack stating he hates mime (this joke is paid off later when an actual mime starts annoying Jack at a concert). Dale at one point says, "How Joe Pesci of you" to Jack and makes the now-overused Lou Gehrig joke, asking what are the odds that Lou Gehrig would die of Lou Gehrig's disease? (The character of Christopher Moltisanti made the same joke on *The Sopranos*.)

Dale's character has a lot of what Woody Allen once described (in *Manhattan*) as "quirks and mannerisms," yet Robin mostly does not overplay them. Sure, his character of Dale is neurotic as hell, but Robin walks the line between authenticity and camp. One of Dale's "quirks" is slamming on the brakes while driving because he believes he just ran over an invisible body, now lying dead on the highway. Dale himself admits to Jack that he "used to be somewhat unstable." He also discusses his musical, *Hello, Doctor, It's Still Swollen,* which is about prostate enlargement. (Now, *that's* a funny bit. Is it Robin's or part of the script? It's unclear, but it's definitely funny. It feels like a bit of Robin improv.) Robin's character is also a reluctant flyer and a plane scene gives the master a chance to hyperventilate, sing, tremble, and act like a nervous maniac (Dale later learns that Scott is also a nervous flyer, which convinces him he must be his son).

There is some slapstick physical comedy in a hotel shower, and a predictable port-o-potty scene involving Scott's "real"(?) father Bob (Bruce Greenwood). Billy Crystal does some physical stuff after he's burned when Scott pours hot coffee on his testicles. Dale/Robin's deposition scene is also funny.

The final section of the film involves a rock concert with Sugar Ray and Scott's two fathers rescuing him from two drug dealers from whom Scott used five thousand dollars of their money to

148

buy the girl who dumped him a diamond pin. Another likely improvised scene is when Robin Williams and Billy Crystal dance to Sly and the Family Stone which, in and of itself, is notable.

Admittedly, some of the jokes wouldn't fly today in our politically correct and hypersensitive cultural climate, especially one in which there's confusion about who took a shower with sixteen-year-old Scott, and there are lines like "the boy and I were in the shower."

At different moments, Robin speaks with an English accent and also pretends to speak German. Plus there's a cameo by Mel Gibson as a body piercer and Mary McCormack as a stranded woman Robin picks up on the way to the airport.

Overall, *Fathers' Day* is an enjoyable romp, and even though it's no *Mrs. Doubtfire* or *The Birdcage*, for Robin fans, it's worth your viewing time. Once.

WHAT THE CRITICS HAD TO SAY

Roger Ebert: "*Fathers' Day* is a brainless feature-length sitcom with too much sit and no com. It stars two of the brighter talents in American movies, Robin Williams and Billy Crystal, in a screenplay cleverly designed to obscure their strengths while showcasing their weaknesses." (from rogerebert.com, May 9, 1997)

Bob McCabe: "Williams and Crystal find their own rhythm with the material and deliver some much needed laughs." (from *Empire Magazine*, July 14, 2014)

Maitland McDonagh: "This smug, formulaic comedy is nominally based on the French *Les Comperes*, but it's really the Billy and Robin Show, and all considerations are secondary to their trademark comic shenanigans. How much you enjoy the film will depend entirely on how much you enjoy the spectacle of Williams spewing forth streams of nonsensical gibberish in an attempt to impersonate a German record producer, and Crystal pitching snit fits." (from *TV Guide*, July 14, 2014)

Flubber

(1997)

I have a queasy gyro.

—Weebo

This remake of Disney's 1961 *The Absent-Minded Professor*, with Robin Williams taking the Fred MacMurray part of the original, is a bit of a bipolar mess: It doesn't know if it wants to be an adult romantic comedy or a wacky kid's movie with loveable, and yes, wacky characters. (Both versions are based on the 1943 short story "A Situation of Gravity" by Samuel W. Taylor.)

Kids will—and do—like the movie. Robin is the absent-minded professor, Philip Brainard, with crazy ideas and a loveable cluelessness, and the character of Weebo, a flying drone-like robot who knows everything and serves as Dr. Brainard's assistant, is irresistible. Plus, the flick is loaded with scads of slapstick and other physical comedy. (Worth noting is that the scene of Flubber insanely bouncing all over the place (and wrecking stuff) suggests a similar scene in the same year's *Men in Black,* in which an alien ball bounces all over the MIB headquarters, leaving destroyed equipment in its wake. Plus, *Flubber* has a *Back to the Future*-es-que flying car.)

So yes, kids like it, but adults will have a few problems with the Professor Brainard character. We're supposed to willfully suspend our disbelief long enough to believe that the Professor is so absent-minded and so caught up in his work that he forgot his own wedding to Sara (Marcia Gay Harden, who is very good in this), not once, not twice, but three times. We're led to believe that his work is *that* all-consuming (which might justify such forgetfulness...*might*), but later, Brainard tells Weebo that he's not distracted because of his work; he's distracted because of his love for Sara. Wait...*what*? The obvious adult response to this would be, "Well, then, if you love her so much, how could you leave her stranded at the altar three times?" But, of course, that question does not get asked, since it would take the attention away from Brainard's battle with his enemies: Chester Hoenicker, the school sponsor to whom he owes money, Hoenicker's hired thugs (wonderfully named Smith and Wesson), and Brainard's "friend" Wilson who wants to steal Sara from him.

There are some attempts at appealing to an adult audience with the use of scientific jargon and the incongruous nude (but not explicit) art class, but the dichotomy doesn't work. Adults will find *Flubber* a bit of a chore to get through; kids will ignore the stuff aimed at their parents.

Robin does what he can with the role. He plays it straight and fairly restrained for the most part and there seems to be very little, if any, trademark Robin improv zaniness (the mambo dance scene is a little Robin-esque, though).

There are a few set pieces in the film, including lots of explosions, an off-the-wall basketball game enhanced by Brainard putting Flubber on the soles of his players' sneakers, as well as several flying car scenes. There's also the aforementioned *Beetlejuice*-like (overly long) scene in which all of Brainard's appliances dance to mambo music.

As a former English professor, there's one particular line that struck a nerve. In a scene in which the financial windfall anyone who owns Flubber can expect, Sara says, "If we were interested in making money, we wouldn't have become teachers." True dat.

There is some sadness in the flick, especially when one of the thugs "kills" Weebo with a baseball bat. But fear not! She had already downloaded herself into a computer and creates for Brainard her "daughter," whom she names Weebette.

There's a Flubber fight in Hoenicker's mansion's library, and in a scene no one probably saw coming, Wilson swallows Flubber and then shoots it out of his ass. Yes. You read that right (kids probably love that scene).

Overall, this is one of Robin Williams's lesser efforts. His adult audience may watch it once (and, as one Robin fan told me, "never watch it again"), but if you've got kids and sit with them watching it, a likely splendid time will be had by all.

WHAT THE CRITICS HAD TO SAY

David Ansen: "A cute, well-meaning, but ultimately disappointing movie. Williams, an enormously busy actor these days, seems tired here—and so does a lot of the slapstick." (from *Newsweek*, November 30, 1998)

Roger Ebert: "How absent-minded do you have to be before they call in the doctors to begin clinical testing?" (from the *Chicago Sun Times*, January 1, 2000)

Owen Gleiberman: "In *Flubber*, the special effects threaten to overwhelm story, character, and emotion, but you don't necessarily mind. There are far less entertaining things to see in a movie than Robin Williams being out-acted by rocketing Jell-O. Williams' bow-tied, shock-haired professor is 'absent- minded' because his entire being is wedged into his brain. ('I love you on a subatomic level!' he tells his fiancée, played by Marcia Gay Harden, whom he keeps forgetting to meet at the altar.)" (from *Entertainment Weekly*, December 5, 1997)

Good Will Hunting

(1997)

Will: *He used to just put a belt, a stick, and a wrench on the table. Just say, "Choose."*

Sean: *Well, I gotta go with the belt there.*

Will: *I used to go with the wrench.*

Sean: *Why the wrench?*

Will: *'Cause fuck him, that's why.*

Sean: *Your foster father?*

Will: *Yeah.*

One of the most powerful elements of Robin Williams's performance in *Good Will Hunting* is that, in the movie, one of the funniest men who has ever lived isn't funny. Even when his character is telling a funny story, he's not funny. Sean the widowed psychiatrist wears sadness like it's one of his beat-up old sweaters or windbreakers. Even when Sean specifically tells a joke in the classroom or at a bar, it falls flat. It takes skill to tank like this, and Robin Williams comes through, providing even more evidence of his skill as a dramatic actor.

Good Will Hunting is its co-writers'—Matt Damon and Ben Affleck—show, but Robin Williams provides a huge, balancing counterpoint to Damon's tortured, arrogant, and super-brilliant Will Hunting (there really are, of course, people as smart as Will in our world, although Will seeming to know everything about everything does stretch credulity at times).

The underlying story is simple: Will gets in trouble—repeatedly—and as a last-ditch effort to keep him out of jail after a multitude of offenses—including assaulting a cop—a math professor at MIT, Gerard Lambeau (Stellan Skarsgård) takes responsibility for him and ultimately sends him to Robin Williams's psychiatrist character Sean as part of a court-ordered program.

At first, Will is *beyond* resistant—and this is why Sean is the sixth therapist Will ended up seeing. The first five walked away after briefly suffering Will's nonsense. But Sean is different and can parry Will in ways the boy genius has never experienced.

Robin's character doesn't appear until thirty-three minutes into the movie. Robin plays the character in a very nuanced way: Sean always seems to have a small smile on his face, but it's also very clear that he is troubled and miserable. We learn this is mainly because he lost his wife to cancer, but also that he was abused as a child, which mirrors much of Will's upbringing.

Sean and Will ultimately bond and, due in large part to Sean's influences, Will decides to take a pass on a high-paying tech job and instead follow the woman he loves, Skylar (Minnie Driver), to California where she will attend medical school.

Robin has some killer speeches, including his most memorable, which he delivers to Will as they sit on a park bench at a lake. It's the one in which he makes Will utterly aware that, even if he knows everything there is to know about Michelangelo and his art, he still has no idea what it smells like in the Sistine Chapel. Or what it's like to watch the person you love die.

There seems to be an interesting nod to Robin's family in a scene in which Professor Lambeau tells Will, "I see you used McLaurin here." "McLaurin" is the name of Robin's brother (and later, his grandson).

The crucial scene for Will and Sean takes place in Sean's office when Sean repeatedly tells Will, "It's not your fault," until Will breaks down and embraces Sean. The performances in this scene are extraordinary, although some critics (including psychotherapists) found the rather sudden resolution of Will's psychological dysfunction a bit too pat.

Good Will Hunting is an excellent film that could have benefited from being a tad shorter. There are a few scenes that come off as unneeded, but that's a small criticism for a film that boasts a superb script, a compelling story, and excellent performances, particularly by Robin Williams.

WHAT THE CRITICS HAD TO SAY

Roger Ebert: "[Robin Williams plays] a community college professor who has messed up his own life, but is a gifted counselor [and] gives one of his best performances, especially in a scene where he finally gets the kid to repeat, 'It's not my fault.'" (from RogerEbert.com, December 25, 1997)

Janet Maslin: "The film strains slightly in creating a set of neatly parallel friendships and by finding too many echoes of Will's problems in Sean's own past. But what it does beautifully is to develop a doctor-patient sparring that becomes affecting and important to both parties. Edgy and sarcastic as he is, Will works overtime to locate the doctor's raw nerves, and the actors play this out passionately. Williams is wonderfully strong and substantial here." (from *The New York Times*, December 5, 1997)

What Dreams May Come

(1998)

Thought is real. Physical is the illusion. Ironic, huh?

—**Albert**

I interviewed Richard Matheson, the author whose 1978 novel *What Dreams May Come* was adapted for this Robin Williams flick, for my book *The Complete Stephen King Encyclopedia* to talk about his enormous influence on King as a writer. By then I had read the novel this film is based on and I remember being overwhelmed by Matheson's depiction of Summerland and his explication of the afterlife.

> Summerland, also called the Astral plane Heaven, is depicted as where souls who have been good in their previous lives go between incarnations.
>
> **Wikipedia**

The *What Dreams May Come* film differs from the novel, but one thing I remember, both from the introduction and bibliography of the book, was that Richard said everything in the novel about heaven and the afterlife is based on concrete scientific evidence. As he tells us, only the characters in the book are fictional.

Let's face it: the single, dominating question in every human being's life is "What happens after we die?" We want to know, is there a heaven? Are we reunited with our loved ones? Will we see our pets?

According to Richard Matheson and *What Dreams May Come* (as well as volumes of research cited in the book's bibliography), the answer is unequivocally "yes" to all of the above.

In a relatively brief, Hallmark-y opening sequence, we meet the family: Chris (Robin Williams), his wife Annie (Annabella Sciorra), and their kids, Ian (Josh Paddock), and Marie (Jessica Brooks Grant). But this "morning/breakfast/rushing out of the house" scene we've seen a million times is a tease: Before long the kids are dead, and it's four years later. Annie is in the depths of depression, and Chris is at a loss as to how to proceed with a completely eviscerated life.

This is not a funny movie, although it does have Robin Williams in it, so some levity is to be expected. Chris is a doctor and Robin pulls out his trusty "Elmer Fudd" impersonation to relax a nervous child. Annie is a curator at an art gallery. Paintings become a dominant thematic metaphor throughout the film, and the Summerland they experience can be described as paintings vividly come to life.

As Chris and Annie both struggle to live in their childless, tragedy-consumed world, Chris is killed by a car hurling through the air when he stops to help at an accident scene on his way home from work. Is this the final straw that breaks Annie's emotional and psychological "back?" It sure as hell is.

After Chris dies, he's met by "Doc" (Cuba Gooding Jr.) who serves as a sponsor of sorts in the afterlife as Chris transitions from living in the empirically real world to living in the afterlife which, he quickly learns, is solely of his own making. We live after death if we want to. We later learn that Doc is actually his son Ian, taking on a different persona to help his father.

Chris can't stay away from his home, or Annie, and his visits torture her. She can sense his presence, and she even does some automatic writing with his influence. He also attends his own funeral.

But ultimately he says goodbye and moves on to the next phase of his post-mortal existence. And the first thing that happens is he is reunited with their dog Katie, who had to be euthanized when she got sick.

Chris also meets Leona, another guide who we later learn is actually his daughter Marie.

Doc ultimately comes to Chris to tell him that Annie killed herself and that he'll never see her again because suicides go to hell and can never escape. Well, we'll just see about that, Chris insists.

Doc takes him to a Tracker (Max von Sydow) who Chris later learns is actually a beloved former professor.

Chris manages to make it to hell and actually find Annie, who does not recognize him or remember him. And if he cannot convince her to choose reincarnation to live another life to pay for her sin of suicide, he will lose his mind and never escape hell either.

The film ends with a heartwarming "family reunion" resolution that some critics and fans found unsatisfying. Chris and Annie—who, we are assured, are unquestionably soul mates—get to start over and find each other in a new life. Their reincarnated selves meet in a scene that mirrors their initial meeting in two boats on a lake.

There is also an alternate ending on the DVD in which we witness each of their rebirths, including Annie's birth in Sri Lanka.

What Dreams May Come is a potent film with a devastating performance by Robin Williams. The duality of his persona—manic comic and dramatic thespian—is powerfully evident in this film.

WHAT ROBIN HAD TO SAY

"I believe in heaven and hell. I've had coming attractions of them in my dreams." (from Canoe.ca, September 20, 1998)

"[*What Dreams May Come*] deals with such emotionally intense issues, I didn't know if I'd want to do this for four or five months, be near this kind of dark pain and loss that are at the core of it. But as we kept doing it, I thought, 'Well, it's certainly interesting.' And it makes you look at your own life and how you live your life—but that's a side effect of being near this kind of intense emotion." (from CNN, October 7, 1998)

WHAT THE CRITICS HAD TO SAY

Roger Ebert: "*What Dreams May Come* is so breathtaking, so beautiful, so bold in its imagination, that it's a surprise at the end to find it doesn't finally deliver. It takes us to the emotional brink but it doesn't push us over. It ends on a curiously unconvincing note—a conventional resolution in a movie that for most of its length has been daring and visionary.... Robin Williams somehow has a quality that makes him seem at home in imaginary universes.... There is a muscular reality about him, despite his mercurial wit, that anchors him and makes the fantastic images around him seem almost plausible. He is good, too, at emotion: He brings us along with him." (from RogerEbert.com, October 2, 1998)

Peter Travers: "Robin Williams plays a good doc who dies in a car wreck. His distraught wife kills herself, which leaves her in hell and him in heaven trying to find her with the help of an afterlife guide. Director Vincent Ward, who handled myth with style in *The Navigator,* flounders here despite dazzling visuals. There hasn't been this much stuporous spiritual overload since Yanni in concert." (from *Rolling Stone*, October 2, 1998)

Patch Adams

(1998)

What's wrong with death sir? What are we so mortally afraid of? Why can't we treat death with a certain amount of humanity and dignity, and decency, and, God forbid, maybe even humor? Death is not the enemy gentlemen. If we're going to fight a disease, let's fight one of the most terrible diseases of all, indifference.

—Patch Adams

It can be tricky doing a film about a real person. The writers, director, and cast need to decide three things: what to leave in, what to leave out, and what to make up.

Dr. Hunter "Patch" Adams's initial reaction to this film was not as enthusiastic nor positive as it became later. In one early comment he made, he said the problem he had with it was that the film only made him out to be a funny doctor. This is a bit of a lopsided assessment since there are many scenes in the movie in which Robin portrays Dr. Adams as a kind, compassionate, and, yes, serious human being.

That said, though, we will look at this film as another Robin Williams movie, and discuss it within the context of Robin as

163

an actor and as an interpreter of the screenwriter's script and the director's vision.

Patch Adams is based on the book *Gesundheit: Good Health is a Laughing Matter* by Adams and Maureen Mylander ("Gesundheit" means "health" in German).

There are a few differences between book and film worth noting. First is Robin's age. He's somewhat older (thirties?) than a typical med student when he starts medical school after checking himself out of a psychiatric hospital. In reality, Patch Adams was around seventeen or eighteen when his mother checked him into the hospital for suicidal tendencies.

Also, in the movie, Patch's girlfriend Carin (Monica Potter) is murdered by a psychiatric patient. In real life, Carin did not exist. The character was very loosely based on Adams's real wife, Linda. However, Patch's male best friend *was* murdered by a psychotic patient. They changed the gender and made Carin a love interest for the movie.

In the movie, Patch patches a patient's leaking coffee cup and the grateful patient called him "Patch." In real life, a patient did give him the nickname, but because he said he "patched up" people's emotional loneliness.

As for Robin's performance in the movie, it is an odd amalgam of zany Robin and heartfelt, serious Robin. When he's entertaining children in the pediatric ward of a hospital with a clown nose and bedpan shoes, he's funny Robin. When he's talking about healthcare or his love for Carin, he's serious Robin. This does work for the most part, although the tone shift can be jarring.

There are some interesting moments in the film. In one scene, Patch's roommate Rudy (Michael Jeter) tells him he's "fuzzier" than his last roommate. That could be a reference to Robin's natural hirsuteness, but what's fun about this is that the year prior to *Patch Adams*, Robin had played a character in Woody Allen's

Deconstructing Harry who was literally out of focus and looked blurry (i.e., fuzzy).

Also, at one point, Patch shouts out "Let's do it!" which may be a nod to Robin's deceased friend John Belushi who shouts the same thing in *Animal House*.

One segment that serves the film but doesn't really work is when Patch crashes a meat-packers' convention and does a whole routine of dumb meat jokes and meat speeches. This sequence (as well as the "giant legs in stirrups" scene) does not seem to be in the book (which—full disclosure—I have not read), and it seems somewhat out of place in the film (the "giant tub of noodles" scene *is* in the book, though, except that Patch himself bathes in it, not a patient).

Some of Robin's bits seem ad-libbed. He does some gags that he's done in his stand-up (the hissing cat, for one), and when he's in zany Robin mode, he's a lot of fun. Serious Robin comes off here as a bit saccharine on occasions, but overall it's worth a viewing if you're a Robin fan. Plus, the movie serves as a good introduction to a more holistic, patient-centered philosophy of medicine that is, thankfully, becoming more a part of mainstream health care. This movie may have had something to do with that.

Dr. Hunter "Patch" Adams's statement on the death of Robin Williams

The terrible news of the passing of Robin Williams reached me here in the Peruvian Amazon late Monday night with tremendous sadness. Surrounded by over 100 friends and clowns on our annual clown trip, we mourn this tragic loss and continue to treasure his comic genius.

Robin Williams was a wonderful, kind and generous man. One important thing I remember about his personality is that he was unassuming—he never acted as if he was powerful or famous. Instead, he was always tender and welcoming, willing to help others with a smile or a joke. Robin was a brilliant comedian—there is no doubt. He was a compassionate, caring human being. While watching him work on the set of the film based on my life—*Patch Adams*—I saw that whenever there was a stressful moment, Robin would tap into his improvisation style to lighten the mood of cast and crew. Also, I would like to point out, Robin would be especially kind toward my children when they would visit the set. Contrary to how many people may view him, he actually seemed to me to be an introvert. When he invited me and my family into his home, he valued peace and quiet, a chance to breathe—a chance to get away from the fame that his talent has [sic] brought him. While early in life, he turned to drug use and alcohol to escape, he replaced the addiction with moments of solitude to help cope with the stress that fame brought. This world is not kind to people who become famous, and the fame he had garnered was a nightmare. While saddened, we are left with the consequences of his death. I'm enormously grateful for his wonderful performance of my early life, which has allowed the Gesundheit! Institute to continue and expand our work. We extend our blessings to his family and friends in this moment of sadness. Thank you for all you've given this world Robin, thank you my friend.

WHAT THE CRITICS HAD TO SAY

Roger Ebert: "*Patch Adams* made me want to spray the screen with Lysol. This movie is shameless. It's not merely a tearjerker. It extracts tears individually by liposuction, without anesthesia. It is allegedly based on the life of a real man named Patch Adams, who I have seen on television, where he looks like Salvador Dali's seedy kid brother. If all of these things really happened to him, they should have abandoned Robin Williams and brought in Jerry Lewis for the telethon." (from Rogerebert.com, December 25, 1998)

Janet Maslin: "Choosing another of the soggier roles he has lately favored, Williams spends a lot of time here smiling gratefully at the compliments heaped on him ('God, Patch, it's amazing what you've done with this place, you know?') and looking significantly older than the medical student he initially plays. To save the material from utter oblivion, he also does his share of clowning, though it bears the stamp of the creative team (the director, Tom Shadyac, and the writer, Steve Oedekerk) behind some Jim Carrey films." (from *The New York Times*, December 24, 1998)

James Berardinelli: "Robin Williams, who won an Oscar for his beautifully-understated role in *Good Will Hunting*, wavers between being effective and going over-the-top. From time-to-time, he has genuinely funny moments (when *Patch Adams* goes for comedy, it's not half bad), but, for the most part, the dramatic aspect of his performance is off. He's forcing the audience's emotional response. And, although attempting to replicate his work in *Dead Poets Society*, Williams is working with a script that isn't as polished, so some of his scenes come across as overwrought instead of heartbreaking." (from *ReelViews*, December 25, 1998)

Jakob the Liar
(1999)

Hitler goes to a fortune-teller and asks, "When will I die?" And the fortune-teller replies, "On a Jewish holiday." Hitler then asks, "How do you know that?" And she replies, "Any day you die will be a Jewish holiday."

—**Jakob**

In the season two episode of the HBO series *The Sopranos*, "D-Girl," Tony Soprano's psychiatrist Dr. Melfi explains the roots of existentialism to Tony:

> After World War II, people were disillusioned by the sheer weight of the horrors. That's when the whole idea took root that there were no absolute truths.

Jakob the Liar is a Holocaust movie, but none of it takes place at the camps. It is set in a Jewish ghetto in Poland during World War II where, every day, the residents live with the fear that the German soldiers will come, round them up, and put them on a train. And they all know where those trains go.

Jakob Heym (Robin Williams) is a latke (potato pancake) maker who hasn't made a single latke in the years after the Germans closed down his restaurant.

One day, he gets trapped outside the boundaries of the ghetto and is caught and brought before the German commandant who calls him "the smart Jew," due to his obvious intelligence and casually facile wit. While in the office, Jakob hears a radio broadcast that recounts that the war is going badly for the Germans, and he sees a wall map that shows the Russians closing in on Jakob's area.

Jakob is allowed to return to the ghetto without punishment, and it isn't long before he spreads the word about what he learned in the commandant's office. People are hungry for news about the war and Jakob becomes something of a celebrity, but for the wrong reason. His neighbors believe he knows what he knows because he has a clandestine radio, which he most assuredly does not.

Jakob "adopts" a ten-year-old girl, Lina (Hannah Taylor Gordon) who was secretly removed from the death train from another ghetto that her parents were on. They snuck her off the train with the hope she might survive. They knew she wouldn't if she remained on the train. Jakob encounters her on his way back to the ghetto and hides her in his attic.

Jakob's nonexistent radio serves as a metaphor for the hope the residents thrive on. As long as the radio continues to tell Jakob important information, they all still have a chance at survival, the frequent ghetto suicides notwithstanding.

Ultimately, the news of Jakob's radio makes its way to the Germans, who torture him—they waterboard him and beat him—and then demand that he admit to everyone that he never had a radio and that everything he told them was a lie. He refuses and he is executed in front of his friends.

In a voiceover, Jakob then tells us…

> So that's how it ended. I never got a chance to be the big hero and make my big speech. I swear, I had a speech all prepared… about freedom and never giving in.

But somehow…Yes, that's how it ended. They all went off to the camps…and were never seen again.

However, Jakob had often talked about the other possible ways that the war might end, including the Russians storming the town, killing the Germans, and setting everyone free. Or perhaps stopping the trains on their way to the camps, letting everyone off, and destroying the Germans.

That's why the next thing we hear Jakob say is…

But maybe it wasn't like that at all. Because, you know, as Frankfurter says: "Until the last line has been spoken, the curtain cannot come down." About fifty kilometers out of town, the train was stopped by Russian troops, who had just taken Bezanika and Pry.

The last scene of the movie is Lina peering out between the wooden slats of the train car and seeing an Andrews Sisters-like trio of singers performing with a band in a field. Fade to black.

Which ending is real? Were the people of the ghetto rescued? Did Lina survive?

Ambiguous endings can be thought-provoking, and the conclusion of *Jakob the Liar* is no exception.

And most come away from the film hoping that Lina saw the singers and heard the music.

WHAT THE CRITICS HAD TO SAY

Roger Ebert: "[Robin] Williams is a talented performer who moves me in the right roles but has a weakness for the wrong ones.… If less is more, then Williams often demonstrates that more is less. Movies as different as *Dead Poets Society* and *Patch Adams* have been brought to a halt by interludes in which Williams darts in a frenzy from one character and accent to another.

Here, in a scene that passes for restrained, he imitates Churchill, and uses a kitchen funnel and a flour can to create sound effects (only sneezing a little because of the flour). These scenes demonstrate that Williams cannot use shtick in a serious movie without damaging the fabric." (from RogerEbert.com, September 24, 1999)

Janet Maslin: "[Robin] Williams's yen to play the clown who cried has served him inexplicably well through some maudlin recent movies. But it certainly isn't bringing out his best." (from *The New York Times*, September 24, 1999)

Scott Tobias: "On paper, the collision of manic/mawkish Robin Williams and a topic as solemn and delicate as the Holocaust suggests a level of tastelessness rivaled only by Jerry Lewis' infamous, never-to-be-released *The Day The Clown Cried*, in which Lewis (as Helmut Doork) plays a Nazi clown who leads children into the gas chamber. But the great relief—or, for camp lovers, the disappointment—of *Jakob The Liar* is that Williams rediscovers the dignity and restraint that's been missing from his work for the last 15 years." (from avclub.com, March 29, 2002)

Bicentennial Man

(1999)

One is glad to be of service.

—Andrew Martin

Bicentennial Man is a terrific movie, some of the critical gibes notwithstanding. Robin Williams plays a robot who becomes an android who becomes a hybrid android/human, and he does it so well, there is almost no need for a suspension of disbelief.

The movie takes place in the "not-too-distant future," and the chronological time span is from 2005, when Andrew is first manufactured, to 2205, when Andrew ceases to function at the age of 200.

Andrew is delivered to the Martin family, and the first thing he does after being unpacked is give them a presentation on the Three Laws of Robotics:

1. A robot may not injure a human being, or, through inaction, cause a human being to come to harm.

2. A robot must obey all human orders, except where those orders come in conflict with the first law.

3. A robot must protect itself, so long as doing so does not conflict with the first two laws.

At first, the two Martin sisters—Little Miss and Grace—do not like Andrew. Grace orders him to jump out a window, which he does; Little Miss is distraught when Andrew accidentally breaks her favorite glass horse figurine. Andrew's relationship with Grace never evolves into closeness, but the same cannot be said for his relationship with Little Miss. To make amends for his clumsiness, Andrew studies woodworking and sculpts a beautiful wooden horse for Little Miss. She is holding it on her deathbed years later.

Sir Richard Martin recognizes that Andrew is unique and encourages him to build things (mostly clocks), and teaches him the "facts of life" (which Andrew says "sounds so messy").

The movie takes us through the passage of time as Andrew remains the Andrew he was when he first became part of the Martin household, but everyone else ages.

Sir Richard, who *did* recognize Andrew's uniqueness, at first did not understand the extent of Andrew's singular identity. Andrew is not, he learns, one of those robots who has a personality chip, a piece of hardware that makes robots more like humans, at least superficially. They're more verbal, they wisecrack, they dance, and so forth. No, Andrew's positronic brain can understand context, and nuance, and, above all, the idea of freedom. And that is the subtextual theme running throughout most of the film. Andrew understands what it means to be human, and to be a free "person," and strives his entire existence to become as human as he can be.

As technology advances over the decades, Andrew works with Rupert Burns (Oliver Platt) to design and create body parts and organs that are both human and bionic. By the time he "dies," Andrew is at least 50 percent human, including possessing a central nervous system and digestive tract.

Another element of human existence that Andrew eventually understands is the concept of love. He falls in love with Portia,

Little Miss's granddaughter, and petitions the World Court to allow him to be declared a human so their marriage can be considered "official." He loses this case, until the end of his life—when the court finally accedes and declares him fully human and his marriage to Portia completely legitimate and official—but he dies before the decision is read:

> Andrew is the oldest living human being in recorded history. For it is by this proclamation that I validate his marriage to Portia Charney and acknowledge his humanity.

If there is one reasonable criticism of *Bicentennial Man*, it's that it might be considered a bit too long. The whole sequence in which Andrew travels the world looking for more "like him" and finding only "deleted" robots could have been shorter—or even eliminated—without harming the film. In fact, such an edit would probably have tightened up the narrative. Also, the wedding dancing scene is ho-hum.

That said, however, the film is a wonderful tale of what might be. And Robin's performance is one of his best: Even when he's telling what he considers "funny" jokes, there's nary a hint of the manic Robin that sometimes surfaces in scenes like this in other movies.

Andrew's original response to "Why did the chicken cross the road?

One does not know, sir. Possibly a predator was behind the chicken. Or, possibly, there was a female chicken on the other side, if it's a male chicken. Or possibly a food source, or, depending on the season, it might be migrating. One hopes there's no traffic.

Andrew's jokes after he learns
about a sense of humor

- Two cannibals were eating a clown. One turns to the other and says, " Does this taste funny to you?"

- How do you make a hanky dance? Put a little boogie in it.

- What is a brunette between two blondes? Translator.

- Do you know why blind people don't like to skydive? It scares their dogs.

- A man with dementia is driving on the freeway. His wife calls and says, "Sweetheart, I heard there's someone driving the wrong way on the freeway." He says, "One? There's hundreds!"

- What's silent, smells like worms? Bird farts.

- It must have been an engineer who designed the human body. Who else would put a waste process-ing plant next to a recreation area?*

- A woman goes into a doctor's office. The doctor says, "Mind if I numb your breasts?" "Not at all." " Num-num-num-num-num."

*This is the same joke Robin, as "President Tom Dobbs," used in Man of the Year.

WHAT THE CRITICS HAD TO SAY

Roger Ebert: "From the first moment we see Andrew, we're asking ourselves, is that really Robin Williams inside the polished alumi-num shell? *USA Today* claims it is, although at times we may be looking at a model or a computer-generated graphic. The robot's body language is persuasive; it has that same subtle courtliness that Williams himself often uses.... *Bicentennial Man* begins with promise, proceeds in fits and starts, and finally sinks into a cornball drone of greeting-card sentiment. Robin Williams spends the first half of the film encased in a metallic robot suit, and when he emerges, the script turns robotic instead. What a letdown." (from RogerEbert.com, December 17, 1999)

Stephen Holden: "As befits a Robin Williams movie, the screenplay (by Nicholas Kazan) pours on the sentimentality in lumpy, mawkish speeches about freedom, the joys of sex and the meaning of life. Not even Williams, pulling out every moist, sad-clown expression in his bag of grimaces, can redeem these speeches from sappiness. But as it lumbers toward a mystical romantic ending in an early-23rd-century hospital, *Bicentennial Ma*n achieves the pop grandiloquence of a *Star Trek* installment. In its warm, fuzzy, self-congratulatory humanistic vision, nothing in the universe beats being a flesh-and-blood mortal." (from *The New York Time*s, December 17, 1999)

A.I. Artificial Intelligence

(2001)

Starving minds, welcome to Dr. Know, where fast food for thought is served up twenty-four hours a day…in 40,000 locations nationwide. Ask Dr. Know. There's nothing I don't.

—Dr. Know

A.I. Artificial Intelligence has a similar theme to *Bicentennial Man*: the quest to become human (i.e., free). In *Bicentennial Man*, it's an adult male robot named Andrew (which became his name after Little Miss mangled the word "android") who wants to be declared a person; in *A.I.*, it's also a robot, but an eleven-year-old boy (a "mecha") named David (Haley Joel Osmont).

Steven Spielberg directs his own screenplay adaptation of Brian Aldiss's short story "Supertoys Last All Summer Long" and the movie is dedicated to Stanley Kubrick, who originally planned on producing it before he fired Aldiss. Spielberg took the reins after Kubrick's death. Kubrick described the film as "a picaresque robot version of *Pinocchio*." That's some lineup, and the expectations were sky high, so to speak.

But rather than a well-constructed sci-fi movie with a connected narrative, *A.I.* is all over the place. As Robin Williams fans, our interest is in the role Robin voiced for the film, that of the animated know-it-all, Dr. Know. Robin does what he can with the dialogue, but the sequence comes off as David and Gigolo Joe (Jude Law) interacting with a voice-activated Google or Alexa of the Future. David does, though, eventually learn where to find the Blue Fairy that will make him a real boy (see: *Pinocchio*), and that's a wrap for Robin.

A.I. has everything sci-fi, including an underwater Manhattan…and even aliens. They come in at the end to grant David his final wish after he's been frozen and deactivated for 2,000 years. Yes, you read that right: he's "asleep" for 2,000 years and awakens with nary a tweak in his appearance or in his single-minded goal, to see his human "mother" (Frances O'Connor) again.

There is one sequence of the film that's worth discussing on its own: the Flesh Fair.

Steven Spielberg has filmed some powerfully disturbing scenes. He did, after all, do *Schindler's List*. But the Flesh Fair in *A.I.* may win the prize for the most disturbing scenes he's ever shot. A Flesh Fair is an exhibition held in an arena in which obsolete, damaged, or unwanted androids are destroyed. They are, after all, just machines, right? As the emcee Lord Johnson-Johnson (Brendan Gleeson) reminds the crowd, "We are only demolishing artificiality."

But what is profoundly upsetting is that the robots all look like human begins. And they are aware of their fate. One pleads to have his "pain receivers" turned off before the "show" begins.

And what is the show? It consists of destruction of the mechas in the most sadistic, horrifying ways possible, done while they're "conscious" and still functioning. They are shot from a cannon into a flaming fan that ignites them and shreds them to pieces.

They are smashed into pieces and they are stood upright and restrained as acid is poured over them, dissolving them as they watch their "bodies" disintegrate.

And the crowd goes wild.

We're back in Rome, watching in the Colosseum as the lions tear slaves apart.

David is ultimately saved from being rended because he is so believable as a young boy that the crowd riots to prevent him from "dying."

For all its flaws, though, *A.I. Artificial Intelligence* is a masterpiece. The special effects, the performances, Spielberg's direction, and, yes, Robin (and even Chris Rock) contributing make it a must-see, and not just for Robin Williams fans.

WHAT THE CRITICS HAD TO SAY

Roger Ebert: "*A.I.* is audacious, technically masterful, challenging, sometimes moving, ceaselessly watchable. What holds it back from greatness is a failure to really engage the ideas that it introduces. The movie's conclusion is too facile and sentimental, given what has gone before. It has mastered the artificial, but not the intelligence." (from RogerEbert.com, June 29, 2001)

Charles Taylor: "*A.I. Artificial Intelligence* is Spielberg's attempt to unite…two strains, the showman and the adult filmmaker. It's a wildly problematic movie: ambitious on a scale that few filmmakers can even contemplate, daring in its attempt to make a break with its director's past work even as it extends the themes of that work, gutsy in its willingness to alienate audiences. It is also a mess of jarring impulses and tones that leaves viewers stranded, with no access to the film that makes emotional sense. Spielberg clearly wants to bring a new element of darkness and pessimism to his work but he's also wary of losing his audience—and perhaps not even philosophically comfortable with pessimism in the first place." (from *Salon*, June 29, 2001)

Death to Smoochy

(2002)

Whose toes do you have to suck to get a drink around here?

—**Rainbow Randolph**

The thing about *Death to Smoochy* is that it is not a movie you can watch without acknowledging that the story is satirical and the characters are caricatures. It's a cartoon come to life. Many reviews—and this is the reason for its notorious reputation as one of Robin's worst films—take the flick seriously.

We simply cannot take *Death to Smoochy* seriously, i.e., as a legitimate workplace comedy, a behind-the-scenes look at the oftentimes grotesque and greedy world of children's TV.

Nobody in real life talks or acts like the characters in Adam Resnick's over-the-top script.

The plot is convoluted, but understandable. Robin Williams plays a beloved kid's TV show host by the name of Rainbow Randolph, a bizarre clown-type, who gets kicked off the air for getting caught taking a bribe to put someone's kid on the show.

The network replaces Rainbow with Smoochy the Rhino, played by Sheldon Mopes (Edward Norton), who actually believes that singing inane folk songs to junkies at a methadone clinic is serving mankind and the greater good.

The rest of the movie consists of bizarre plot points, including a charity helmed by sleazy Merv Green (Harvey Fierstein), who is only looking to exploit Smoochy and skim his group's profits; the Irish Mob wanting to protect Smoochy so their "mascot," the too-many-punches-to-the-head demented Spinner Dunn (Michael Rispoli), can get a role on Smoochy's show; Rainbow Randolph's often-psychotic attempts to both kill Smoochy and get his own show back (including a Times Square attempted suicide scene in which Rainbow pours gasoline on himself and is saved from immolation by a little girl who blows out the match); and an assassination attempt by a disgraced former kid's show host named Buggy Ding Dong (Vincent Schiavelli).

The movie is, as Roger Ebert astutely notes in his review below, made by very talented people (you have to very good to be this bad), but the movie is not an enjoyable or entertaining watch. It's a chore.

One bright spot is the extremely gifted Catherine Keener, who plays Smoochy's love interest Nora and a shark-like network executive.

The movie ends, unexpectedly to say the least, with Rainbow and Smoochy becoming partners in a show. *After* what is probably the most bizarre ice show ever set on skates.

WHAT THE CRITICS HAD TO SAY

Roger Ebert: "Only enormously talented people could have made *Death to Smoochy*. Those with lesser gifts would have lacked the nerve to make a film so bad, so miscalculated, so lacking any connection with any possible audience.... We begin with Rainbow Randolph, played by Robin Williams, an actor who should never, ever, play a clown of any description, because the role writes a license for him to indulge in those very mannerisms he should be striving to purge from his repertory." (from RogerEbert.com, 2002)

Peter Travers: "*Death to Smoochy* allows Robin Williams to bust out of his sappy *Patch Adams* image by playing Randolph Smiley, a kiddie TV star with a preference for Johnnie Walker, backstage blow jobs and egofests in which he tells his staff, 'I'm Rainbow Fucking Randolph.' …This black-comic assault on family entertainment is going to set a lot of teeth on edge." (from *Rolling Stone*, March 29, 2002)

Claudia Puig: "The world of kids TV is ripe for parody, but Robin Williams's dark comedy *Death to Smoochy* doesn't have enough of the black humor one wants in such a farce. However good it is to see Williams in a comedic endeavor after his maudlin missteps *Patch Adams* and *Bicentennial Man*, it's too bad he isn't funnier." (from *USA Today*, Match 28, 2002)

Insomnia
(2002)

You and I share a secret. We know how easy it is to kill someone.
That ultimate taboo. It doesn't exist outside our own minds.
—Walter Finch

Insomnia is a great movie. And it is one of Robin Williams's utterly unfunny performances. His character Walter Finch barely cracks a smile, let alone cracks a joke.

The film is Christopher Nolan's remake of the 1997 Norwegian film, *Insomnia*, and also stars Al Pacino and Hilary Swank.

Robin's performance is considered to be one of his best, but he doesn't even show up in the film until an hour has passed. His voice is on two phone calls before we actually see him, and the first time we see his image is actually in a photograph.

Robin is a crime novelist who "accidentally" killed a seventeen-year-old girl to make her stop laughing at him. Al Pacino is a Los Angeles detective named Will Dormer who is currently being investigated by internal affairs for tampering with evidence. He is sent to Nightmute, Alaska, to investigate the girl's murder, and after he "accidentally" shoots his partner (who has decided to cut a deal with internal affairs that would implicate Will), he starts hearing from Walter, who is completely forthcoming about murdering Kay. But he didn't mean to do it, you see, and he has a plan to save Will's lifetime of work and also get off the hook for Kay's murder by framing her cheating boyfriend.

Complicating matters for outsider Will is that Nightmute is one of those Alaskan towns that never gets dark for several months each year. In an early scene that takes place in what seems to be broad daylight, Will asks to be taken to the high school the boyfriend attends to arrest him in front of his friends. Detective Ellie Burr (Swank) has this exchange with him:

> **Will:** I want to go to the school. Pull him out in front of friends. Catch him off guard. It will get people talking. So how far away is the school?
>
> **Ellie:** It's ten o'clock, Detective Dormer.
>
> **Will:** You bet.
>
> **Ellie:** At night.

Will's subsequent devastating insomnia plays a role in how he deals with the case, but also seems to fine-tune his detective's intuition, allowing him to come to conclusions, as well as moral decisions, that provide a satisfying if bloody, conclusion.

The dialogue, cinematography, performances, and editing are as close to flawless as is possible, and the film has a solid 92 percent rating on Rotten Tomatoes's Tomatometer. *Insomnia* is one of Robin Williams's best films.

WHAT THE DIRECTOR HAD TO SAY

Christopher Nolan: "What I thought of Robin, was, well, he is an extraordinary guy to work with and he really gave what I consider to be a flawless performance. I wound up watching the film hundreds of times as we cut it, and I never hit that point with the performance where you start to see the acting. Most performances, at a point, bits start to peel off and away, but with Robin's he was very much in that character. Not that he's a very dark person to work with—he's very lively and friendly and amusing to work with. He really found something within himself. I think it's a very underrated bit of work on his part." (comment made at the Hero Complex Film Festival, June 14, 2010)

WHAT THE CRITICS HAD TO SAY

Roger Ebert: "[Al] Pacino and [Robin] Williams are very good together. Their scenes work because Pacino's character, in regarding Williams, is forced to look at a mirror of his own self-deception. The two faces are a study in contrasts. Pacino is lined, weary, dark circles under his eyes, his jaw slack with fatigue. Williams has the smooth, open face of a true believer, a man convinced of his own case." (from RogerEbert.com. May 24, 2002)

Peter Travers: "As Walter Finch, a novelist who befriended the murdered girl, [Robin] Williams doesn't enter the film until near the midpoint, but he brings a scary intensity to the role that's electrifying." (from *Rolling Stone*, May 8, 2002)

One Hour Photo

(2002)

According to The Oxford English Dictionary...the word "snap-shot" was originally a hunting term.

I just took pictures.

—Sy Parrish

One Hour Photo might be a perfect thriller. Why? Because everything you think you know about the behavior of photo guy Sy Parrish (Robin Williams), and how you think the movie will end, is turned on its head by the end of the film. And even with its images of violence and threatening scenes of peril, nobody dies.

Once upon a time, people took pictures on film, and then the pictures had to be developed. That's the period in which *One Hour Photo* takes place. There's an interesting exchange between Nina Yorkin (Connie Nielsen) and Sy as she's dropping off her film. She tells him her husband is trying to convince her to go digital, i.e., buy a digital camera. Sy tells her not to do that because then he'd lose his job. He ignores the potential convenience, quality, and cost elements of getting away from film and (as a deranged narcissist) only worries about himself.

One Hour Photo is *unnerving*. Robin Williams disappears into his character quite effectively, and even when Sy smiles, it's a thin, creepy smile.

Sy the photo guy has been developing people's pictures at SavMart for eleven years. He is meticulous about the quality of the prints he creates and considers even a tiny percentage of color inaccuracy a huge problem—which does not endear him to the equipment techs who he summons to the SavMart for what is essentially a wasted trip.

Sy's favorite customers are the Yorkins, an all-American, seemingly perfect family who have been bringing their film to Sy forever, and who consider him a weird but friendly guy. One of the most horrifying things we learn about Sy is that he has a photo collage consisting of almost 900 photographs covering a wall of his apartment—and they're all of the Yorkins. After Sy gets fired for making extra copies of photos for himself and giving away cameras to favorite customers (like Jakob Yorkin), he decides to target Will for vengeance. The cops discover that he has scratched out Will's face in every single photo on his wall.

Sy learns that the truth about the Yorkins is a little different— Will Yorkin (Michael Vartan) is having an affair with one of Sy's customers—Sy sees a lot in the pics he develops—and this upsets Sy to no end.

After getting fired by his boss, Bill (Gary Cole), Sy snaps. He begins stalking Nina Yorkin and her son Jake, and slips a picture of Will kissing his lover Maya (Erin Daniels) into pics Jake took and that Nina picked up (he developed Maya's pictures and saw the incriminating shot). After losing his job, Sy felt that Will should be the one to receive punishment. This makes no sense, but Sy is a sociopath and logic is not his default mode when it comes to the Yorkins.

Sy tracks Will and Maya to a hotel, manages to get into their room, and forces them to perform sexually explicit acts, which he photographs. He then leaves, and is caught, arrested, and questioned by Detective James Van Der Zee (Eriq La Salle). We then realize that we've already seen this interrogation scene: It is the opening scene of the movie.

During a return to the questioning scene that takes place at the end of the film, Sy goes off on a rant that suggests he may have been a victim of child abuse by his father, and that might have been the traumatic psychological injury that triggered his sense of alienation and moved him toward isolation and avoiding relationships—except for the superficial ones with his idealized customers. He tries repeatedly to be considered as "Uncle Sy" to the Yorkins, but they make it clear they'd like to keep him at a distance and are content dealing with him only over the photo counter.

The twist at the end of the movie is that, even though Sy threatened Maya and Will with a knife, he didn't harm either of them, other than psychologically and emotionally. Maya is found naked and in the tub; Will is found in a robe sitting on the edge of the hotel bed.

At the end of the interview session, Sy asks if he can see the pictures he took in the hotel. We obviously think they're going to be pics of Maya and Will naked and having sex. But they're not. They're pictures of the bathroom fixtures, the shower curtain, and other mundane objects in the hotel room.

Sy did what he did solely to emotionally torture Will and Maya. He had to destroy what he could not have. A final scene shows Will returning home, his son Jake hugging him, and his wife Nina just staring at numbly at him.

In the special features on the DVD, Robin talks about why he wanted to do *One Hour Photo*: "This is something different from anything I've done…doesn't look like anything I've done…doesn't feel like anything I've done … This is fascinating. It's worth being a part of." On an episode of *The Charlie Rose Show* included in the special features, Robin talks about what some people called his "triptych of evil," which consisted of *Death to Smoochy, Insomnia,* and *One Hour Photo*, all of which came out in 2002. He also mentioned two previous characters he considered "dark," which were his roles in *Dead Again* and *The Secret Agent*.

WHAT ROBIN HAD TO SAY

"[Sy] is nice, but with a dark side. He does things that are creepy, that are bizarre…. He's almost like a creature that blends into its environment. You see the clothes…the hair, everything is designed to be part of it." (from the "Making of *One Hour Photo*" featurette in the special features on the DVD)

WHAT DIRECTOR MARK ROMANEK HAD TO SAY

"We tried to make a non-judgmental and un-ironic movie." (from the "Making of *One Hour Photo*" featurette in the special features on the DVD)

WHAT THE CRITICS HAD TO SAY

James Berardinelli: "*One Hour Photo* is an actor's triumph—a fitting destination for Robin Williams to reach after essaying increasingly darker and more dysfunctional characters in films like *Death to Smoochy* and *Insomnia*. The actor, who once was known almost exclusively for his comedic roles, has painstakingly reworked his image over the past few years, following in the footsteps of other funny men who have displayed impressive dramatic ability and range. Any lingering doubts about Williams's ability to play a role completely straight (and there shouldn't be any after *Good Will Hunting* and *Insomnia*) are erased by *One Hour Photo*." (from reelviews.net, 2002)

Peter Travers: "It would have been easy for Robin Williams to play Sy Parrish—Sy the Photo Guy to his customers—as the monster at the mall. Going the psycho route is a ham actor's dream. But Williams, following the spare lead of director Mark Romanek (the video whiz bringing a striking style to the film), gives a performance that is riveting in its recessiveness and, as a consequence, truly, deeply scary.... Williams handles the gradations of Sy's madness with subtle skill—we're a long way here from the soppy excesses of *Patch Adams* and *Bicentennial Man*." (from *Rolling Stone*, September 13, 2002)

Roger Ebert: "Robin Williams plays Sy, another of his open-faced, smiling madmen, like the killer in *Insomnia*. He does this so well you don't have the slightest difficulty accepting him in the role. The first time we see Sy behind his counter, neat, smiling, with a few extra pounds from the diner routine, we buy him. He belongs there." (from RogerEbert.com, August 23, 2002)

Elvis Mitchell: "Mr. Williams plays Sy as all middle-brow vanity; for him, cleanliness is not only next to godliness, it's also a form of integrity." (from *The New York Times*, August 21, 2002)

When asked by Charlie Rose if he ever wanted to direct, Robin replied, "My only wish is to cater."

The Rutles 2: Can't Buy Me Lunch

(2002)

The lunch you make is equal to the lunch you take.

—**Tom Hanks**

This is a chapter about a sequel to a Beatles mockumentary in a book about the work of Robin Williams?

Yes, because Robin makes a short appearance in *The Rutles 2: Can't Buy Me Lunch* as German rockologist and sexologist Hans Hänkie.

At around fifteen minutes into *Can't Buy Me Lunch*, Robin Williams appears as Hänkie, speaking fake German to someone off-screen. Then he launches into this obviously improvised monologue:

> That was Hitler's original design for a plane called the Shtupa, which was designed to drop large penises on the enemy. Screaming penises. The Shtupa would fall from the skies dropping penises. But they changed it to the Shtuka because they are afraid. Because Hitler only had one ball. And Göring had no balls.

Melvin the interviewer (Eric Idle) then asks, "What about the Rutles?":

> Oh, the Frauleins. Crazy for them. Yelling at them "[fake German]." Sounds like, "I want dick." But no, it means, "I love you. I love you." And they loved them. More than just love. They wanted them.

Melvin thanks him and Hänkie replies, "Oh, it's great to talk with you. And will the check clear?" Melvin replies, "It'll be a small one from the BBC."

Hänkie responds:

> Oh, BBC. I remember listening to them as a child. "The chicken has no lips." We would hear your broadcasting. "The fox is in a nightgown. I repeat. The fox is in a nightgown." You are crazy people. I wonder how you won the war with these strange riddles you're broadcasting. But yet the French blew up a train afterwards. I remember my uncle said, "The fox is in a nightgown," and the train blew up. Yeah, I have bad memories.

Robin appears later on in the film, at around the fifty-one-minute mark. This is his second monologue:

> Could you think of any Communist rock bands? No, I don't think so. There was nothing called the Village People's Republic, you know. There was no bands of two million gay Chinese.

Robin was a lifelong Beatles fan, but was just starting out in his career when the first mockumentary *The Rutles: All You Need is Cash* was produced in 1978, so he wasn't in that film. But twenty-four years later, he was able to pay tribute to the Pre-Fab Four and make a (somewhat bizarre) appearance in *Can't Buy Me Lunch*.

WHAT THE CRITICS HAD TO SAY

Nathan Rabin: "*The Rutles: All You Need Is Cash* was a Beatles satire by people who clearly loved and understood their source material and bothered to get the details right. *Rutles 2* qualifies as little more than an overly reverent tribute to the 1978 original, and it barely bothers with the details at all. (Robin Williams's footage, in particular, looks as if it belongs in a different film, though nagging aesthetic concerns are always a secondary irritation when dealing with Williams.)" (from film.avclub.com, March 29, 2005)

House of D

(2004)

If you make a wish, and don't tell nobody, it could come true.

—**Pappass**

Where the prison once was, there is now a garden.

—**On-screen text from the**
***House of D* alternate ending**

David Duchovny says he wrote the script for *House of D*, his directorial debut, in six days. The snarky among us would likely offer as a retort, "We can tell," or some such other denigrating insult about his screenplay. Well, not here, and not today.

House of D is a touching—and, yes, well-written—coming of age story with excellent performances by Anton Yelchin (Tommy Warshaw), Téa Leoni (Mrs. Warshaw), and, of course, Robin Williams (Pappass). Also worth noting is that Tommy Warshaw's love interest Melissa is played by Robin's real daughter, Zelda Williams. She delivers a first-rate performance, although knowing that the character of "Pappass" is her real-life dad, a couple of the scenes come off as a bit cringy. Especially the scene in which Pappass tells Melissa, "I have a huge penis."

Duchovny plays the adult Tommy Warshaw in the beginning and end segments of the movie—scenes that are set in the present day. The rest of the movie is an extended flashback to 1973 New York that tells fourteen-year-old Tommy's story during a critical and tragic period of his young life.

Robin Williams plays Tommy's best friend Pappass, a mentally-challenged janitor who works at Tommy's school. Robin's face, which took two hours of makeup each day to achieve, looks weird. Of it, Robin said, "I had fake teeth and my ears pushed forward to transform the face. There's a certain disorder where people look very elf-like, and we went with that one" (robin-williams.net). In the final scenes of the film, which take place in the present time, he also wore a fat suit.

Frequently, Yelchin's character Tommy talks to "Lady" (Erykah Badu) from the street beneath her window in the Women's House of Detention. She advises him and serves as a surrogate mom, just as Pappass sometimes serves as a surrogate dad, even though Tommy is the more mature and intellectually capable person in that relationship.

Tommy goes to school on a scholarship and delivers meat as an afterschool job. Pappass pedals the bike and accompanies Tommy on all his deliveries. Their bond is tight and neither have positive home lives. Pappass's father (Mark Margolis) is a drunk and makes Pappass turn over any money he makes every day. Tommy's mother (Téa Leoni) is a nurse, a widow, and almost certainly addicted to tranquilizers. She has invested her entire sense of self in the hoped-for success of her son, yet she is clearly in psychological trouble. She overdoses on purpose one night and ends up brain dead, and Tommy is the one who furtively pulls the plug on her breathing machine in the hospital. Making a decision like that is difficult enough as an adult; making it as a fourteen-year-old is earth-shattering.

After his mom's death, distant relatives come to "take care" of Tommy. Lady tells him to run. He says goodbye to Pappass and spends the next couple of decades in Paris, where he marries and has a son.

He returns to New York and sees Pappas, Lady, and his old school. He tells his wife to come to New York with their son, and he introduces them to Pappass.

The movie ends with all of them standing in the garden where the House of Detention once stood.

House of D is a worthy entry in Robin's filmography. He does not deliver an over-the-top performance, as some critics had expected he would.

(Also worth mentioning is that *House of D* has an awesome '70s soundtrack, including the songs "Hold Your Head Up" by Argent; "China Grove" by the Doobie Brothers, "Melissa" by the Allman Brothers Band; "Funk #49" by the James Gang; "As" by Stevie Wonder; and "Harmony" by Elton John.)

WHAT ROBIN HAD TO SAY

"It has a lot of nice truths in it. For me that's the most interesting thing about the script." (from the special feature "Building the House of D" on the DVD)

WHAT THE CRITICS HAD TO SAY

Rex Reed: "It's a warm, nostalgic mood piece that recaptures a time and place when people were friendlier and more human, things were more positive, movies were more creative and life was more fun." (from *The Observer*, April 14, 2005)

Roger Ebert: "Sappy, inane, cornball, shameless...Tommy's [David Duchovny] best friend is Pappass...played by Robin Williams. Pappass is retarded. He is retarded in 1973, that is; when

Tommy returns many years later, Pappass is proud to report that he has been upgraded to 'challenged.' In either case he is one of those characters whose shortcomings do not prevent him from being clever like a fox as he (oops!) blurts out the truth, underlines sentiments, says things that are more significant than he realizes, is insightful in the guise of innocence, and always appears exactly when and where the plot requires." (from RogerEbert.com, April 28, 2005)

Peter Travers: "In his feature debut as a director, *X-Files* David Duchovny shows a sharp eye for composition. It's his tin ear for dialogue that dulls this nostalgia piece about Tom Warshaw (Duchovny), an artist living in Paris with his French wife and remembering his life in Manhattan, circa 1973, when he turned thirteen…Tommy partners with a retarded delivery guy named Pappass, played by Robin Williams without dodging any of the role's many mawkish pitfalls." (from *Rolling Stone*, April 15, 2005)

A. O. Scott: "The reasons to avoid *House of D*, David Duchovny's earnest, unwatchable coming-of-age drama, can best be summarized in a simple declarative sentence. Robin Williams plays a retarded janitor. For some reason, Mr. Williams, a comedian of prodigious gifts who occasionally shows himself to be a more than capable character actor, is fatefully drawn to a particular kind of sentimentality. The character of Pappass, a wise, kindly, mentally disabled man who helps guide a troubled boy on life's difficult journey, must have been irresistible to him, given his track record of crinkly, heartfelt mugging." (from *The New York Times,* April 15, 2005)

The Final Cut

(2004)

Is suicide under Self-Help?

—**Alan Hakman**

Think about everything you've seen and heard during your life. Yes, even *that* stuff. Now imagine that someone could watch any, or all of that material, on video, and on demand, so to speak.

That is the premise of *The Final Cut*.

In the not-so-distant future, the technology exists to implant a two-millimeter wide organic device into an unborn child's brain. This implant will record anything and everything that child sees and hears from the moment of birth until his or her death.

The implant is called the Zoe Implant and, upon the person's death, an editor, known as a Cutter, is given the complete recording of that person's life and he or she is tasked with cutting it down (using, we kid you not, a device called The Guillotine) into a two-hour or so movie called a Rememory.

The Cutters have a code:

I.   A Cutter cannot sell or give away Zoe footage.

II. A Cutter cannot have a Zoe implant.

III. A Cutter cannot mix Zoe footage from different lives for a
Rememory.

Robin Williams is Alan Hakman, one of the most respected
and sought-after Cutters in the business. His Rememories are legendary and also, what families love the most, empathetic. He is
careful to edit out the ugly stuff: the beatings, the visceral obscen-
ity and, of course, the crimes.

The Guillotine organizes a person's hundreds of thousands of
hours of life (a seventy-five-year-old man would have recorded
657,000 hours at the time of their death, for example) into
categories, including sleep, eating, career, education, etc., and
includes categories like violence, masturbation, travel, and more.
The Cutter then scans and edits until a presentation that can be
viewed in one sitting is finalized.

This is an intriguing concept and an entire movie could have
been made just on the lives and experiences of various Cutters,
i.e., what they leave in, what they leave out, and how they make
determinations as to what to preserve and what to obliterate from
a person's life.

But *The Final Cut* seems to want to be a murder mystery
instead of a tech-driven sci-fi film. The movie opens with Alan
witnessing the death of his ten-year-old friend Louis Hunt. Louis
fell from a high board in a barn. Alan remembers leaving bloody
footprints in the dirt as he flees the barn after checking Louis's
body. This event has haunted him throughout his life, and he uses
Louis's rabbit foot necklace as a bookmark in his Cutter notebook.

The second subplot in the movie involves anti-implant activists who want the Zoe footage of a recently deceased wealthy
tycoon named Bannister, believing he abused his daughter, and
that if they reveal this information, the Zoe implant would be
banned. The activists protest outside Rememory ceremonies and

carry signs with slogans like "Remember for Yourself," "Live for Today," "Open Your Eyes," and "Consent Not Control." Hakman agrees to do Bannister's Rememory.

These are a lot of plots to juggle and the script cannot, by necessity, treat each equally. The whole Hakman and Delila (Mira Sorvino) relationship thread is given short shrift, as is the stunning revelation that Hakman has a Zoe implant and that the death of Louis Hunt is on it.

The immediate problem with Hakman having a Zoe implant is that the company who hired him as a Cutter would have known he had one and disqualified him. (Remember Part II of the Cutter's Code?) How do we know they know? Hakman steals his original Zoe implant records from the company.

The story gets a little muddy, but ultimately anti-implant activist and former Cutter Fletcher (Jim Caviezel) conspires to have Hakman killed and it is revealed he plans to use Hakman's Zoe implant (which, remember, has seen everything Hakman has seen in his years as a Cutter, including the Bannister stuff) to expose and destroy Bannister's legacy.

This is after, though, Hakman manages to access his own Zoe implant and discover that Louis did not die in the barn and that the bloody footprints were actually made by him stepping in paint.

The Final Cut is an enjoyable sci-fi movie and features a non-comedic, intensely dramatic performance by Robin that is the epitome of "restrained." Even when Hakman smiles, he looks, as critic Mick LaSalle described it, "incurably depressed."

The Zoe Implant

The Zoe Implant is a tiny chip, just two millimeters wide, that is implanted into an unborn child's brain. It interacts

> with the surrounding nerve endings, "plugging in" to the impulses that control seeing and hearing. By doing so, it is able to record both sight and sound, keeping a permanent record of the subject's life for posterity.
>
> *From the Zoe Implant promotional material*

WHAT ROBIN HAD TO SAY

"When you read something this good and this unique, you wanna do it, and that's why everyone's here."

"There is still that thing about human memory vs. computer memory that is still quite unique and adaptable and malleable according to what emotions have affected you."

"Eventually these interviews will be conducted by two A.I.s. Thank you for coming." (All quotes are from an interview with Robin on the special features on the DVD.)

WHAT THE CRITICS HAD TO SAY

Roger Ebert: "Robin Williams stands apart from the problems of *The Final Cut*, just as he stands apart from the other characters. It's been said that inside every comedian is a sad man refusing to weep. Williams has extraordinary success in channeling this other person. How strange that the same actor can play some of the most uninhibited of all characters, and some of the most morose." (from RogerEbert.com, October 14, 2004)

Mick LaSalle: "Robin Williams plays an expert cutter, a role that makes good use of Williams's tendency to look incurably depressed. Like a priest or an emergency room doctor, a cutter is forced into a daily confrontation with human frailty and perfidy. With Williams—whose aura of misery doesn't seem self-indulgent but rather the result of a heightened sensitivity to others' suffering—we understand the toll this takes. It's in his haunted eyes, in his tentativeness and his inability to engage with people. He sees entire lives, but he sees only the surfaces of those lives, not the thoughts or the imagination, where most of life is lived." (from SFGate.com, October 15, 2004)

Noel
(2004)

I don't want to be alone when I die.

—**Charlie Boyd**

Noel does not seem like a Christmas movie even though it is set on Christmas Eve and Christmas Day in New York City.

Why? Because the denizens of its world are, for the most part, sad—Christmas carols (sung by nuns, of course), Christmas lights, and the tree at Rockefeller Plaza notwithstanding.

Susan Sarandon plays Rose Collins, a book editor who is single, childless, and alone on Christmas Eve.

Rose's mother is lost to her from Alzheimer's, but that doesn't stop Rose from decorating her room with family photos, visiting her daily, and talking to her as though she was still cognizant of her presence, which, until the end, she most assuredly is not.

One day, Rose steps into the room across the hall from her mother's room to pay a visit to the bedridden man there who never gets any visitors. He just *lies there*, and this troubles Rose. She is surprised to find a man sitting in the corner of the room. He greets her and we learn that this is Charlie Boyd, played by Robin Williams in one of his occasional uncredited roles.

Rose later again runs into Charlie as she stands on the dock of the East River staring down into the icy water. Is she considering suicide? Possibly, but Charlie tells her he'll have to go in after her if she jumps, so they end up going to her apartment. He tells her he was once a priest, and he spends the night there (platonically). The next morning he tells her that her mother "spoke" to him and told him she wants Rose to be happy. This horrifies Rose and she throws him out.

Later, she finds her mother eating and more aware of her surroundings. Rose also asks the nurse about the visitor the man across the hall had the previous day and learns that no one had visited him. *But I'm looking for Charlie Boyd*, she insists. *He was here*. And that's when *Noel* morphs into a supernatural fable. That's when the nurse tells Rose that Charlie Boyd is the guy lying in the bed. Suddenly understanding that Charlie had one last mission to fulfill in his earthly life, Rose squeezes his hand and tells him he can leave now. And his wish to her that he not be alone when he dies was granted. His spirit had physically manifested to help a soul in trouble and Rose, thus, has a happy—if tear-jerking—ending to her Christmas story.

Noel has a couple of other concurrent stories running throughout, but they're not as interesting or emotionally satisfying as the story of Rose's redemption and Charlie Boyd's peaceful transition to the next life.

Alan Arkin is very good as the widower who searches for the reincarnation of his late wife every Christmas Eve, and Paul Walker and Penelope Cruz are a standard youngish couple troubled by jealousy and trust issues.

The movie belongs to Susan Sarandon, though, and while, at first, *Noel* comes off as somewhat depressing, it does end on a relatively happy note.

WHAT THE CRITICS HAD TO SAY

Roger Ebert: "In Chazz Palminteri's new film, the most miserable character is probably Rose (Susan Sarandon), a divorced, middle-age book editor whose mother has disappeared into Alzheimer's. At one point she stands on the banks of a river, looking longingly at the icy water, but she's talked back from the edge by Charlie (Robin Williams), who she met in her mother's nursing home, where he was sitting in the corner in the dark in a room with an unmoving body on the bed—a body that Rose, in her desperation, one night told, 'I love you!'…Only a cynic could dislike this movie, which may be why I disliked it. I can be sentimental under the right circumstances, but the movie is such a calculating tearjerker that it played like a challenge to me." (from RogerEbert.com, November 11, 2004)

Dave Kehr: "The various stories swirl together, some drifting into the realm of the supernatural (where we encounter an unbilled Robin Williams, in one of his sad clown roles) and others into the more prosaically therapeutic." (from *The New York Times*, November 12, 2004)

Noel Murray: "Actor Chazz Palminteri lined up an amazing cast for *Noel*, his feature directorial debut. He's got Susan Sarandon as a New York book editor dealing with her Alzheimer's-stricken mother, Robin Williams as the mysterious stranger who hangs out in the hospital room next to Sarandon's mom…. But no matter how good the actors or how sweet the premise, *Noel*'s characters never become more than characters. Everything they say and do happens because they're in a movie." (from *The AV Club*, November 8, 2004)

Robots

(2005)

When in Robot City, guests of the Rusties—that's us—stay at Aunt Fanny's boarding house, where our motto is: "Beats rustin' outside."

—Fender

Robots is a movie for kids, but it has a few double entendre jokes ("Grow some bolts," for example) that might keep the adults amused enough to watch the whole thing without getting too bored.

As with the majority of kids' films these days, *Robots* comes with a message. Multiple messages, actually.

The first is "be true to yourself"; i.e., follow your dream. Rodney wants to be an inventor, so his parents encourage him to travel to Robot City to apply for a job with Bigweld Industries, helmed by the "greatest robot in the world," Mr. Bigweld, Rodney's idol.

While there, he meets Fender, a red robot who preys on tourists and who shepherds Rodney to Bigweld using a transportation system that offers what might be the most entertaining sequence of the movie. Tubes, and spring-loaded catapults, and all manner of contraptions and roller coaster-like devices speed Rodney to Bigweld, where he is refused entry by a puppet-like guard straight out of *The Wizard of Oz*.

Rodney and Fender manage to sneak their way in, where they learn that the malevolent and money-hungry Phineas Ratchet has taken over the company and secreted Mr. Bigweld away from everyone.

Ratchet's evil plan is simple: no more robot repairs. Expensive upgrades only. This will mean the "demise" of countless older and broken-down robots. Thus, the second message: corporations are greedy and evil and will place profit over "people" (robots) at every opportunity. Robots needing spare parts will instead be sent to the Chop Shop where they will be destroyed and melted down to be used to make new, profitable robots.

And thus we learn the mission of Rodney, Fender, and their entire crew of motley machines: rescue Mr. Bigweld, remove Ratchet from power, and provide all the spare parts and repairs the robot population of the world needs.

They, of course, succeed, and after bringing his dishwasher (literally) father the spare parts he needs to survive, the movie ends with all the residents of Rodney's hometown dancing to "Get Up Offa That Thing" by the legendary James Brown.

Robin's performance as Fender serves the script well and there are occasional flashes of comedian Robin, particularly when he does a few voices, including a Spanish accent and Britney Spears singing "…Baby One More Time."

WHAT THE CRITICS HAD TO SAY

Roger Ebert: "The thing that struck me first of all about *Robots* was its pictorial beauty. I doubt that was the intention of the filmmakers, who've made a slapstick comedy set in a futurist city that seems fresh off the cover of a 1942 issue of *Thrilling Wonder Stories*." (from RogerEbert.com, March 10, 2005)

James Berardinelli: "Leave it to Robin Williams to save the day. While his vocal performance isn't quite up to the standard he established in *Aladdin*, it's only a rung lower. It brings life and energy to *Robots*. Most of Williams' dialogue has an improvisational quality to it—as if he was told the substance of his dialogue, but was given carte blanche as far as word choice and delivery. The result is a sense of spontaneity. We're never quite sure what Williams' animated alter-ego is going to say or do next. That element of the film will keep adults interested long after the storyline has shifted into autopilot." (from reelviews.net, March 11, 2005)

The Big White

(2005)

Margaret Barnell: *Tastes like a rectal polyp.*

Jimbo: *How would she know?*

In an interview with Marc Maron, Robin said that *The Big White* was the movie that made him go back to drinking. After twenty years of sobriety, the isolation and cold during the making of the film were too much to handle, so he fell off the wagon.

So, was it the movie? Or the miserable ordeal of spending weeks in a frozen, bone-chilling landscape? Maybe both?

The Big White seems to want to be a hybrid of *Fargo* and *Raising Arizona*, but it falls short of both, for the most part. It fails to achieve the comedic brilliance of *Raising Arizona* and the twisted darkness of *Fargo* (David Mattin of the BBC said the film "wants to be a cross between small-screen hits *Northern Exposure* and *Frasier*").

It's got dark themes, as Robin Williams noted. But he also said it was funny, but that's something individual viewers will have to decide. Robin is notably not funny in this flick. The one scene in which Robin's character Paul Barnell tries to tell a joke to an insurance executive, he gets cut off. (The joke was "This grasshopper walks in a bar. And the bartender says, 'We have a drink named after you.' And the grasshopper says…" And that's where Barnell got interrupted in the movie. The usual punchline for this joke is, "No kidding? You have a drink named Steve?")

The plot's what we might call "textbook wacky." Ever since *A Weekend at Bernie's*, any movie that involves a dead guy being a main character and being carted all over the place is usually considered de facto wacky.

Paul Barnell (Robin Williams) owns a struggling ("failing" is actually more accurate) travel agency and is married to Margaret, who has Tourette's Syndrome. Broke and desperate, he attempts to cash in a life insurance policy he has on his brother Ray (Woody Harrelson), who has been missing for five years. The problem, though, is that a person has to be missing for seven years before they can be declared legally dead.

Faced with towering financial woes, Barnell is at his wit's end until—and here's where the "wacky" kicks in—he happens to find a corpse in the dumpster outside his travel agency. The dead guy was a mob hit, and Barnell decides to pass him off as his dead brother Ray.

The guy who ordered the hit wants to see the dead guy as proof of the hit, so the hitmen track the missing-from-the-dumpster corpse to Barnell (he kept it in his basement refrigerator) and when they invade Barnell's home, they're confronted by his wife Margaret, who they take hostage until they get the body back. The hostage scenes allow Holly Hunter to method act Tourette's, complete with cursing, bizarre behavior, and absolutely zero fear.

The discovery of the eaten-by-wolves body of the mob hit (yes, Barnell went all out to convince authorities that the body was his brother) ends up being written about in *USA Today* and Ray shows up from Florida, beats up Paul, and demands half of the insurance settlement.

Claims adjuster Ted Waters (Giovanni Ribisi) doesn't believe that the body is Ray, and much of the movie revolves around his multiple tries to uncover the fraud perpetrated by Barnell. (And Waters's girlfriend Tiffany (Alison Lohman) runs a psychic hotline from their apartment. Remember? "Wacky.")

The movie ends with Ray dying, Paul keeping the money (and possibly paying off Waters?), and Paul and Margaret taking off for a vacation in Hawaii, which they can now afford since they were able to keep the million-dollar payoff on Ray's life insurance policy.

The Big White is competently directed (Mark Mylod went on to direct both *Games of Thrones* and Golden Globes winner *Succession* episodes), very well-acted, and the snow-covered landscapes are gorgeous. But the parts in this case do not conspire to make for a memorable whole.

Robin Williams talks about suicide

WTF Podcast with Marc Maron, April 26, 2010

When I was drinking there was only one time, even for a moment, where I thought, "Fuck life."...Then even my conscious brain went like "Did you honestly just say "Fuck life"? You know you have a pretty good life as it is right now. Have you noticed the two houses? Yes. Have you noticed the girlfriend? Yes. Have you noticed that things are pretty good even though you're not working right now? Yes. Let's put the suicide over here and discuss it. Let's put that in the discussion area.

First of all you don't have the balls to do it. I'm not going to say it out loud. Have you thought about buying a gun? No. What were you going to do, cut your wrist with a water pick? Maybe...

Can I put that here in the "What the Fuck!" Category? Can I ask you what you're doing right now? You're sitting in a hotel room with a bottle of Jack Daniels. Is this maybe influencing your decision? Possibly.

OK. And who's that in the bed over there? I don't know. Well don't discuss that with her cuz she may tweet it. This may not be good...let's put that over here. We can talk about that in therapy or maybe a podcast two years from now. You wanna talk about it in a podcast? No. I feel safe. You're talking about it in a podcast. Who is this? It's your conscience, Asshole.

WHAT ROBIN HAD TO SAY

"[*The Big White*] is a really interesting dark comedy...with darker themes, but funny." (from the special features on *The Big White* DVD)

WHAT THE CRITICS HAD TO SAY

Philip French: "Giovanni Ribisi is rather good as the claims investigator, but the picture is never funny, only occasionally exciting and not very convincing." (from theguardian.com, March 25, 2006)

Stella Papamichael: "Despite being an A-List star, Robin Williams occasionally likes to mix it up with low-budget features like *The Big White*. Unfortunately, this dark comedy about a man trying to pass off a random corpse as his dead brother for the insurance payout was a good idea marred by 'cheap and obvious' gags." (from bbc.co.uk/films, August 4, 2006)

RV

(2006)

Whenever a big white man picks up a banjo, my cheeks tighten.

—Bob Munro

RV is one of Robin Williams's better mid-period comedies. It's got a strong pedigree, with Robin starring in a script directed by Barry Sonnenfeld of the *Men in Black* franchise, and co-starring Jeff Daniels, Cheryl Hines, Kristin Chenoweth, and Will Arnett.

RV is a rather broad (there are a couple of over-the-top "poop" bits), somewhat formulaic comedy, but there are several laugh-out-loud moments, the type of scenes sometimes missing from some of Robin's less-than-funny comedies.

Bob Munro (Robin) works for a soda company that is trying to convince another company to merge with them. Robin's germophobic boss Todd (Will Arnett) insists that Robin make a presentation to the two brothers who own the company, requiring Bob to cancel his family's planned trip to Hawaii. Bob decides to rent an RV and drive to the company in Colorado rather than fly—and he deceitfully doesn't tell his family the reason for this sudden change of plans. He instead paints a picture of them all going on a wonderful family road trip, even though he's never driven an RV before, and his wife and kids have no desire to embark on such a "vacation."

"Robin Williams driving an RV" is, let's face it, a comedy high concept, and Robin, Sonnenfeld, and company milk it for every laugh they can find. Robin, a master of physical comedy, right off the bat does a seatbelt bit that's very funny, and he almost wrecks the neighborhood just pulling away from his house.

The tagline for the movie is "One family. Eight wheels. No brakes."—and that pretty much sums it up. Just the notion of Bob taking his family on a road trip, having never done such a trip before, suggests the possible complications and problems they will almost certainly encounter. And they do, beginning with breaking the parking brake so that the RV rolls away whenever it's parked, and Bob not knowing how to empty the sewage tank (thus, giving us the aforementioned poop bits).

Bob and fam run into the Gornicke family, who live on a bus and travel the country. They're like the Partridge family on ecstasy, but dad Travis (Jeff Daniels) is a Stanford graduate and mom Mary Jo (Kristin Chenoweth) runs a highly successful makeup products franchise business from the bus.

Avoiding the Gornickes becomes a part of the Munros' agenda, but they ultimately end up saving Bob and family from some rather crazy predicaments.

There is physical comedy galore in *RV*, but there are also some heartfelt and genuine moments between Bob and his family, and between the Munros and the Gornickes.

Bob screws up the presentation and gets fired for it, but then is offered a big job with the company with which they wanted to merge. The brothers were so impressed with Bob's sincerity and him advising them to keep their family company in the family that they end up offering him a job.

And then the RV rolls over the brothers' cars and crushes them flat. Bob, you see, never got the parking brake fixed.

RV is a genuinely enjoyable and funny film. Robin plays it straight for the most part, except for the scene when he comes to the aid of his bullied son and does a whole hip-hop dude monologue, which was obviously improvised by Robin during shooting (there's a deleted scene in the special features which has Robin doing the same scene, but improvising a whole bit as a Kung Fu master).

WHAT THE CRITICS HAD TO SAY

Digby Lewis: "Robin Williams…gives a refreshingly entertaining performance.… *RV* is a well written comedy and welcome evidence of Williams's talent as a comic actor." (from BBC.com. June 17, 2006)

Roger Ebert: "There is nothing I much disliked but little to really recommend. At least the movie was not nonstop slapstick, and there were a few moments of relative gravity, in which Robin Williams demonstrated once again that he's more effective on the screen when he's serious than when he's trying to be funny." (from RogerEbert.com, April 27, 2006)

Jeannette Catsoulis: "Playing Bob Munro, an overworked soda-company executive, Robin Williams tricks us into believing he can control his inner maniac beyond the film's first 15 minutes; when he fails, any hopes of *RV* going off-formula are dashed." (from *The New York Times*, April 28, 2006)

The Night Listener

(2006)

I'll lay out the events exactly as I remember them. I want you to believe this, after all. That'll be hard enough as it is. This one is called "The Night Listener."

— **Gabriel Noone**

There is a pre-crawl end title at the conclusion of *The Night Listener* that reads:

> This film was inspired by a telephone friendship with what is believed to be a 14-year-old boy. To this day the existence of that boy has never been conclusively proven. He would be 28 years old today.

And the beginning of the movie tells the viewer it was inspired by true events.

Based on the novel by Armistead Maupin, the movie tells precisely that story, with Robin Williams as Gabriel Noone, the radio host who ends up engulfed in what was ultimately determined to be a faux relationship with a dying teenage boy.

In an interview with Maupin by Rob Vaux (Flipside Movie Emporium, August 7, 2008), Vaux writes:

[Maupin's book *The Night Listener*] is based on the real-life case of Anthony Godby Johnson, a young boy supposedly dying of AIDS who penned a memoir entitled *A Rock and a Hard Place*. In the 13 years since its publication, it has been uncovered as a likely hoax and Johnson appears to have been a fabrication of his "guardian," despite maintaining long-distance friendships with a number of prominent people.

Robin Williams is fiercely in his "not only am I not funny, I couldn't be funny if I tried" mode for his performance as Noone. Like Robin's character Nolan Mack in *Boulevard*, Noone is gay, but unlike Mack, Noone is openly gay and experiencing the sadness and trauma of the end of a long relationship he had with Jess (Bobby Cannavale) as the film begins.

Ashe (Joe Morton), an editor friend of Gabriel's, gives him a copy of a book that's coming out and encourages him to read it. It tells the sordid story of Pete Logand, who was sexually abused for years as a child—*with* his parent's knowledge and participation—and who is now in hiding to prevent his mother from finding him.

Gabriel is fascinated by the story and becomes somewhat obsessed with Pete when he gets a call from Pete's adoptive mother Donna, who puts Pete on the phone. Except, as Jess reminds him, Pete and Donna sound an awfully lot alike.

Gabriel becomes fully obsessed when he learns that no one has ever actually seen Pete, and he flies to Wisconsin to see him for himself.

Things do not go as Gabriel plans—Donna is blind, for one thing, and Pete is in some hospital that Gabriel can't find—and he eventually accepts that Pete, in all likelihood, was a fabrication of Donna.

The epilogue of the film shows Donna looking at a condo. She's now sighted, doesn't have a seeing-eye dog, and, she tells the realtor, is looking forward to having her son get out of the hospital tomorrow. "How," the realtor asks, "did your son lose his leg?"

We can add *The Night Listener* to the list of Robin Williams thrillers, which also includes *One Hour Photo, The Secret Agent, Insomnia*, and *The Final Cut*. These films highlight that even though he is known for being a wonderful comedian and comic actor, he should also be heralded for his powerful dramatic work.

WHAT THE CRITICS HAD TO SAY

James Berardinelli: "*The Night Listener* is an eerie, occasionally disturbing motion picture focused on the differences between perception and reality. The film exists in the gray area separating drama from psychological thriller, although the mood is in many ways more appropriate to the latter than the former, and it doesn't take much of a stretch to apply the word 'noir' to what's on hand." (from reelviews.net, August 4, 2006)

A. O. Scott: "Mr. Williams, in one of his blessedly shtick-free performances, effectively conveys Gabriel's weary, worried stoicism, but the movie limits his character to a few easy, literal motivations. A scene with Gabriel's bluff, Southern father (John Cullum) is intriguing without being especially illuminating, and Mr. Cannavale's character seems more functional than real." (from *The New York Times*, August 4, 2006)

Everyone's Hero

(2006)

Without that bat, he's just fat!

—**Napoleon Cross**

The animated *Everyone's Hero* was the last project Christopher Reeve and his wife Dana Reeve worked on before their deaths. Christopher Reeve died of sepsis in October 2004 at age 52; Dana Reeve died of lung cancer at age 44 in March 2006. Neither of them lived to see the film's September 2006 release.

Robin Williams, Chris Reeves's longtime friend, voiced the character of the owner of the Cubs, Napoleon Cross, but Robin rejected being credited for his role reportedly out of respect for his friend.

These facts alone imbue the movie with a tinge of sadness, yet it's still a decent kid's movie with a very positive, uplifting message: "Keep on swinging."

Everyone's Hero is set during the Great Depression. A kid named Yankee Irving is a big Yankees fan (his father is a janitor at Yankee Stadium), but he's a terrible baseball player. He comes across an abandoned baseball that can talk and he names it Screwie (voiced by Rob Reiner). Screwie has an attitude.

The Yanks are in the World Series, and everyone is hoping Babe Ruth will hit enough home runs to win the Series against the Chicago Cubs. However, Napoleon Cross, the Cubs' evil owner, plots to have Babe Ruth's bat Darlin' (voiced by Whoopi Goldberg) stolen and thus, hopefully, screw up the chances of the Yankees winning.

Yankee Irving manages to steal the Babe's bat back from the Cubs pitcher Lefty Maginnis (voiced by William H. Macy)—who Cross tasked with stealing it—and the rest of the movie is about Yankee's mission to get it to Chicago in time for the final game of the World Series.

Yankee encounters all manner of obstacles and challenges (the train scenes are particularly nerve-wrecking and very well-animated), but finally manages to find Babe Ruth and deliver the bat to him.

Incredibly, Yankee ends up being put in as a pitch hitter for the Yankees and, using Darlin' with Babe's blessing, he hits a home run (Lefty pitches Screwie at him) and he wins the World Series for the Yankees.

Everyone's Hero is a fun movie with some adult references put in (without moving out of the G rating, though), presumably, to prevent the parents from not getting too bored.

Robin has five or six scenes and is predictably capable at playing one of the villains in the flick. His character ends up getting caught and being arrested after the game ends.

It's an enjoyable movie for the younger crowd, but it's most memorable and noteworthy as the Reeves' final project.

WHAT THE CRITICS HAD TO SAY

Peter Hartlaub: "*Everyone's Hero* is a strange film, because it seems designed specifically for extremely old moviegoers to see with their great-great-grandchildren. With its 1930s setting, several of the jokes are so dated they may even go over the heads of some grandparents. ("Hey, there's a horse jumping off a diving board," a train passenger says while reading a newspaper. "Oh, wait, that's Eleanor Roosevelt.")" (from sfgate.com, September 15, 2006)

Jeannette Catsoulis: "Given that this is the last creative collaboration of Christopher and Dana Reeve (Christopher Reeve directed, along with Colin Brady and Dan St. Pierre, while Dana Reeve provided the voice of Yankee's mother), *Everyone's Hero* enters multiplexes already shadowed by tragedy. And while that may not be the best start for a kiddie feature, the movie's sentimental provenance could earn it a critical pass it doesn't deserve." (from *The New York Times*, September 15, 2006)

Man of the Year

(2006)

If Mama Cass had shared a lunch with Karen Carpenter, both would still be alive today...

—Tom Dobbs

The first third or so of *Man of the Year* is disconcerting to watch in this time of Trump, since a lot of what happens in the movie anticipated Trump's ascendancy as a candidate and his eventual election. Robin Williams plays Tom Dobbs, a comedian and talk show host who ends up running for president, essentially because he makes people laugh. He ends up winning the election, an event presented as far-fetched in the film, yet the viewer is expected to believe that it could actually have happened (considering the election of 2016, there is now some validity to that narrative conceit).

But Dobbs doesn't actually win the election because of a glitch (intentional?) in the new Delacroy voting systems installed all over the country. It isn't long before Eleanor Green (Laura Linney), a whistleblower who is fired from Delacroy, is being drugged and smeared in an attempt to save the company's enormous profits from the perceived success of the new system.

So is it a political satire? A thriller? A comedy? Yes and no to all three.

It does satirize modern politics, but only superficially. It does morph into a thriller after Eleanor starts telling people about the computer glitch, but the resolution is pat and implausible. And it is a comedy, if only because Robin Williams is in it, and there are set pieces in which he's allowed to let loose. The bonus features on Robin's stand-up performances in the film reveal lots of Robin jokes that didn't make it to the final cut.

Man of the Year is one of those movies in which the viewer may suddenly realize, "Everything would be made clear if she just said *this…*" or "All would be understood if he just did *that…*" But if they did, then there probably wouldn't be a movie.

All of the plot issues aside, though, the movie works particularly well on one specific level: the acting. The cast is comprised of A-List players and, in addition to the great Robin Williams, viewers are also treated to terrific performances by Christopher Walken, Laura Linney, Jeff Goldblum, and Lewis Black, as well as appearances by Faith Daniels, Tina Fey, Amy Poehler, James Carville, and Catherine Crier, all playing themselves.

Man of the Year is no *Wag the Dog* (another Barry Levinson political film), but it's definitely watchable, especially because of Robin Williams—and the outtakes thoughtfully provided add to the enjoyment. We can never get enough Robin Williams stand-up, and between the film and the bonus features, fans will consider watching *Man of the Year* time well spent.

WHAT THE DIRECTOR BARRY LEVINSON HAD TO SAY

"Working with Robin is great, because you have, you might say, a Ferrari, and then sometimes you wanna say, 'OK, let's hit the gas and just take off.'...It's not what you might call free improvisation. It has been worked on." (from the bonus features on the *Man of the Year* DVD)

WHAT THE CRITICS HAD TO SAY

Anna Smith: "*Man Of The Year* is rarely dull, but it's never compelling and ultimately unconvincing." (from bbc.co.uk, October 26, 2007)

Stephanie Zacharek: "It's a comedy, a political thriller, a love story: Barry Levinson's *Man of the Year* tries to be all things to all people and fails on every count—a little like the generic, ineffectual politicians it's pretending to excoriate." (from Salon.com, October 13, 2006)

Keith Phipps: If there's anything sadder than a satire without teeth, it's a thriller without thrills. Even sadder is the rare movie that fails at both genres simultaneously. That, and that alone, makes *Man Of The Year* exceptional. Actually, make that three genres: Might as well throw in science fiction, since the film stars Robin Williams as a *Daily Sho*w-like comedy-news-program host who becomes an unexpectedly viable political candidate based on his sheer hilarity." (from avclub.com, October 12, 2006)

Happy Feet

(2006)

There is a wisdom, brothers and sisters, that stands above all others. Never, ever, no matter what, drop your egg.

—**Lovelace**

How can you not love a movie that begins with the Beatles "Golden Slumbers," ends with a new Prince song, and features hundreds of tap-dancing and singing penguins, including a full-fledged production of Queen's "Somebody To Love"?

Happy Feet won an Academy Award for Best Animated Feature and the accolade was well-deserved. Writer/Director George Miller and his massive team of animators, voice artists, computer whizzes, and dancers created a completely immersive experience in which penguins talk, sing, dance, have accents, and believe in a penguin deity known as the "Great 'Guin."

Robin Williams voices the characters of Ramón and Lovelace and his performances add a lot of fun to the film. Mumble (Elijah Wood), the star of the show, is born without the ability to sing. Because he can't sing, he can't create his heartsong, which is what female penguins use to decide with whom they will mate. In penguin society, the females go fishing and the dads stay home on egg duty. The male's job is to keep the egg safe and warm until the little tyke pokes its way out of its shell. However, Mumble's dad Memphis (Hugh Jackman) accidentally dropped Mumble's egg, a blunder that resulted in Mumble not being able to sing, but instead being able to dance, a skill not welcomed or highly valued (initially) in penguin culture.

Mumble is ensorcelled with Gloria, but without a heartsong, the relationship seems to have no future. Also, Mumble's colony is experiencing problems with their food supply. A seabird wearing an electronic ankle band tells Mumble the story of aliens abducting him and blames them for the lack of fish in their habitat. The aliens are, of course, humans, and the lack of fish is due to over-fishing in the penguins' natural environment.

Mumble decides to seek out the aliens and talk to them. He wants to convince them to leave their food supply alone. During his voyage he washes up on a beach and ends up captured and placed at Marine World in Australia. He's imprisoned for months and just as he is about to completely lose his mind, a little girl taps on the glass to draw his attention. This inspires Mumble to tap dance for her. Humans are stunned by this development and determine that the penguins are trying to send a message. They return Mumble to his colony with a tracker on his back and they ban all maritime fishing in his area, thereby providing Mumble and his "people" a bountiful supply of fish.

In addition to highlighting the perils of over-fishing, the movie also takes a few well-aimed swipes at organized religion. One of the elder penguins is a religious leader and a demagogue who doesn't want to accept Mumble's assurance that if they all dance, the "aliens" will understand their plea and stop stealing their food. He uses language that could easily be interpreted in a religious context and he refers to angering the Great 'Guin the way many modern preachers speak about angering God.

The effects in *Happy Feet* are incredible; the production numbers are amazing; and the movie serves as an animated adventure, a cautionary tale, and a musical. And it does it all in an hour and forty-six minutes.

No wonder it won an Oscar.

And no wonder they did a sequel.

WHAT THE CRITICS HAD TO SAY

James Berardinelli: "As usual, Robin Williams adds spontaneity and humor to the proceedings (including at least one line that had me laughing out loud)." (from reelviews.net, November 17, 2006)

David Edelstein: "You should see *Happy Feet*—not only because it's stupendous, but also because it features the best dancing you'll see on the screen this year. Mumble comes tap-tap-tapping out of his egg, and all I could think as I watched was that somewhere Ray Bolger was smiling." (from *New York*, December 1, 2006)

Ron Yamauchi: "I've been enjoying the *Happy Feet* fruit snacks for several weeks and am pleased to report that the movie leaves an equally bizarre and artificial, yet strangely addicting, aftertaste." (from straight.com, November 22, 2006)

John Hayes: "*Happy Feet* will be remembered for its animation breakthroughs and fine voicing by a cast that includes Elijah Wood, Robin Williams, Hugh Jackman and Nicole Kidman." (from the *Pittsburgh Post-Gazette*, November 17, 2006)

Happy Feet Two

(2011)

You, me, beautiful egg, right now.

—**Ramon**

Remember when Andy Griffith left *The Andy Griffith Show* after eight seasons and CBS retitled it *Mayberry R.F.D.* and put Ken Berry in the lead as the head of the town council? *Happy Feet Two* kind of feels like that.

Mayberry R.F.D. did well and ran for three seasons, but it just wasn't the same. Mayberry was still supposed to be Mayberry, but it was undeniably *less than*.

Happy Feet Two did close to $160 million in box office receipts worldwide (less than half of *Happy Feet*'s $385 million, though) and that may not bode well for the possibility of a threequel. (In an interview with Christina Radish in 2011, director George Miller said, "If something comes up that's really exciting and I can convey that enthusiasm to other people, then there would be a third one.")

The narrative of *Happy Feet Two* is a bit all over the place, but the main plot point is that due to global warming, an iceberg has broken off an ice shelf and trapped the penguins in a crevice, separating them from their food source. Thus, the goal—and somewhat blatant ecological message—is save the penguins.

The penguins are still living in frozen Antarctica, and they can still dance, only now Mumble and Gloria from the first film have had a son named Erik (voiced by Ava Acres) and Erik—oh no—can't dance. He sure as hell can sing though, and his rendition of a Tosca-inspired aria late in the film kind of saves the day by convincing Bryan the elephant seal to come and help them remove the iceberg that's trapping the penguins.

Robin Williams is as good as ever in the dual roles of Ramon and Lovelace, and it's clear he sticks to the script. There isn't a lot of obvious verbal riffing by Robin, although he may have made contributions to the dialogue as filming progressed.

There are two new characters in this sequel: Will and Bill the Krills, voiced by Brad Pitt and Matt Damon respectively. They're clever, and funny, and add a new element to the story.

Overall, *Happy Feet Two* is very well done and impeccably animated, but the overall impact is, as mentioned, less than the original.

WHAT THE CRITICS HAD TO SAY

Bill Clark: "*Happy Feet Two* should keep younger kids reasonably entertained, especially if they're too young to fully comprehend the peril that the penguins are in. The animation is outstanding, with lush environments and great attention to detail." (from fromthebalcony.com, November 22, 2011)

Louise Keller: "Robin Williams and Hank Azaria provide much of the humor with their funny voices and kooky characters, while Richard Carter, as the broad-Aussie accented elephant seal is a formidable addition. The mish-mash of accents is not necessarily successful and tends to detract from the reality rather than complement it. Considerable screen time is given to two tiny pink crustacean characters voiced by Matt Damon and Brad Pitt, whose Bill and Will Krill are caught on the wave of change in a bid to move up the food chain. Visually, the krills are exquisite, with delicately described glistening features, although some may find their shrill quibbling and repeated clichés a tad irritating." (from urbancinefile.com, December 26, 2011)

Laura Clifford: "There will be plenty of negative reviews for *Happy Feet Two*, but I have to appreciate an animation that segues from a baby penguin singing a Tosca-based aria to a giant elephant seal into a rescue stampede set to 'Rawhide.' *Happy Feet Two* is two cards short of a deck, but in a good way." (from reelingreviews.com, November 11, 2011)

Night at the Museum

(2006)

Anything's possible, Lawrence. If it can be dreamed, it can be done. Hence the twenty-foot jackal staring right at you.

—**Teddy Roosevelt**

It took more than 1,200 people to make *Night at the Museum* at a cost of $110 million. The skill of the creative team and all that money are visible on the screen since this is, essentially, a special effects-driven movie in which the actors are there to support the premise that everything in the Museum of Natural History in New York comes to life at night.

The secondary story is that of divorced dad Larry (Ben Stiller) needing to prove himself to his son Nicky (Jake Cherry). Larry has a reputation of losing jobs and apartments; Nicky's new stepdad is a highly successful bond trader; and the comparison is unsettling for both Larry and Nicky.

The makers of *Night at the Museum* take the cliché "history comes to life" seriously. Boy, do they. We get to meet Teddy Roosevelt, played by Robin Williams; and also Civil War soldiers (both North and South); Attila and his Huns; Wild West cowboys; Roman soldiers; Lewis and Clark and, of course, their guide,

Sacagawea; Chinese rail workers; Vikings; and Neanderthals, as well as a literal zoo of animals, ranging from a Tyrannosaurus Rex to capuchin monkeys, rhinos, lions, tigers, a stampeding mastodon, and a whale. An Easter Island head statue comes to life and speaks, mostly to demand chewing gum. Also, the Egyptian Pharaoh Ahkmenrah comes alive. It is his magical Table of Ahkmenrah that provides the power for everything to come to life.

The film also features appearances by three Hollywood legends, Dick Van Dyke, Mickey Rooney, and Bill Cobbs. They all play security guards who are retiring and plan on stealing from the museum anything they can fence, including the Tablet of Ahkmenrah.

Robin Williams plays his role straight. Teddy Roosevelt has a few humorous lines, but there is no signature Robin mugging or comedic mania. He does a great job, but many actors could have played the role and done an equally effective job. There's nothing that suggests this was a role that could not have been played by anyone but Robin, like in *Good Morning, Vietnam* or *Mrs. Doubtfire*. He made those roles his own.

Night at the Museum is a fun family movie, and it has a happy ending. It is quite something to see exhibits in a museum come alive, and it is particularly satisfying when the ones who Larry needs to believe that all of it actually happens—his son Nicky and his possible love interest, museum docent Rebecca (Carla Gugino)—end up believers.

WHAT THE CRITICS HAD TO SAY

James Berardinelli: "*Night at the Museum* is put together like a live-action cartoon. At times, it feels like *Jumanji* (the participation of Robin Williams enhances the sense of déjà vu) and there are some obvious steals from *Gulliver's Travels*. What's missing, however, is a sense of magic.... Robin Williams [has] just enough screen time to avoid 'cameo' status." (from reelviews.net, December 22, 2006)

Robert Wilonsky: "The first half-hour's too slow; the last half-hour's too manic, as if to compensate. But at least it entertains... Stiller's almost irrelevant to the proceedings; his best scene involves a smartass monkey slapping him stupid, which is as dumb as it sounds. But he's boring because he has to be, lest Teddy Roosevelt (Robin Williams) run off with Sacajawea (Mizuo Peck) while Dick Van Dyke and Mickey Rooney (not wax figures—really) get away with the goods. Yeah, it's that kind of holiday movie." (from VillageVoice.com, December 12, 2006)

Scott Tobias: *"Night At The Museum* [is] content to just populate its CGI world with kid-friendly slapstick, anachronistic gags and movie references, and stretches of fruitless improvisation from Ben Stiller and Robin Williams. And when it pauses from the chaos and noise for a heartwarming pro-family message, that's when it really gets deadly." (from film.avclub.com, December 24, 2006)

Night at the Museum: Battle of the Smithsonian

(2009)

I hate to ask, but, as you see, I'm missing a few body parts. Could you please give us a scratch?

—**Teddy Roosevelt Bust**

Yes, the success of the first *Night at the Museum* movie spawned this movie, which is the second in the trilogy. But so what? Movie franchises exist to allow viewers to revisit a world they enjoyed and, yes, it serves to make the creators money. Again, so what?

The *Night at the Museum* movies boast fun stories and incredible special effects. The Wright Brothers' plane flying over Washington, D.C.? Abraham Lincoln coming alive and rising up out of his Lincoln Memorial throne and walking around? These are amazing scenes and the movies are worth watching just to see the impossible come to life.

Perhaps more importantly, though—and this is touched on by director Shawn Levy in the special features—the movies have spurred young people to look into some of the historical events and historical figures depicted in the films. That can only be good in this day and age.

Robin Williams revisits his Teddy Roosevelt role in *Battle of the Smithsonian*, this time as both the Teddy on horseback from the first movie, and also as a bronze bust with no arms or body.

The movie picks up a couple of years after the first movie. Larry Daley (Ben Stiller) is now the successful founder of a company called Daley's Devices. He does infomercials with George Foreman (played by the real Foreman), and offers products like the Glow-in-the-Dark Flashlight, the Unlosable Key Ring, and the Super Big Dog Bone. He is making lots of money and is obviously no longer a night guard at the Museum of Natural History.

He visits the Museum and learns that the museum board has decided to remove all the exhibits and store them in the Federal Archives at the Smithsonian Institution. They will be replaced by holographic displays providing visitors with information, but there will be no more physical displays. Larry discovers that the magical Tablet of Ahkmenrah will remain in New York and, thus, once the exhibits leave the museum, they'll never come to life again.

But wait! The story needs a complication and one conveniently appears. Jedediah the cowboy calls Larry to tell him that Dexter the monkey stole the Tablet and is bringing it to the Smithsonian. Yikes! This means that *everything* in the Smithsonian's nineteen buildings will come to life when the sun goes down. Larry decides he must travel to Washington, prevent this earth-shattering event, and, of course, rescue his friends.

Thus, the "battle" of the title: Larry wages that battle against a malevolent Egyptian Pharaoh named Kahmunrah (Hank Azaria) who wants the Tablet so he can control the world.

There is also a romantic element (albeit minor) to the story. Larry meets none other than Amelia Earhart (Amy Adams) who is quite game to do whatever is necessary to help Larry achieve his victory. Plus, there's some smooching between the two that goes nowhere, mainly because Amelia Earhart will go back to being a mannequin as soon as the sun comes up (as Kurt Loder noted in his MTV review of the film, Amy Adams has one of the best lines in the script: She tells Larry, "You haven't been able to take your cheaters off my chassis since we met").

The story has a happy ending. Amelia and Larry fly the exhibits back to New York, Larry sells his company, donates the money to the museum on the condition that nothing changes, and they open for evening hours. The hook, though, is that all the exhibits can legitimately come to life and interact with the patrons because the cover story is that Larry's money went toward creating and installing incredibly lifelike animatronic displays of all the exhibits.

This second installment is well-done and, as acknowledged, the special effects are extraordinary. Watch it with kids and you'll see what a great job the creative team did revisiting the Museum.

WHAT THE CRITICS HAD TO SAY

Kurt Loder: "I was surprised by how funny and well-made the sequel is, especially for a 'family film.' *Battle of the Smithsonian* is packed with set-piece scenes of a sometimes uproarious nature and intricately constructed digital action sequences." (from MTV. com, May 22, 2009)

Roger Ebert: "Oh, did I dislike this film. It made me squirm. Its premise is lame, its plot relentlessly predictable, its characters with personalities that would distinguish picture books, its cost incalculable (well, $150,000,000). Watching historical figures enact the clichés identified with the most simplistic versions of their images, I found myself yet once again echoing the frequent cry of Gene Siskel: 'Why not just give us a documentary of the same actors having lunch?'" (from RogerEbert.com, May 20, 2009)

James Berardinelli: "The best thing that can be said about the second *Night at the Museum* (which bears the unnecessarily long full title of *Night at the Museum: Battle of the Smithsonian*) is that it's harmless. And pointless. And dumb. This is a perfect example of a motion picture that exists exclusively because its predecessor made a lot of money. And, like most movies that fit into that category, the filmmakers have been careful not to change the formula. Keep potential viewers in their comfort zone. The hope is that those who enjoyed the first installment will appreciate the sequel. Well, I didn't like the first one. So what about the bigger budgeted, more hyped sequel? Well, I didn't hate it." (from reelviews. net, May 22, 2009)

Peter Travers: "Adults who see this movie unaccompanied by a child should sign up pronto for therapy with Gabriel Byrne on [HBO's] *In Treatment*. Ben Stiller, my satiric comic hero last summer in *Tropic Thunder*, has the dull-edged look of a man taking a paycheck job in a downsized economy. I swear I could see his ass dragging." (from *Rolling Stone*, May 21, 2009)

Night at the Museum: Secret of the Tomb

(2014)

Smile, my boy. It's sunrise.

—Teddy Roosevelt

How often is it that the third film in a franchise is considered the best?

Not very often, right? In fact, it's sometimes the opposite situation: The third film in a franchise (the "threequel") can be so poorly received that it occasionally sinks the franchise. (*The Godfather: Part III* comes to mind, as does *Die Hard with a Vengeance* and *Superman III,* although both the *Die Hard* and *Superman* franchises continued. There's no *Godfather IV,* though—yet.)

In many ways, *Night at the Museum: Secret of the Tomb* is the best of the *Night at the Museum* franchise, although part of its appeal is that we already know the characters and the seminal plot point: the Tablet of Ahkmenrah brings inanimate objects to life after sunset.

This time around, the setting is London. The Tablet is corroding and that is screwing everything up and Larry needs to get to

London and the Egyptian artifacts section of the British Museum to figure out how to fix it. He persuades the fired (but ultimately reinstated) Dr. McPhee (Ricky Gervais) to authorize shipping Ahkmenrah to London and, when Larry gets there, he discovers that Teddy Roosevelt (Robin Williams), Sacajawea (Mizuo Peck), Octavius (Steve Coogan), Jedediah (Owen Wilson), Attila the Hun (Patrick Gallagher), Rexy the T Rex, Dexter the monkey (Crystal), and a Neanderthal christened Laaa (Ben Stiller, in a dual role) have also come along. So, let the mayhem begin!

It seems that Ahkmenrah's father Merenkahre knows the secret of the Tablet, which is that it was created by—and is charged by—moonlight and, after centuries of being in the basement of the Museum in New York, it is decaying and will eventually fail, unless it is recharged by the moon.

That's the goal: expose the Tablet to moonlight so that all the living exhibits will not end up frozen for all time. The problem, though, is that Sir Lancelot (Dan Stevens) has stolen the Tablet because he believes it is actually the Holy Grail.

There is a scene in which Lancelot bursts into a theater where a performance of—what else?—*Camelot* is being staged. He runs right up on the stage and confronts King Arthur, played by Hugh Jackman and Queen Guinevere, played by Alice Eve. They try to remain in character, but then eventually tell Lancelot who they actually are and that the play is being staged, and everything is fake. This is one of most fun scenes in the flick.

Lancelot ultimately gives back the Tablet and it is charged by the moon, and everything goes back to normal. It is decided, though, that the Tablet should remain in London with Ahkmenrah's parents, which means, sadly, that the New York Museum exhibits will never come to life again. Larry accepts this and walks away from the Museum one last time.

We jump to three years later. We learn that Larry is now a teacher, and that the British Museum is bringing its Egyptian displays to the New York Museum. That's right: the Tablet will return to New York, and when it does, everyone comes alive in a final scene in which they all dance to "Got to Be Real."

The last scene is Larry standing on the sidewalk outside the museum with a wistful smile on his face as he listens to the music and knows that all his friends have been reunited. At least for now.

As for Robin Williams as Teddy Roosevelt, he has a large presence in the film and is in many scenes. Unlike the first two films, where he popped up for a couple of scenes, here Teddy is a major character throughout. This was Robin's last onscreen role. The film is dedicated to Robin and Mickey Rooney.

WHAT THE CRITICS HAD TO SAY

Louise Keller: "A zippy script injects renewed life to the *Museum* franchise, offering a crowd-pleasing mix of inventive ideas, quirky humor and impressive visual effects to its star-studded cast. With director Shawn Levy once again at the helm, *Dinner for Schmucks* screenwriters David Guion and Michael Handelman have cleverly incorporated a twist to the premise of the Museum of National History's exhibits coming to life by moving the characters from New York to London. Smart move; well executed." (from urbancinefile.com, December 25, 2014)

Simon Reynolds: "Thanks to its nifty blend of high-concept and wide-appeal comedy, the *Night at the Museum* series has established itself as dependable family entertainment. Third time around the magic is wearing thin, however, with the bulk of the action relocating to London as Ben Stiller's security guard Larry attempts to revive the magical tablet that brings exhibits to life." (from digitalspy.com, December 16, 2014)

License to Wed

(2007)

Anybody who kicks a reverend's ass for his woman, you're A-okay in my book.

—**Reverend Frank**

The performances in *License to Wed* are precisely what they should be for this particular movie. Every actor, ironically, takes the script seriously and brings their mostly-A game. They obviously know the script is ludicrous, but—and this can be considered a mark of their professionalism (and goal of getting paid, too, of course)—they go with it.

The reason *License to Wed* is an overwhelmingly disliked and excoriated Robin Williams movie—take a look at the negative reviews—is because of the premise. *License to Wed* is one of those comedies in which the audience is expected to accept and believe one important principle: stuff happens in the movie that would *never* happen in real life, in the real world.

Never.

The filmmakers attempt to create a fictitious world in which ridiculous events and behaviors occur and the goal is for the viewer to buy into it and, thus, enjoy the movie.

Once you accept that a seemingly sadistic, manipulative reverend would insist on a wedding prep program that incorporates illegal activities before being allowed to marry in his church, well, then everything else falls into place—but only if that suspension of disbelief is *first* in place.

One of the dominant tropes of this type of movie is that laws don't exist.

Illegally bugging the couple's apartment—and by a child? Sure…why not?

Illegally making the bride drive blindfolded through city traffic? Sure…why not?

Bringing two kids on leashes and two defecating robot babies into Macy's for a wedding registry visit and terrorizing the place without getting arrested? Sure. This is a wacky movie, right?

Insisting the couple not have sex until the honeymoon? Imagine how that "requirement" would go over in the real world.

Having a creepy little kid sidekick who seems to revel in the almost mob-inspired tutelage from his mentor? Sure…why not? (Where's child services when you need them?)

The groom writing the last paragraph of *Ulysses*, all 3,680 words of it (just kidding—he actually writes out his wedding vows) in the beach sand outside his fiancé's hotel window, and doing it perfectly, and, it is assumed, in the dark? Sure…why not?

Robin Williams, for all his *Family Feud*-inspired *Commandments Challenge* routine and Reverend Frank wisecracks, plays it straight, for the most part. He says ostensibly funny things (which aren't really funny) but they're never delivered by the comic persona we know and love. They're darker and the tone is more, again, sadistic and manipulative. Original Robin, in this movie, we barely knew ya…

The movie includes outtakes over the ending credits that are funnier than the movie. Truth be told, that fact may sum up any honest review of *License to Wed*.

WHAT THE CRITICS HAD TO SAY

James Berardinelli: "No matter how hard I try, I'm finding it difficult to write anything positive about *License to Wed*. This movie is bad from top to bottom, front to back, and start to finish. Many romantic comedies sacrifice humor in favor of romance; this one isn't romantic either. If this was the debut outing for Robin Williams or Mandy Moore, neither would get another job. Williams is as unfunny as he has ever been and Moore shows no evidence of charisma or charm." (from reelviews.net, July 3, 2007)

Mick LaSalle: "There's bad, there's awful and there's horrible, and then somewhere beyond that, in its own Kingdom of Lousy—where all the milk curdles and the jokes aren't funny—is *License to Wed*, the latest ghastly exercise starring Robin Williams." (from sfgate.com, July 3, 2007)

Christy Lemire: "Here's how bad *License to Wed* is: Even the outtakes at the end are lame. It's exactly what it looks like from the commercials—a one-joke movie, and that one joke isn't even funny to begin with. Robin Williams is constantly straining as Reverend Frank, the minister from hell who forces the newly engaged Ben (John Krasinski) and Sadie (Mandy Moore) to undergo a sadistic marriage prep course before they can say 'I do.' You'll wish you'd said: 'I don't.'" (from the Associated Press, July 2, 2007)

Cindy Pearlman: "Robin Williams at his best." (from the *Chicago Sun-Times*, July 3, 2007)

August Rush

(2007)

You know what music is? God's little reminder that there's some-thing else besides us in this universe, a harmonic connection between all living beings, everywhere, even the stars.

—**Wizard**

Robin Williams plays his character Wizard in *August Rush* as a Fagin-esque figure from Dickens's *Oliver Twist*. He is said to have modeled the character on U2 legend Bono, and he dresses, as Roger Ebert described it, like a drugstore cowboy.

That said, admittedly, it's somewhat unpleasant to see Robin playing such a conniving, selfish, and, at times, mean character. We've seen him play dramatic roles quite successfully, but this role leaves a bad taste. (He doesn't appear in the movie until almost forty minutes into its 113-minute running time.)

August Rush is about an eleven-year-old musical prodigy named Evan (he's later christened August Rush by Wizard) who is trying to find his birth parents. He was put up for adoption after his mother Lyla's father forged her name on an adoption form and told her the baby had died during an emergency deliv-ery. Lyla (Keri Russell) had hooked up one night with an Irish musician named Louis (Jonathan Rhys Meyers), and Evan (Freddie Highmore) was conceived. Lyla is a concert cellist; Louis had a rock band: *Voila!* Musical genes abound in little lost Evan. And that's the set-up for a somewhat preposterous ending in which now-twelve-year-old August conducts his own symphonic composition in a Juilliard-sponsored concert in Central Park in front of thousands of people.

Robin's character Wizard is something of a guardian/sponsor for young homeless kids who can play music. They all live in an abandoned church, and Wizard sends them out every day as "buskers," street musicians who perform on corners, in parks, and anywhere else there are pedestrians who might throw a buck or two into their cigar box or open guitar case.

After Evan escapes from the residential school where he's lived for eleven years and fifteen days, he ends up in New York, where he meets one of Wizard's street musicians, Arthur (Leon Thomas III), who brings him home to Wizard.

Wizard recognizes the enormous musical potential in Evan, renames him "August Rush," and tries to exploit his talent any way he can.

Through a series of far-fetched coincidences and contrived situations, Evan/August ends up studying at Juilliard. In the meantime, his mother and father are both on a mission to find him, and each other, with neither knowing anything about the whereabouts of anyone, including Evan. (His mother learned August was alive from a deathbed confession by her father.)

During a rehearsal of August's symphonic piece, Wizard interrupts and claims he's August's father, making him leave the Juilliard hall and putting him back on the street.

Evan escapes—again—and Wizard is left empty-handed, so to speak. Evan gets to the concert, conducts his own composition like Leonard Bernstein, and, it is assumed, is reunited with his birth parents, who just so happen to make it to the front row of the concert simultaneously. Dad holds Mom's hand; she recognizes him. Evan turns to the audience, bows, locks eyes with his parents, and recognizes them. The end. We don't get to see the reunion, which is an absolutely infuriating way to end the movie.

WHAT THE CRITICS HAD TO SAY

James Berardinelli: "As Wizard, Robin Williams hits all the wrong notes. There's potential here for a genuinely creepy, frightening character but, in order to get a PG rating, the gloves are on, making Williams more cartoonish than menacing." (from reelviews.net, November 21, 2007)

Roger Ebert: "Here is a movie drenched in sentimentality, but it's supposed to be. I dislike sentimentality where it doesn't belong, but there's something brave about the way *August Rush* declares itself and goes all the way with coincidence, melodrama and skillful tear-jerking." (from RogerEbert.com, November 20, 2007)

Stephen Holden: "To describe *August Rush* as a piece of shameless hokum doesn't quite do justice to the potentially shock-inducing sugar content of this contemporary fairy tale about a homeless, musically gifted miracle child." (from *The New York Times*, November 21, 2007)

Shrink

(2009)

God, I love Susan. She's amazing. She's fucking incredible.
—Jack Holden

Robin Williams has four scenes in *Shrink*, and none of them are all that memorable. His appearance in the film is uncredited.

Robin plays Jack Holden, an actor whose career is faltering and who sees Dr. Carter (Kevin Spacey) for sex addiction. At least he thinks he's a sex addict, but Dr. Carter makes it very clear to him that his real problem is that he's an alcoholic. Holden's reaction to repeatedly being told he's an alcoholic is to respond, "Functional."

In the first scene Jack has with Dr. Carter—which occurs about fourteen minutes into the film and lasts about three minutes—it's hard to tell how much of it Robin improvised. He delivers Robin-esque lines like:

- He says that after he married Susan, he "hung up my spurs" and "put the pony in the paddock."
- He also says "no more chasing strange" and no more "French wrestling."
- He says his wife "makes me harder than Chinese algebra."

- He tells the doctor he (Jack) should go to Cock Enders.

- He tells Carter that one way of dealing with his sex addiction is to call a friend he calls the Admiral who "sees more puss than a litter box" and have him describe his previous night's sexual activity—"sort of a coitus descriptus," Jack says.

- He also describes masturbation as buttering the corn, punching the clown, and "beef strokinoff."

These are all Robin-like lines. So perhaps the director let him wing it a bit.

His second scene is him being interviewed with his co-star about their latest movie and some of it sounds like Robin was ad-libbing a bit.

His third scene is him riding in a cart and urinating off the side.

His final scene is him being hit on at a bar by a young blonde and turning her down, telling her, "Ten years ago, that would've been a yes."

The rest of the movie is Kevin Spacey's "shrink" story. He is a shrink to the stars in Hollywood, a best-selling author, and undeniably clinically depressed. His wife committed suicide, and he seems to be suffering from PTSD big time. His solution is to smoke huge amounts of weed, never step into his bedroom, and sleep in his clothes. He hangs out with his weed dealer Jesus (Jesse Plemons), but still manages to see patients.

Some of the other stories involve his dealings with Hollywood types, except for one patient referred to him pro bono by his father (Robert Loggia), who is also a shrink. Jemma (Keke Palmer) is a teenage high school student whose mother killed herself and left a note which she has yet to read.

Dr. Carter's "step-godbrother" Jeremy (Mark Webber), an aspiring screenwriter, steals Jemma's file, reads it, and writes a screenplay based on her story. Of course it's brilliant, of course she finally endorses it after initially feeling betrayed, of course it will be made into a movie, and of course Dr. Carter gets clean and returns to sleeping in the marital bed.

Robin Williams did small independent films like this throughout his career, but he could have passed on this one. His character doesn't have enough to do or say and his appearance is perfunctory. It is worth noting, though, that it is yet another Robin film with a suicide theme.

WHAT THE CRITICS HAD TO SAY

Roger Ebert: "We meet a movie star past his sell-by date (Robin Williams, unbilled), who thinks his problem is sex addiction, although Henry assures him it is alcoholism (the sex addict's running mate).… [We] sense Williams restraining himself from bolting headlong into his descriptions of sexual improbabilities …" (from RogerEbert.com, July 29, 2009)

Claudia Puig: "Robin Williams has a small and nearly pointless part as a has-been star who claims he is a sex addict, though the good doctor insists that he's an alcoholic. He has some clever dialogue, referring to enjoying the escapades of a randy friend vicariously as 'coitus descriptus.'" (from *USA Today*, July 23, 2009)

World's Greatest Dad

(2009)

If you're that depressed, reach out to someone, and remember, suicide is a permanent solution to temporary problems.

—**Lance Clayton**

Personal Note from the Author: I do illustrated lectures at libraries in Connecticut based on my books. One of my most popular talks is about Robin Williams, based on my 1997 book *The Robin Williams Scrapbook* and this book. After Robin's suicide in 2014, a frequent question at my Robin Williams talks and during interviews was, "Do you think the movie *World's Greatest Dad* inspired Robin in the way he chose to end his life?" It's an inevitable question since Robin committed suicide by hanging himself off a closet doorknob with a black nylon belt around his neck. The son in the movie, Kyle, accidentally dies from autoerotic asphyxiation by choking himself with a scarf while masturbating. Is it a coincidence? Robin could have overdosed, used a gun, drowned himself, etc., but he chose hanging, and in a similar way to the method used by the character in the movie. The answer I offer is, "We don't know," and I leave it at that.

World's Greatest Dad is as black as a black comedy can get.

Robin Williams plays English teacher Lance Clayton. His poetry class is very unpopular at the high school where he teaches, and it is likely to be cancelled. He is clandestinely dating art teacher Claire Reed. He is also a failed novelist several times over. According to a stack of rejected manuscripts, he is the author of the following unpublished novels:

Darwin's Pool

The Speed of Bad News

Invisible Dog's Teeth

The Narcissist's Life Vest

Lance also has a fifteen-year-old son named Kyle who is an absolute creep. He is a chronic masturbator, he says vulgar things to the girls at school, he is horrifically rude and cruel to his father, and he has precisely one friend, Andrew the vegetarian.

One night, Lance comes home to find Kyle dead at his computer with a scarf around his neck. He died from suffocation while masturbating. Lance is distraught, but after a few moments of grief, he hatches a plan that will ultimately benefit him in ways he could never have hoped for.

He makes Kyle's death look like a suicide. He removes the scarf, zips up Kyle's pants, and hangs him in the closet. He also writes a suicide note.

When Kyle's autopsy report and suicide note get posted on the internet, Kyle becomes an idealized icon and tragic hero at the high school. Suddenly, kids who despised him are calling him their best friend. Girls who would either ignore him or give him the finger suddenly start wearing his picture in a locket around their neck.

Lance sees an opportunity in this posthumous idolization and "writes" Kyle's journal. He has it printed and gives out copies to anyone and everyone: students, teachers, and eventually an agent and publishers.

The journal is a beautifully written, heartfelt cry for love, as well as being an exegesis on teenage angst and loneliness to which every student at the school can relate.

The book becomes famous, Kyle becomes posthumously famous, and Lance becomes real-world famous. This insanity peaks when Lance is invited to be on the *Dr. Dana Show* (an *Oprah*-like talk show) to talk about his son and the crisis of teenage suicide. Publishers are waiting to talk to him about publishing Kyle's journal, now titled (thanks to Claire) *You Don't Know Me*. They also want to simultaneously publish one of Lance's own novels. Lance's dreams are coming true—and all due to a hoax he perpetrated following the tragic death of his only son. Does he feel guilty? Hell, yeah, he does.

At a ceremony changing the name of the high school's library to the Kyle Clayton Memorial Library—a ceremony which includes a live performance by "Kyle's favorite" Bruce Hornsby (he's actually Lance's favorite)—Lance gives the following speech:

> You guys didn't like Kyle. But that's okay, I didn't either. I loved him. He was my son, but he was also a douchebag. He wasn't very smart. And he didn't kill himself. Kyle died accidentally while masturbating. I made it look like a suicide And I wrote a suicide note. I also wrote his journal. Thank you.

The principal calls him an asshole, Claire slaps him across the face, and students give him the finger.

But now, suddenly free, he strips naked and dives into the school pool.

In a sort of epilogue, Kyle's friend Andrew visits Lance and tells him, "I knew you wrote the book. I liked it. You're a good writer. I think you should keep writing."

Lance then asks him if he'd like something to eat, to which Andrew says yes, and tells him he's a vegetarian.

"I know," Lance says to the polite, respectful young man who will likely now become his surrogate son.

World's Greatest Dad is a well-done look at high school drama, teenage anxiety, and the depression that comes with being a failed artist.

It's a pretty good comedy, too.

WHAT THE CRITICS HAD TO SAY

Roger Ebert: "Robin Williams is the star, demonstrating once again that he's sometimes better in drama than comedy. He has that manic side he indulges, and he works better (for me, anyway) when he's grounded." (from RogerEbert.com, September 2, 2009)

Claudia Puig: "At its best, *World's Greatest Dad* is reminiscent of the cutting humor of *Heathers* or *Donnie Darko*. At its worst, it's exploitative and shocking in its treatment of an essentially taboo subject and its tragic aftermath.... Williams is excellent and convincing as a discouraged artist who makes some unlikely but understandable choices after decades of feeling creatively stifled. It's his best performance since 2002's creepy *One Hour Photo*." (from *USA Today*, August 8, 2009)

Old Dogs

(2009)

Scat happens, man.

—**Dan**

Yes, indeed, scat does happen, but it's too easy to make that joke and apply it to *Old Dogs*. Even if it kind of fits.

Old Dogs is not a very good movie for many reasons, and it had a troubled and somewhat schizophrenic labor and birth. It was repeatedly delayed due to Bernie Mac's death, Robin Williams's heart surgery, and the death of John Travolta's son Jett, plus it was originally R-rated, with adult jokes, but that version failed with test audiences. They went back into the cutting room and turned it into a lame, PG hodgepodge of weak jokes, bad slapstick, and dumb scenarios. This *Old Dogs 2.0* renovation did not fix it. They thought they could make it a kid's movie, but it's hard to imagine any kid enjoying it.

There is no denying that John Travolta and Robin Williams are team players. They gave their all to the movie and did the best they could. But the script is all over the place and it just doesn't end up working.

The premise is weak: Dan (Robin Williams) married Vicki (Kelly Preston) seven years prior to the beginning of the story, and they were divorced a day later. However, they did consummate the marriage and now, because Vicki has to spend two weeks in prison for civil disobedience, the twins Dan and she conceived, now seven, have to stay with Dan because Vicki's best friend, hand model Jenna (Rita Wilson) who was supposed to take them, ended up disabled after Dan slams her hands in the trunk of a car. *Whew.*

Complicating this situation is the big deal Dan and his partner Charlie (John Travolta) are in the middle of trying to finalize with a Japanese corporation. So, of course, the kids wreak havoc at Charlie's apartment and their business office, with the added bonus of fart and poop jokes thrown in for bad measure.

And if the predictable and dumb scenarios (Robin in a jetpack?) that then play out aren't enough, Charlie's dog dies and they stage a dog funeral in a pet cemetery. *Sure, add a dead dog to the script. Can't hurt, right?*

If there is any redeeming value to *Old Dogs*, it's the all-star cast. Robin, John Travolta, Kelly Preston, Rita Wilson, Seth Green, Lori Loughlin, and Bernie Mac all do what they can and their star power and charisma are present in all their scenes. (John Travolta's daughter Ella Bleu Travolta plays one of Robin Williams's kids.)

Old Dogs is a silly, slapstick-y comedy that fails more than it works, but as Robin Williams fans, it's worth a watch to witness Robin mugging it up (he does some physical comedy with faces and golf-ball-to-the-balls gags) and to watch his and Travolta's undeniable chemistry (they were reportedly good friends in real life and it shows).

WHAT THE CRITICS HAD TO SAY

James Berardinelli: "Here's a primer for how to endure *Old Dogs* if an unfortunate series of circumstances should place you where seeing it is unavoidable. Arrive late and leave early." (from reelviews.net, November 24, 2009)

Claudia Puig: "The chemistry between Robin Williams and John Travolta, playing business partners and best pals, makes this formulaic comedy a notch better than its premise indicates." (from *USA Today*, November 25, 2009)

Roger Ebert: "*Old Dogs* is stupefying dimwitted. What were John Travolta and Robin Williams thinking of? Apparently their agents weren't perceptive enough to smell the screenplay in its advanced state of decomposition, but wasn't there a loyal young intern in the office to catch them at the elevator and whisper, 'You've paid too many dues to get involved with such crap at this stage in your careers.'" (from RogerEbert.com, November 24, 2009)

Carrie Rickey: "Predictable as the premise is, Travolta's and Williams's unpredictability makes for some chortle-worthy slapstick, less of Laurel & Hardy vintage than of Abbott & Costello swill." (from the *Philadelphia Inquirer*, November 24, 2009)

The Big Wedding

(2013)

Oscar Wilde once said that marriage is a triumph of imagination over intelligence.

—**Father Moinighan**

The Big Wedding is billed as a romantic comedy with a wacky premise, boasting an Oscar-winning cast and, of course, Robin Williams as (again) a priest. (Robin also played a priest in the 2007 flick, *License to Wed*.) Robin's role amounts to maybe seven or eight minutes of total screen time.

The problem with that description, and thus moviegoers' expectations, is that there's not that much romance, the movie's not that funny, and the zany premise seems a bit shopworn.

The premise is that the future-mother-in-law of the main couple's (Robert De Niro and Diane Keaton) daughter is a strict Catholic from Colombia and her son (the fiancé) Alejandro (Ben Barnes) never told her that his future in-laws had divorced ten years ago. She's coming for the wedding—even though she has never traveled and hates the idea of flying—and so Don and Ellie (De Niro and Keaton) must pretend they're still married, while

Bebe (Susan Sarandon), Don's live-in girlfriend for a decade, must likewise pretend to just be the caterer. Wacky, right?

Admittedly, the Oscar-winning cast excels. And any movie with four Academy Award winners is worth your time, regardless of other considerations. Robert De Niro, Diane Keaton, Susan Sarandon, and Robin Williams are all very good.

Robin plays his role as Father Moinighan as a toned-down and calmed-down Reverend Frank from the aforementioned *License to Wed*. In that film, Reverend Frank and his marriage "requirements" made the guy come off as certifiable. In *The Big Wedding*, Robin plays Father Moinighan pretty straight. Ironically, since it's a comedy, Robin plays the priest *non*-comedically, for the most part.

De Niro, Keaton, and Sarandon all show why they've won Academy Awards. They're all very good. The younger cast members—Ben Barnes, Topher Grace, Amanda Seyfried, Ana Ayora—all hold their own. It had to be pretty intimidating to show up on the set and know you're working with such a stellar main cast.

Ultimately the madcap situation is resolved after a humiliating and loud psychodrama that family members don't know is being overheard by the entire contingent of wedding guests. Alejandro's mother scolds her son for thinking her so inflexible; Don finally proposes to Bebe; and Alejandro and Missy "elope" to the side of the lake, where Robin marries them in what might be the fastest marriage ceremony ever depicted on film.

Considering the elements involved—the script based on a very popular French movie; the cast; the beautiful setting—*The Big Wedding* could have been better. It's still an enjoyable hour and a half, though, and it's always a pleasure to see Robin in a priest's Roman collar (which, at one point, after falling in the lake, he wears with a bathrobe).

WHAT ROBIN HAD TO SAY

"Just a lot of good people. I mean, it's a wonderful ensemble. It's like a paid vacation. Don't tell anybody. But it's lovely." (from the "Coordinating *The Big Wedding*" special feature on the DVD)

WHAT THE CRITICS HAD TO SAY

James Berardinelli: "Robin Williams has what amounts to a very odd cameo (reminiscent of Rowan Atkinson's turn as a priest in *Four Weddings and a Funeral*)." (from reelviews.net, April 26, 2013)

Sandy Schaefer: "Father Moinighan…is portrayed by an uncharacteristically buttoned-down Robin Williams. There's not much satirical bite to any of [the supporting characters'] scenes, but the moments with Williams are worth a few chuckles." (from screenrant.com, April 26, 2013)

Lee Daniels' The Butler
(2013)

I have today issued an Executive Order directing the use of troops under federal authority to aid in the execution of federal law at Little Rock, Arkansas.

—**President Dwight D. Eisenhower**

I know the way.

—**Cecil Gaines**

In *Lee Daniels' The Butler*, Robin Williams plays President Dwight D. Eisenhower, and he doesn't appear in the film for very long. Robin has two scenes, and a third in which he is heard on television. His first is in the Oval Office discussing the ongoing school segregation tumult, and then there is one of him also in the Oval Office, painting at an easel, while talking to Cecil about where Cecil's kids go to school.

And since the movie moves chronologically, it isn't long before the Kennedys are in the White House and Ike is not a part of the story any longer.

Director Lee Daniels, in the documentary included in the bonus features on the DVD, says that his movie chronicles the civil rights story from the beginning to Obama, and that's accurate. And the device he uses to tell this history is that it is all seen through the eyes of a black White House butler who served under eight Presidents, and who witnessed firsthand the massive changes America went through establishing true civil rights for all of its people.

The movie is mostly historically accurate (they even have the LBJ "chairing" (ha) a meeting while sitting on the toilet) but the story of butler Cecil Gaines has been somewhat fictionalized by screenwriter Danny Strong. Nonetheless, this odd hybrid of fact and fiction works for the most part and it presents what one critic called *Civil Rights for Dummies* for a modern audience. (Personal Note: As the author of four of the acclaimed "For Dummies" books, I'm not sure if that's a smear or an accolade. I'm leaning toward it being, right or wrong, a bit of a dig.)

Robin's performance is good and there's nary a hint of comedic Robin anywhere—except in the outtakes when he makes the joke that he was "caught between a Little Rock and a hard place."

Lee Daniels' The Butler is an important movie, criticisms and flaws notwithstanding. It is stunning to witness what happened to African-Americans in America during the sullied pre-civil rights decades, and young people who may not be fully aware of what actually happened in the country they call home are in for a visceral wake-up call.

WHAT ROBIN HAD TO SAY

"You realize how violent, how provocative it was, and these changes which now, having a black president, that's kind of the whole purpose of this script is: do you remember? Do you remember what it was like?"

"I play Ike. He's a fascinating guy. He's kind of a quiet ego among large egos." (both from the special features on the DVD)

WHAT FOREST WHITAKER HAD TO SAY

"The thing about Robin Williams was his stillness and simplicity in the role. I enjoyed working on the scenes with him. He was actually very delicate in his painting scenes, and his contemplation. I think he did a beautiful job of that." (from the special features on the DVD)

WHAT THE CRITICS HAD TO SAY

Steven Boone: "Everybody decries comparing mainstream 'black' directors, but everybody secretly does it, so, what the hell, let's play: On the evidence of *The Butler* alone, I'd say Daniels will grow in greater esteem with cineastes than either pioneer Spike Lee or box office champ Tyler Perry." (from RogerEbert.com, August 15, 2013)

James Berardinelli: "Stunt casting undermines the White House scenes. Three presidents don't have actors stand in for them: Truman isn't mentioned and Ford and Carter are briefly seen only in old news footage. The other five are portrayed by well-known actors and there's not an unqualified casting success among them…. Robin Williams (as Eisenhower) and Alan Rickman (as Reagan) are completely wrong, with ludicrous makeup that never hides the actor." (from reelviews.net, August 17, 2013)

Andrew O'Hehir: "*Lee Daniels' The Butler* is big, brave, crude and contradictory, very bad in places and very good in others, and every American should see it." (from Salon.com, August 15, 2013)

The Face of Love

(2013)

I give great friend.

—**Roger Stillman**

One critic said *The Face of Love* had a preposterous premise; another said the premise was definitely possible when factoring in biology and evolution.

The premise in question is this: A widow can run into a man who doesn't just *look like* her late husband, but is his *exact double*. How exact? Ed Harris plays both roles. *That's* how exact.

Nikki (Annette Bening) is still grieving for her dead husband, Garret, five years after he drowned in Mexico. She decides to visit an art museum they enjoyed when he was alive and, while there, sees a guy sitting on a bench who looks exactly like Garret. So she stalks him, learns he's an art teacher named Tom Young, and crashes his class, telling him she wants to take his course. It's the middle of the semester, he tells her, so she finagles him into giving her private art lessons at her home, which she has stripped of photos of her late husband.

The relationship between Nikki and Tom grows, but she does not, of course, even hint that she's living out her ultimate fantasy:

that her husband never died and she is back together with him. She doesn't even tell Tom she's a widow. She tells Tom that Garret left her.

Robin Williams plays Roger, Nikki's next-door neighbor. He has been asking her out forever, but she considers him to be just a friend. Conveniently, each time there's a possibility that Roger might discover Tom, it doesn't happen.

The person in Nikki's life who first sees Tom is Summer, Nikki and Garret's daughter. Seeing Mom "dating her dead dad," so to speak, freaks Summer out and she screams at Tom to get out of the house.

In a dramatic climactic scene, Tom discovers he looks just like Garret by seeing a photograph of Nikki and Garret on a picture wall of the couple's favorite Mexican restaurant; Nikki actually calls him Garret at one point, and then she apparently tries to drown herself at the beach. Tom swims after her, saves her, discovers the truth, and they break up.

A year later, Nikki gets a postcard to an event at an art gallery. It's not an opening, though; it's a memorial for Tom Young, who died within the past year. He had been terminally ill (heart trouble, according to his ex-wife), but never told Nikki. She attends the memorial and sees a painting of herself walking up out of the pool at her house, with Tom watching from the house. His face is also reflected in the glass. The title of the painting? "The Face of Love," of course. The movie ends with Roger still being her friend and Nikki finally swimming in her pool after so many years of avoiding the water.

One of the reviewers cited below asserts that Robin is wasted in this movie. That's fair to say. He has very few scenes, and he's not funny at all. He plays the role as mostly a sad widower longing for a new love from afar (even if he is only next door).

The Face of Love is a bit thematically schizophrenic in a sense. Is it a love story? A thriller? Both? An argument can be made that it's actually both *and* neither, but it is still a watchable effort, if only for the consummate performances by Annette Bening, Ed Harris, and Robin Williams.

WHAT ROBIN HAD TO SAY

"When you play with someone like [Annette Bening] you have to get your chops together."

"To me, what affected me most about it was the idea of a second chance. And the idea of an exact duplicate second chance…how extraordinary would that be."

(Both from the cast featurette bonus feature on the DVD.)

WHAT THE CRITICS HAD TO SAY

Susan Wloszczyna: "Neighbor and needy widower Roger (a wasted Robin Williams) clearly would like to be closer to this lonely lady but he practically has 'Just a Friend' stamped on his forehead." (from RogerEbert.com, March 7, 2014)

Betty Jo Tucker: "When the film opens, we see Nikki (Bening) thinking about past moments with Garrett, her husband of 30 years. It's obvious she still misses him terribly. Her neighbor Roger (Robin Williams) seems to care about her—but she just wants to be friends." (from reeltalkreviews.com, July 15, 2014)

Kaori Shoji: "There's a whiff of horror here, enhanced by the presence of the late Robin Williams, playing Roger—Garret's best friend and Nikki's admirer, who's always lurking about the place. A bit scary." (from *The Japan Times* (japantimes.co.jp), February 4, 2015)

Brice Ezell: "On the surface, *The Face of Love* wants to be a touching romantic drama, but the nature of the narrative is such that no amount of feel-good moments (or the occasional presence of Robin Williams) can mask the darkness of Nikki's suffering, and indeed the premise of the film itself." (from popmatters.com, August 14, 2014)

The Angriest Man in Brooklyn

(2014)

*My tombstone will say, "Henry Altmann, 1951 dash 2014." I
never knew till now, it's not the dates that matter...it's the dash.*

—Henry Altmann

Robin Williams shot *The Angriest Man in Brooklyn* approximately a year prior to a worsening of symptoms that would later
be identified as manifestations of his Lewy body disorder. In an
essay for the medical journal *Neurology*, his wife Susan Williams
said that late October 2013 was the time when Robin's symptoms worsened, and a new array of psychological symptoms also
began cropping up, including paranoia, delusions, insomnia, and
memory troubles.

The Angriest Man in Brooklyn was filmed in New York from
September 10, 2012, through October 14, 2012, and Robin was
still functioning as an actor at a very high level.

It was one of the last performances of his body of work that
he was apparently able to handle as perfectly as he had his other

seminal roles throughout his decades-long professional career. It was also the last film released while he was still alive.

The DVD of the movie has a "making of" featurette in which Robin is interviewed, and also a gag reel, in which he seems happy, animated, and loving.

And *The Angriest Man in Brooklyn* holds notoriety as yet another Robin Williams film which has suicide as a theme. Robin's character, Henry Altmann, jumps off the Brooklyn Bridge in an attempt to kill himself, but he survives.

The Angriest Man in Brooklyn, a remake of the 1997 Israeli film *The 92 Minutes of Mr. Baum*, immediately puts its main character, Henry Altmann in the nightmarish position of knowing he has ninety minutes to live (a time frame his doctor got off the cover of a magazine—it's the time it takes to cook a turkey breast) which, even though it isn't true, drives him to anger and madness over the things he regrets in life and what he needs to do before he dies.

Henry frantically traverses New York to get to his brother, his wife, and, most importantly, his estranged son Tommy, before his watch shows 6:22 p.m., which he believes will be his time of death. While all this is going on, his doctor, Dr. Sharon Hill (Mila Kunis), is pursuing him to tell him she exaggerated and that he needs to get to the hospital.

Robin Williams and Mila Kunis are very good together, and, as high-octane as their individual performances are, they never veer into implausible territory.

There is humor in this dark comedy, some from Robin, some from characters Henry and Dr. Hill interact with, but the funniest scene in the movie—as politically incorrect as it undeniably was—is the scene with James Earl Jones as Ruben the electronics store clerk. Henry runs into Ruben's store to buy a video camera to record a final message to his son. Ruben, Henry quickly learns, stutters:

Henry: I need a camcorder, and I need one quick.

Ruben: W-W-W-W-W-W-W-W-W-What type are you interested in?

Henry: It doesn't matter. Just one of those. That one! The little one right there.

Ruben: P-P-P-P-P-P-P-Panasonic or the...F-F-F-F-F-F-F-Fujitsu?

Henry: No, that one!

Ruben: Oh, the Samsung.

Henry: Yeah, the Samsung. I'll take it.

Ruben: W-W-W-W-W-W-W-W- Warranty?

Henry: No, definitely not. How do I get it to work?

Ruben: F-F-F-F-F-F-F-F-F-first, you have to charge the...B-B-B-B-B-B-B-B-B-B-

Henry: Batteries?

Ruben: Batteries.

Henry: Yeah, okay. How long will that take?

Ruben: F-F-F-F-F-F-F-F-F-F-four hours.

Henry: Do you have one that's ready to go right now?

Ruben: Well, the, um...F-F-F-F-F-F-F-F-F-F- Fujitsu-or the...F-F-F-F-F-F-F-F-F-F-F-F-F-F-F-F-F-F-F-F-F-F-F-F-F-F-F-F-F-Fuji.

Henry: Which one do you recommend...the F-F-F-F-Fujitsu or the F-F-F-F-F-Fuji?

Ruben: F-F-F-F-F-F-F-F-F-F- Fuck you!

Henry: Bravo!

How these two thespian legends kept a straight face and ultimately got through this scene is incredible.

Henry is eventually persuaded by Dr. Gill to go to the hospital and, in a voiceover, we're told that he lived another eight days before suffering a hemorrhagic stroke. We see him reconciling with his entire family in the hospital, and the final scene is them all gathering to scatter his ashes into the East River off the Staten Island Ferry. The ferry's captain angrily confronts them for what they did (which violates the law that ashes can only be scattered at sea if you're more than three miles from shore) and, in memory of Henry, they all lace into the mariner, asking him, "What do you think we're doing, littering?" and, "Have you no humility? No fucking manners?" And telling him, "It's ashes, you moron!"

And thus, as Henry's last voiceover assured us, he did, indeed, live on in the hearts of those who loved him.

WHAT THE CRITICS HAD TO SAY

David Cantu: "The cast was so perfect with Williams providing a dramatic performance with comedy thrown in to ease the tension and Kunis with the way her most intense moments showed her vulnerability. It really was a treat to see them on screen together." (from cinemadeviant.com, July 22, 2014)

Drew Hunt: "Playing an intensely agitated New Yorker in the scatterbrained dark comedy *The Angriest Man in Brooklyn*, Robin Williams once again proves he can insufferably crank the energy to 11 without batting an eye, only this time his frenzied comic demeanor is replaced with equally harried contempt." (from slantmagazine.com, May 22, 2014)

Boulevard

(2014)

I drove down a street one night. A street I didn't know. It's the way your life goes sometimes. I'll drive down this one and another. And now, another.

—**Nolan Mack**

Boulevard was the last feature film of Robin Williams's career and it is a ferociously unpleasant viewing experience.

Robin plays Nolan Mack, a closeted gay man who, at sixty, decides to be true to himself and come out of the closet. He and his wife Joy (Kathy Baker) have lived separate lives for decades, but they do truly love each other. It's clear, though, that Joy has suspected that her husband was not the man he pretended to be for a long time.

Nolan's infatuation with a young male hooker (with whom he doesn't have sex) destroys the life he spent years building. A violent physical confrontation in the parking lot of the bank where Nolan works involving his consort Leo (Roberto Aguire), Leo's pimp, Nolan, and, ultimately, the police—with everyone at Nolan's work watching—is excruciatingly uncomfortable and paints in vivid strokes the mess Nolan has created.

Robin plays Nolan dark. Even when he's seemingly happy, or at least not unhappy, there's an aura of misery and dissatisfaction permeating his every expression, word, and action.

Boulevard was filmed from May 19, 2013, through June 23, 2013, and Robin seems in control of his acting powers and is effective and compelling. Robin's wife Susan revealed in an essay for the medical journal *Neurology* that Robin's Lewy body disorder symptoms began becoming seriously problematic around October of 2013, so it's likely that that played a part in why this was his final dramatic film.

Boulevard Blunder?

In a scene at the end of the movie with Robin Williams and Bob Odenkirk, Nolan (Robin) has just told his best friend Winston (Odenkirk) that he was splitting with his wife, that he left his job, and, it is assumed, he is moving to New York. When Odenkirk asks Robin about his ailing father, he replies, "I'll still visit. Some things remain, you know." But then Odenkirk says, "I'll write to you *from* [emphasis added] New York, unless they have Wi-Fi there.... Then I'll email you." So who's going to New York? Nolan or Winston? The final scene shows Robin in a restaurant meeting a man for, we assume, a date, and it looks like he could be in New York. Possible explanation? It's feasible that Odenkirk's "from" should have been "in" and it got overlooked in post-production. There was no indication throughout the film that Odenkirk's character was considering moving to New York.

WHAT THE DIRECTOR DITO MONTIEL HAD TO SAY

"Robin Williams had a problem on the last day of shooting the drama *Boulevard*: He couldn't figure how to play out his final scene. We walked for an hour and talked it through," says director Dito Montiel. "Then after we shot it, Robin was like, 'We got it!' I remember that in particular. It was such a great way to end it all." (from *USA To*day, July 8, 2015)

WHAT THE CRITICS HAD TO SAY

Roger Ebert: "The ingredient [Robin Williams] brings most to *Boulevard* is heartfelt empathy, which makes this portrayal heroic. In such a peaceful performance, Williams achieves layers with muted expressions of angst or defeat, and a confident stillness. In his everyman presence, which he achieves before even stepping into the movie's generic suburban setting, Williams is as gentle as he is compassionate for those who live with their secrets daily. Just like with his rambunctious comedy, he plays this character as an accomplished entertainer with nothing to lose." (from RogerEbert.com, July 10, 2015)

Total Film Staff: "The Verdict: A flimsy, contrived drama, sure—but as Robin Williams's sensitive final lead performance the story gains a weight it scarcely deserves and a resonance nobody ever wanted." (from gamesradar.com, April 4, 2016)

A Merry Friggin' Christmas

(2014)

No matter how this pans out, you tried your best. Bottom line, you're one hell of a good dad, Boyd.

—Virgil "Mitch" Mitchler

"Robin Williams and Christmas." Apparently, that was enough of a high concept to get this movie made (the success of *National Lampoon's Christmas Vacation* may have had something to do with it as well).

Robin Williams plays the patriarch of an odd amalgam of a family, but the story mainly focuses on his non-relationship with his eldest son Boyd (Joel McHale). Boyd despises his father. His loathing is such that he actually Photoshopped him out of a family photo he displays in his home.

Robin plays Virgil "Mitch" Mitchler so that, throughout the film, you can understand why his son can't stand him. He's a drunk, and an obnoxious, foul-mouthed, loudmouth who clips his toenails on the kitchen counter, thinks nothing of serving squirrel to his son for Christmas dinner, and continually mocks

Boyd's career success as being unmanly. After all, Mitch owns a Porta Potty company, which is a real man's job. And he'll smoke in his own goddamned house if he wants to!

For some idealistic reason, Boyd agrees to travel from Wisconsin to his parents' home in Chicago for Christmas—but then forgets his son Doug's presents at home. Hello, inciting incident. Doug is on the cusp of no longer believing in Santa Claus and Boyd wants to give him at least one more Christmas as a believer.

So he has to drive back to Wisconsin to retrieve Doug's presents before the kids wake up on Christmas morning. He ends up making the trip with his father Mitch in Mitch's truck loaded with Porta Potties.

Obvious attempts at including moments and scenes of humor and holiday wackiness abound in the film, but most of them fall flat. A kid eats out-of-date pickles and hallucinates; Hobo Santa (Oliver Platt) is run over and there's a discussion of getting rid of his body with acid; Boyd finds an entire Afghani family camped out in his living room due to a misunderstanding of the term "house sit"; and the same cop keeps stopping Boyd and giving him tickets. None of these situations are all that funny, but the cast are team players and they do their best. Robin's character is married to none other than Candice Bergen, and she is very game playing the supportive wife-to-a-Neanderthal in scenarios that many wives wouldn't tolerate from their husband for a second (see the aforementioned "toenails" scene).

A Merry Friggin' Christmas was filmed in March and April of 2013 and, as we know from an essay written by Robin's wife Susan, Robin's Lewy body symptoms didn't become a real problem for him until October of that year, so his performance is the best it can be considering the material. There aren't many Robinisms in the film, although at one point he does his snake tongue gag, and in another scene he mimics a robot. But the laughs are few and far between in this odd film. (Interestingly, Robin was able to record the voiceover for Dennis the Dog in March 2014 for 2015's *Absolutely Anything* despite his symptoms (see next chapter), but he insisted on re-recording the lines after the first session because he said he suddenly understood the character better. It isn't known what, if anything, this "do over" had to do with his cognitive state at the time.)

Ultimately, Boyd, Mitch, and Hobo Santa make it back in time for Christmas morning, giving Doug one more year delighting in the miracle of Christmas—and he ends up loving his "Bridge for Juniors" game that mom and grandma found in the attic and wrapped, on the chance that Mitch and Boyd didn't make it back in time.

Weird Coincidence(?) Department

In *A Merry Friggin' Christmas*, Robin's daughter-in-law (Boyd's wife), played by Lauren Graham, teaches an English as a Second Language course. In 2014's *Boulevard*, Robin's wife, played by Kathy Baker, teaches an English as a Second Language course.

WHAT THE DIRECTOR TRISTRAM SHAPEERO HAD TO SAY

"You can't help but look at it now with a sense of fondness and sadness and all of these emotions. Perhaps if we'd had just a little more time, it would have been great, but I'm sure everybody says that…. I'm glad that it turned out the way that it did, but I wish, especially as the circumstances have dictated, that I had fought harder for the film…. So many people could learn so much from someone like Robin," he said. "It's not about fame and fortune and all of that stuff. What really matters is how you interact with people, and what matters most of all is your work." (from *The New York Times*, November 4, 2014)

WHAT THE CRITICS HAD TO SAY

Matt Zoller Seitz: "*A Merry Friggin' Christmas* is being sold as a parting gift from its late co-star, Robin Williams, but it's a better example of Williams's tendency to enliven rather slapdash films by imbuing his characters with more sincerity and soul than they might have otherwise had." (from RogerEbert.com, November 7, 2014)

Jason Clark: "Even if Robin Williams were still among us, the limp, drearily derivative *A Merry Friggin' Christmas* would feel like it had a pall cast over it. A home-for-the-holidays comedy that dreams of being both a *National Lampoon*-ish feature and *Bad Santa*—with a dash of *Home Alone* schmaltz for good measure—*Christmas* not only never comes close to the highs of those titles, but squanders a cast of actors usually able to elevate weak material." (from *Entertainment Weekly*, November 19, 2014)

Absolutely Anything

(2015)

*But I worship you, master! I love you so much! I can't bear
displeasing you! My whole world collapses when you're cross
with me!*

—Dennis the Dog

Considering the artistic lineage of the talents involved in *Absolutely Anything*, this movie—the final Monty Python effort—could have and should have been better. But it is in no way as bad as some of the reviews would have you believe.

It's a fun premise: a Galactic Council decides whether or not to destroy a planet and its occupants based on what one of the inhabitants does with limitless power.

Simon Pegg plays Neil, a hapless high school teacher who is bequeathed with the power to do absolutely anything (get it?) by simply stating what he desires and waving his hand. It takes him a while to figure out that he does, indeed, have these powers, but once he does, he proceeds to change his life, himself, and the world in ways that are selfish, silly, stupid, and, ultimately as noble as he can conceive.

Some of the jokes made as he experiments with his powers are lame, and possibly even a bit racist:

> Let me have a penis that women find exciting…can I have it in white?

Neil is ensorcelled with his neighbor Catherine, he hates his head teacher boss, and he loves his dog Dennis, which brings us to Robin Williams, who voices Dennis.

Neil gives Dennis the ability to talk, but we don't hear Robin's voice until forty-five minutes into an eighty-five-minute movie. Robin managed to record the lines in March 2014, a few months before he took his own life, but he did ask for a "do-over" to re-record the lines after he figured out how to play Dennis (he said he suddenly realized that Dennis was like a thirteen-year-old boy).

The subplots are a bit lame: an ex-boyfriend stalks Catherine; a teacher, Ray, ends up terrorized by a woman he likes because Neil made her worship him.

Eventually, we learn that the aliens consider that doing good is cause for destruction—not the other way around—but Neil gives Dennis his powers and Dennis orders that whoever controls the abilities be destroyed forever. And everything goes back to normal.

Absolutely Anything is the last performance by Robin Williams, and because of that circumstance alone, the flick is worth a watch. Once.

WHAT THE CRITICS HAD TO SAY

MaryAnn Johanson: "This is a movie that is subjuvenile and offensive, then sentimental and ridiculous, and then it totally falls apart at the end in a way that negates everything we've just endured. Every attempt at a joke falls flat. Every talent here is wasted...and that's a considerable amount of talent." (from flick-filosopher.com, August 18, 2015)

William Thomas: "Sadly, proof that they will make absolutely anything these days." (from *Empire*, August 11, 2015)

Alec Pridgen: "After around four decades, this may be the final Monty Python project. Are they going out in the best way?... Honestly, the film's biggest problem is just the pedigree of the people involved and the expectations it brings. All of the living members of Monty Python. Simon Pegg. Robin Williams. This has to be great, right? Well, it is good. Were the same film featuring less-renowned people it would be a different story." (from mondobizarrocinema.blogspot.com, January 12, 2016)

CREDITS

Note: This list of film credits for Robin's movies comes primarily from IMDb.com, and we express our sincerest thanks to all involved in that extraordinary site that has served movie fans so well since 1990, and continues to do so.

We have taken the liberty of listing Robin as the first credit for every movie since this is, after all, a book about his films. For the sake of space we have eschewed listing uncredited actors and actors whose characters have minor roles in the films, except in specific instances when we felt readers would be interested to learn that so-and-so was in a certain movie.

CAN I DO IT 'TIL I NEED GLASSES? (1977)

Director: I. Robert Levy
Cast: Robin Williams, Roger Behr, Deborah Klose, Moose Carlson, Walter Olkewicz.
Writers: Mike Callie, Mike Price
Music: Bob Jung
Rated R
73 minutes

POPEYE (1980)

Director: Robert Altman

Cast: Robin Williams (Popeye), Shelley Duvall (Olive Oyl), Ray Walston (Poopdeck Pappy), Paul Dooley (Wimpy), Paul L. Smith (Bluto), Richard Libertini (Geezil), with Linda Hunt, Donald Moffat, MacIntyre Dixon, Roberta Maxwell, Bill Irwin, Valerie Velardi.
Writer: Jules Feiffer
Music: Harry Nilsson
Rated PG
114 minutes

THE WORLD ACCORDING TO GARP (1982)

Director: George Roy Hill
Cast: Robin Williams (T.S. Garp), Mary Beth Hurt (Helen Holm), Glenn Close (Jenny Fields), John Lithgow (Roberta), Hume Cronyn (Mr. Fields), Jessica Tandy (Mrs. Fields), Amanda Plummer (Ellen James), Swoosie Kurtz (Hooker), James McCall (Young Garp), Warren Berlinger (Stew Percy), Brandon Maggart (Ernie Holm), Jenny Wright (Cushie), John Irving (Wrestling Coach).
Writer: Steve Tesich, based on the novel by John Irving
Music: David Shire
Rated R
136 minutes

THE SURVIVORS (1983)

Director: Michael Ritchie
Cast: Robin Williams (Donald Quinelle), Walter Matthau (Sonny Paluso), Jerry Reed (Jack Locke), John Goodman (Commando), James Wainwright (Wes Huntley), Kristen Vigard (Candice Paluso), Anne Pitoniak (Betty), Annie McEnroe (Doreen), Bernard Barrow (TV Station Manager),

Marian Hailey (Jack's Wife), Joseph Carberry (Detective Matt Burke), Marilyn Cooper (Waitress), Skipp Lynch (Wiley), Meg Mundy (Mace Lover).

Writer: Michael Leeson
Music: Paul Chihara
Rated R
103 minutes

MOSCOW ON THE HUDSON (1984)

Director: Paul Mazursky
Cast: Robin Williams (Vladimir Ivanoff), Maria Conchita Alonso (Lucia Lombardo), Cleavant Derricks (Lionel Witherspoon), Alejandro Rey (Orlando Ramirez), Savely Kramarov (Boris), Elya Baskin (Anatoly), Oleg Rudnik (Yury), Aleksandr Benyaminov (Vladimir's Grandfather), Paul Mazursky (Dave), Yakov Smirnoff (Lev).

Writers: Leon Capetanos and Paul Mazursky
Music: David McHugh
Rated R
115 minutes

THE BEST OF TIMES (1986)

Director: Roger Spottiswoode
Cast: Robin Williams (Jack Dundee), Kurt Russell (Reno Hightower), Pamela Reed (Gigi Hightower), Holly Palance (Elly Dundee), Donald Moffat (The Colonel), Margaret Whitton (Darla), M. Emmet Walsh (Charlie), Donovan Scott (Eddie), R.G. Armstrong (Schutte), Dub Taylor (Mac), Carl Ballantine (Arturo).

Writer: Ron Shelton
Music: Arthur B. Rubinstein

Rated PG-13
104 minutes

SEIZE THE DAY (1986)

Director: Fielder Cook
Cast: Robin Williams (Tommy Wilhelm), Richard B. Shull (Rojax), Glenne Headly (Olive), Jerry Stiller (Dr. Tamkin), Tony Roberts (Bernie Pell), Jayne Heller (Mrs. Adler), Katherine Borowitz (Margaret), John Fiedler (Carl), William Duell (Joey), Saul Bellow (Man in Hallway), Fyvush Finkel (Shomier), Tom Aldredge (Rappaport), William Hickey (Perls), Eileen Heckart (Funeral Woman #1).
Writer: Ronald Ribman, based on the novel by Saul Bellow
Music: Elizabeth Swados
Not Rated
93 minutes

CLUB PARADISE (1986)

Director: Harold Ramis
Cast: Robin Williams (Jack Moniker), Peter O'Toole (Governor Anthony Cloyden Hayes), Rick Moranis (Barry Nye), Jimmy Cliff (Ernest Reed), Twiggy (Phillipa Lloyd), Eugene Levy (Barry Steinberg), Joanna Cassidy (Terry Hamlin), Andrea Martin (Linda White), Brian Doyle-Murray (Voit Zerbe).
Writers: Harold Ramis, Brian Doyle-Murray
Music: David Mansfield, Van Dyke Parks
Rated PG-13
96 minutes

GOOD MORNING, VIETNAM (1987)

Director: Barry Levinson

Cast: Robin Williams (Adrian Cronauer), Forest Whitaker (Edward Garlick), Bruno Kirby (Lt. Steven Hauk), Richard Edson (Pvt. Abersold), Robert Wuhl (Marty Lee Dreiwitz), J.T. Walsh (Sgt. Major Dickerson), Noble Willingham (Gen. Taylor), Floyd Vivino (Eddie Kirk), Tung Thanh Tran (Tuan), Chintara Sukapatana (Trinh).

Writer: Mitch Markowitz
Music: Alex North
Rated R
121 minutes

THE ADVENTURES OF BARON MUNCHAUSEN (1988)

Director: Terry Gilliam
Cast: Robin Williams as Ray D. Tutto (King of the Moon), John Neville (Hieronymus Karl Frederick Baron von Munchausen), Eric Idle (Desmond/Berthold), Sarah Polley (Sally Salt), Valentina Cortese (Queen Ariadne/Violet), Oliver Reed (Vulcan), Uma Thurman (Venus/Rose), Sting (Heroic Officer), Jonathan Pryce (The Right Ordinary Horatio Jackson), Bill Patterson (Henry Salt), Peter Jeffrey (Sultan), Alison Steadman (Daisy), Charles McKeown (Rupert/Adolphus), Ray Cooper (Functionary), Winston Dennis (Bill/Albrecht), Jack Purvis (Jeremy/Gustavus), Terry Gilliam.

Writers: Charles McKeown, Terry Gilliam
Music: Michael Kamen
Rated PG
126 minutes

PORTRAIT OF A WHITE MARRIAGE (1988)

Director: Harry Shearer

Cast: Robin Williams (Air Conditioning Salesman (uncredited)), Martin Mull (Martin Mull), Mary Kay Place (Joyce Harrison), Fred Willard (Hal Harrison), David Arnott (Staffer #1), Kate Benton (Mrs. Enid Fletcher), Lew Brown (Mayor Norman Sturgeon), Marcia Bures (Audience Woman #1), Helen Page Camp (Audience Woman #2), Beatrice Colen (Mrs. Peaco), Jimmy Cremona (Gas Station Attendant), Jeff Doucette (Darryl Spencer), Conchata Ferrell (Mrs. Sturgeon), Isabel Grandin (Pittsburgh Girlfriend), Christian Jacobs (Tommy Harrison), Lance Kinsey (Staffer #2), Kimberley D. Labelle (Campaign Worker / Waitress), Stephen Lee (Frenchy Kandinsky), Amy Lynne (Debbie Harrison), Michael McKean (Reverend Prufrock), Gabriele Morgan (Female Convict #2), Beans Morocco (Wilbur Neubauer), Marianne Muellerleile (Roxanne), Wendy Haas-Mull (Female Convict #1), Julie Payne (Mrs. Prufrock), Jack Riley (Roy Bloomer), Harry Shearer (Al Silvers), Gidget Swanson (Woman in Crowd), Berel Weinberg (Stage Manager), Kimberley Kates (Young Beauty Queen (uncredited)).
Writers: Martin Mull, Allen Rucker
Music: Wendy Haas-Mull
101 minutes

DEAD POETS SOCIETY (1989)

Director: Peter Weir
Cast: Robin Williams (John Keating), Robert Sean Leonard (Neil Perry), Ethan Hawke (Todd Anderson), Josh Charles (Knox Overstreet), Gale Hansen (Charlie Dalton), Dylan Kussman (Richard Cameron), Allelon Ruggiero (Steven Meeks), James Waterston (Gerard Pitts), Norman Lloyd (Mr. Nolan), Kurtwood Smith (Mr. Perry), Lara Flynn Boyle (Ginny Danburry (scenes deleted), Carla Belver (Mrs. Perry), Leon Pownall

(McAllister), George Martin (Dr. Hager), Joe Aufiery (Chemistry Teacher), Matt Carey (Hopkins), Kevin Cooney (Joe Danburry), Jane Moore (Mrs. Danburry), Colin Irving (Chet Danburry), Alexandra Powers (Chris Noel), Melora Walters (Gloria), Welker White (Tina), Steve Mathios (Steve), Alan Pottinger (Bubba), Pamela Burrell (Directing Teacher), Allison Hedges (Actor / Fairy), Christine D'Ercole (Titania), John Cunningham (Mr. Anderson), Debra Mooney (Mrs. Anderson), John Martin Bradley (Bagpiper), Charles Lord (Mr. Dalton), Kurt Leitner (Lester), Richard Stites (Stick), James J. Christy (Spaz), Catherine Soles (Stage Manager), Hoover Sutton (Welton Professor), James Donnell Quinn (Procession Alumnus), Simon Mein (Welton Vicar), Ashton W. Richards (Phys. Ed. Teacher), Robert Gleason (Father of Spaz), Bill Rowe (Dormitory Porter), Robert J. Zigler III (Beans), Keith Snyder (Russell), Nicholas K. Gilhool (Shroom), Jonas Stiklorius (Jonas), Craig Johnson (Dewey), Chris Hull (Ace), Jason Woody (Woodsie), Sam Stegeman (Sam), Andrew Hill (Senior Student).

Writer: Tom Schulman
Music: Maurice Jarre
Rated PG
128 minutes

CADILLAC MAN (1990)

Director: Roger Donaldson
Cast: Robin Williams (Joey O'Brien), Tim Robbins (Larry), Pamela Reed (Tina), Fran Drescher (Joy Munchack), Zack Norman (Harry Munchack), Lori Petty (Lila), Annabella Sciorra (Donna), Paul Guilfoyle (Little Jack Turgeon), Bill Nelson (Big Jack Turgeon), Lauren Tom (Helen the Dim Sum

Girl), Paul Herman (Tony Dipino), Elaine Stritch (Widow), Chester Drescher (Chester).

Writer: Ken Friedman

Music: J. Peter Robinson

Rated R

97 minutes

AWAKENINGS (1990)

Director: Penny Marshall

Cast: Robin Williams (Dr. Malcolm Sayer), Robert De Niro (Leonard Lowe), Julie Kavner (Eleanor Costello), John Heard (Dr. Kaufman), Penelope Ann Miller (Paula), Alice Drummond (Lucy), Anne Meara (Miriam), Richard Libertini (Sidney), Bradley Whitford (Dr. Tyler), Max Von Sydow (Dr. Peter Ingham), Vinny Pastore (Ward #5 Patient #6), Vin Diesel (Hospital Orderly (uncredited)).

Writer: Steve Zaillian, screenplay, based on the book *Awakenings* by Oliver Sacks, M.D.

Music: Randy Newman

Rated PG-13

121 minutes

DEAD AGAIN (1991)

Director: Kenneth Branagh

Cast: Robin Williams (Dr. Cozy Carlisle), Kenneth Branagh (Roman Strauss/Mike Church), Emma Thompson (Grace/Margaret Strauss), Andy Garcia (Gray Baker), Lois Hall (Sister Constance), Richard Easton (Father Timothy), Jo Anderson (Sister Madeleine/Starlet), Derek Jacobi (Franklyn Madson), Raymond Cruz (Supermarket Clerk), Hanna Schygulla (Inga), Campbell Scott (Doug O'Malley), Wayne

Knight ("Piccolo" Pete Dugan), Christine Ebersole (Lydia Larson), Yvette Freeman (Rest Home Nurse).

Writer: Scott Frank
Music: Patrick Doyle
Rated R
107 minutes

THE FISHER KING (1991)

Director: Terry Gillam
Cast: Robin Williams (Parry), Jeff Bridges (Jack), Amanda Plummer (Lydia), Mercedes Ruehl (Anne), David Pierce (Lou Rosen), Ted Ross (Limo Bum), Kathy Najimy (Crazed Video Customer), Harry Shearer (Sitcom Actor Ben Starr), Melinda Culea (Sitcom Wife), James Remini (Bum at Hotel), Dan Futterman (Second Punk), Bradley Gregg (Hippie Bum), Michael Jeter (Homeless Cabaret Singer), Richard LaGravenese (Strait Jacket Yuppie), Tom Waits (Disabled Veteran (uncredited)).

Writer: Richard LaGravenese
Music: George Fenton
Rated R
137 minutes

HOOK (1991)

Director: Steven Spielberg
Cast: Robin Williams (Peter Banning), Dustin Hoffman (Captain Hook), Julia Roberts (Tinkerbell), Bob Hoskins (Smee), Maggie Smith (Granny Wendy), Charlie Korsmo (Jack "Jackie" Banning), Caroline Goodall (Moira Banning), Amber Scott (Maggie Banning), Phil Collins (Inspector Good), Arthur Malet (Tootles), Dante Basco (Rufio), Gwyneth Paltrow (Young Wendy), David Crosby (Tickles), Glenn

Close (Gutless), Jimmy Buffett (Shoe-Stealing Pirate (uncredited)), Carrie Fisher (Woman Kissing on Bridge (uncredited)), George Lucas (Man Kissing on Bridge (uncredited)).

Writers: James V. Hart and Malia Scotch Marmo, based on the story by J.M. Barrie

Music: John Williams

Rated PG

142 minutes

SHAKES THE CLOWN (1991)

Director: Bobcat Goldthwait

Cast: Robin Williams as Marty Fromage (Mime Class Instructor Jerry), Bobcat Goldthwait (Shakes), Julie Brown (Judy), Adam Sandler (Dink the Clown), Paul Dooley (Owen Cheese), Blake Clark (Stenchy the Clown), Melissa Hurley (Producer at Big Time Cartoon Circus), Tom Kenny (Binky the Clown), Sydney Lassick (Peppy the Clown), Tim Kazurinsky (1st Party Dad), Florence Henderson (The Unknown Woman), La Wanda Page (Female Clown Barfly), Kathy Griffin (Lucy), Tasha Goldthwait (Little Girl Playing on Lawn (uncredited)).

Writer: Bobcat Goldthwait

Music: Tom Scott

Rated R

87 minutes

FERNGULLY: THE LAST RAINFOREST (1992)

Director: Bill Kroyer

Voices: Robin Williams (Batty Koda), Tim Curry (Hexxus), Samantha Mathis (Crysta), Christian Slater (Pips), Jonathan Ward (Zak), Grace Zabriskie (Magi Lune), Geoffrey Blake

(Ralph), Robert Pastorelli (Tony), Cheech Marin (Stump), Tommy Chong (Root), Tone-Loc (The Goanna).

Writer: Jim Cox, based on original stories by Diana Young

Music: Original score by Alan Silvestri, with songs written by Thomas Dolby, Jimmy Webb, Jimmy Buffet, and Elton John

Rated G

76 minutes

ALADDIN (1992)

Directors: Ron Clements, John Musker

Voices: Robin Williams (Genie), Scott Weinger (Aladdin), Linda Larkin (Jasmine), Jonathan Freeman (Jafar), Frank Welker (Abu), Gilbert Gottfried (Iago), Brad Kane (Aladdin singing voice (uncredited)), Lea Salonga (Jasmine singing voice (uncredited)).

Writers: Ron Clements, John Musker, Ted Elliott, Terry Rossio

Music: Alan Menken, Howard Ashman, Tim Rice

Rated G

90 minutes

TOYS (1992)

Director: Barry Levinson

Cast: Robin Williams (Leslie Zevo), Joan Cusack (Alsatia Zevo), LL Cool J (Captain Patrick Zevo), Michael Gambon (Lt. General Leland Zevo), Robin Wright (Gwen Tyler), Donald O'Connor (Kenneth Zevo), Jack Warden (Old General Zevo), Debi Mazar (Nurse Debbie), Jamie Foxx (Baker).

Writers: Valerie Curtin, Barry Levinson

Music: Trevor Horn, Hans Zimmer

Rated PG-13

118 minutes

MRS. DOUBTFIRE (1993)

Director: Chris Columbus

Cast: Robin Williams (Daniel Hillard/Mrs. Doubtfire), Sally Field (Miranda Hillard), Pierce Brosnan (Stu), Harvey Fierstein (Frank), Robert Prosky (Mr. Lundy), Mara Wilson (Natalie Hillard), Lisa Jakub (Lydia Hillard), Matthew Lawrence (Chris Hillard), Polly Holliday (Gloria), Martin Mull (Justin Gregory).

Writers: Randi Mayem Singer, Leslie Dixon, based on the novel *Alias Madame Doubtfire* by Anne Fine

Music: Howard Shore

Rated PG-13

125 minutes

BEING HUMAN (1994)

Director: Bill Forsyth

Cast: Robin Williams (Hector), John Turturro (Lucinnius), Anna Galiena (Beatrice), Vincent D'Onofrio (Priest), Hector Elizondo (Dom Paulo), Lorraine Bracco (Anna), Ewan McGregor (Alvarez), Lindsay Crouse (Janet), Kelly Hunter (Deirdre), Jonathan Hyde (Francisco), William H. Macy (Boris), Grace Mahlaba (Thalia), Theresa Russell (The Storyteller), David Proval (George), Robert Carlyle (Priest), Bill Nighy (Julian).

Writer: Bill Forsyth

Music: Michael Gibbs

Rated PG-13

122 minutes

NINE MONTHS (1995)

Director: Chris Columbus

Cast: Robin Williams (Dr. Kosevich), Hugh Grant (Samuel Faulkner), Julianne Moore (Rebecca Taylor), Tom Arnold (Marty Dwyer), Joan Cusack (Gail Dwyer), Jeff Goldblum (Sean Fletcher), Joey Simmrin (Truman), Ashley Johnson (Shannon Dwyer), Mia Cottet (Lili), Zelda Williams (Little Girl #3 in Ballet Class).

Writer: Chris Columbus, based on the film *Neuf Mois*, written and directed by Patrick Braoudé

Music: Hans Zimmer

Rated PG-13

103 minutes

TO WONG FOO, THANKS FOR EVERYTHING! JULIE NEWMAR (1995)

Director: Beeban Kidron

Cast: Robin Williams (John Jacob Jingleheimer Schmidt (uncredited)), Wesley Snipes (Noxeema), Patrick Swayze (Vida), John Leguizamo (Chi-Chi), Stockard Channing (Carol Ann), Blythe Danner (Beatrice), Arliss Howard (Virgil), Jason London (Bobby Ray), Alice Drummond (Clara), Chris Penn (Sheriff Dollard), RuPaul (Rachel Tensions), Julie Newmar (Herself), Naomi Campbell (Girl), Quentin Crisp (NY Pageant Judge).

Writer: Douglas Carter Beane

Music: Rachel Portman

Rated PG-13

109 minutes

JUMANJI (1995)

Director: Joe Johnston

Cast: Robin Williams (Alan Parrish), Jonathan Hyde (Van Pelt/ Sam Parrish), Bebe Neuwirth (Nora Shepherd), Kirsten Dunst

(Judy Shepherd), Bradley Pierce (Peter Shepherd), Bonnie
Hunt (Sarah Whittle), Patricia Clarkson (Carol Parrish).
Writers: Jonathan Hensleigh, Greg Taylor, Jim Strain, based on
the book by Chris Van Allsburg
Music: James Horner
Rated PG
104 minutes

THE BIRDCAGE (1996)

Director: Mike Nichols
Cast: Robin Williams (Armand Goldman), Nathan Lane (Albert/
Starina), Gene Hackman (Senator Keeley), Dianne Wiest
(Louise Keeley), Hank Azaria (Agador), Dan Futterman (Val
Goldman), Calista Flockhart (Barbara Keeley), Christine
Baranski (Katharine).
Writer: Elaine May
Music: Arranged and adapted by Jonathan Tunick
Rated R
117 minutes

JACK (1996)

Director: Francis Ford Coppola
Cast: Robin Williams (Jack Powell), Diane Lane (Karen Powell),
Jennifer Lopez (Miss Marquez), Brian Kerwin (Brian Powell),
Fran Drescher (Dolores Durante), Bill Cosby (Lawrence
Woodruff), Michael McKean (Paulie), Don Novello (Bar-
tender), Allan Rich (Dr. Benfante), Adam Zolotin (Louis
Durante), Keone Young (Dr. Lin), Todd Bosley (Edward),
Seth Smith (John-John), Mario Yedidia (George), Jer Adri-
enne Lelliott [as Jeremy Lelliott] (Johnny Duffer), Rickey
D'Shon Collins (Eric), Hugo Hernandez (Victor), Irwin
Corey (Poppy).

Writers: James DeMonaco, Gary Nadeau
Music: Michael Kamen
Rated PG-13
113 minutes

ALADDIN AND THE KING OF THIEVES (1996)

Director: Tad Stones
Voices: Robin Williams (Genie), Gilbert Gottfried (Iago), Val Bettin (Sultan), Jerry Orbach (Sa'luk), Jim Cummings (Razoul), Linda Larkin (Princess Jasmine), John Rhys-Davies (Cassim), Frank Welker (Abu/Rajah/Fazahl), CCH Pounder (The Oracle), Brad Kane (Aladdin singing voice (uncredited)), Liz Callaway (Jasmine singing voice (uncredited)).
Writers: Mark McCorkle, Robert Schooley
Music: Mark Watters and Carl Johnson; Songs by David Friedman; Randy Petersen and Kevin Quinn
Not rated
81 minutes

THE SECRET AGENT (1996)

Director: Christopher Hampton
Cast: Robin Williams (The Professor (uncredited)), Bob Hoskins (Verloc), Patricia Arquette (Winnie), Gérard Depardieu (Ossipon), Jim Broadbent (Chief Inspector Heat), Christian Bale (Stevie), Roger Hammond (Mr. Michaelis), Eddie Izzard (Vladimir), Ralph Nossek (Yundt), Neville Phillips (Ticket Clerk), Elizabeth Spriggs (Winnie's Mother), Peter Vaughan (The Driver), Julian Wadham (The Assistant Commissioner).
Writer: Christopher Hampton, based on the novel by Joseph Conrad
Music: Philip Glass

Rated R
95 minutes

HAMLET (1996)

Director: Kenneth Branagh

Cast: Robin Williams (Osric), Riz Abbasi (Attendant to Claudius), Richard Attenborough (English Ambassador), David Blair (Attendant to Claudius), Brian Blessed (Ghost of Hamlet's Father), Kenneth Branagh (Hamlet), Richard Briers (Polonius), Michael Bryant (Priest), Peter Bygott (Attendant to Claudius), Julie Christie (Gertrude), Billy Crystal (First Gravedigger), Charles Daish (Stage Manager), Judi Dench (Hecuba), Gérard Depardieu (Reynaldo), Reece Dinsdale (Guildenstern), Ken Dodd (Yorick), Angela Douglas (Attendant to Gertrude), Rob Edwards (Lucianus), Nicholas Farrell (Horatio), Ray Fearon (Francisco), Yvonne Gidden (Doctor), John Gielgud (Priam), Rosemary Harris (Player Queen), Charlton Heston (Player King), Ravil Isyanov (Cornelius), Derek Jacobi (Claudius), Rowena King (Attendant to Gertrude), Jeffery Kissoon (Fortinbras's Captain), Sarah Lam (Attendant to Gertrude), Jack Lemmon (Marcellus), Ian McElhinney (Barnardo), Michael Maloney (Laertes), John Spencer-Churchill (Fortinbras's Captain (as Duke of Marlborough)), John Mills (Old Norway), Jimi Mistry (Sailor Two), Sian Radinger (Prologue), Simon Russell Beale (Second Gravedigger), Andrew Schofield (Young Lord), Rufus Sewell (Fortinbras), Timothy Spall (Rosencrantz), Tom Szekeres (Young Hamlet), Ben Thom (First Player), Don Warrington (Voltimand), Perdita Weeks (Second Player), Kate Winslet (Ophelia), David Yip (Sailor One).

Writers: Kenneth Branagh (screenplay), William Shakespeare (play)

Music: Patrick Doyle
Rated PG-13
242 minutes, 150 minutes (abridged version)

DECONSTRUCTING HARRY (1997)

Director: Woody Allen
Cast: Robin Williams (Mel), Woody Allen (Harry Block), Richard Benjamin (Ken), Kirstie Alley (Joan), Billy Crystal (Larry/ The Devil), Julie Kavner (Grace), Judy Davis (Lucy), Bob Balaban (Richard), Elisabeth Shue (Fay Sexton), Tobey Maguire (Harvey Stern), Jennifer Garner (Woman in elevator), Paul Giamatti (Prof. Abbott), Stanley Tucci (Paul Epstein), Julia Louis-Dreyfus (Leslie), Mariel Hemingway (Beth Kramer), Hazelle Goodman (Cookie Williams), Eric Bogosian (Burt), Demi Moore (Helen), Caroline Aaron (Doris Block), Eric Lloyd (Hilliard Block), Amy Irving (Jane), Viola Harris (Elsie), Shifra Lerer (Dolly).
Writer: Woody Allen
Music: Songs only
Rated R
96 minutes

FATHERS' DAY (1997)

Director: Ivan Reitman
Cast: Robin Williams (Dale Putley), Billy Crystal (Jack Lawrence), Julia Louis-Dreyfus (Carrie Lawrence), Nastassja Kinski (Collette Andrews), Charlie Hofheimer (Scott Andrews), Bruce Greenwood (Bob Andrews), Charles Rocket (Russ Trainor), Patti D'Arbanville (Shirley Trainor), Mary McCormack (Virginia Farrell (uncredited)), Mel Gibson (Scott the Body Piercer (uncredited)).

Writers: Lowell Ganz, Babaloo Mandel
Music: James Newton Howard
Rated PG-13
98 minutes

FLUBBER (1997)

Director: Les Mayfield
Cast: Robin Williams (Professor Philip Brainard), Marcia Gay Harden (Dr. Sara Jean Reynolds), Christopher McDonald (Wilson Croft), Ted Levine (Wesson), Clancy Brown (Smith), Raymond Barry (Chester Hoenicker), Wil Wheaton (Bennett Hoenicker), Edie McClurg (Martha George), Jodi Benson (Weebo (voice)), Leslie Stefanson (Sylvia), Malcolm Brownson (Father), Benjamin Brock (Window Boy), Dakin Matthews (Minister), Zack Zeigler (Teenage Boy), Samuel Lloyd (Coach Willy Barker), Scott Michael Campbell (Dale Jepner), Bob Sarlatte (Rutland Coach), Bob Greene (Referee), Tom Barlow (Medfield Basketball Player), Scott Martin Gershin (Flubber (voice)), Julie Morrison (Weebette (voice)).
Writers: John Hughes, Bill Walsh; based on the short story "A Situation of Gravity" by Samuel W. Taylor
Music: Danny Elfman
Rated PG
93 minutes

GOOD WILL HUNTING (1997)

Director: Gus Van Sant
Cast: Robin Williams (Sean), Matt Damon (Will), Ben Affleck (Chuckie), Stellan Skarsgård (Lambeau), John Mighton (Tom), Rachel Majorowski (Krystyn), Colleen McCauley (Cathy), Casey Affleck (Morgan), Cole Hauser (Billy), Alison

Folland (M.I.T. Student), Derrick Bridgeman (M.I.T. Student), Vic Sahay (M.I.T. Student), Shannon Egleson (Girl on Street), Rob Lyons (Carmine Scarpaglia), Steven Kozlowski (Carmine Friend #1), Minnie Driver (Skylar), Jennifer Deathe (Lydia), Scott William Winters (Clark), Philip Williams (Head Custodian), Patrick O'Donnell (Assistant Custodian), Kevin Rushton (Courtroom Guard), Jimmy Flynn (Judge Malone), Joe Cannon (Prosecutor), Ann Matacunas (Court Officer), George Plimpton (Psychologist), Francesco Clemente (Hypnotist), Jessica Morton (Bunker Hill College Student), Barna Moricz (Bunker Hill College Student), Libby Geller (Toy Store Cashier), Chas Lawther (M.I.T Professor), Richard Fitzpatrick (Timmy), Frank Nakashima (Executive #1), Chris Britton (Executive #2), David Eisner (Executive #3), Bruce Hunter (NSA Agent), Robert Talvano (2nd NSA Agent), James Allodi (Security Guard).

Writers: Matt Damon, Ben Affleck
Music: Danny Elfman
Rated R
126 minutes

WHAT DREAMS MAY COME (1998)

Director: Vincent Ward
Cast: Robin Williams (Chris Nielsen), Cuba Gooding Jr. (Albert Lewis), Annabella Sciorra (Annie Collins-Nielsen), Max von Sydow (The Tracker), Jessica Brooks Grant (Marie Nielsen), Josh Paddock (Ian Nielsen), Rosalind Chao (Leona), Lucinda Jenney (Mrs. Jacobs), Maggie McCarthy (Stacey Jacobs), Wilma Bonet (Angie), Matt Salinger (Reverend Hanley), Carin Sprague (Best Friend Cindy), June Lomena (Woman in Car Accident), Paul P. Card IV (Paramedic), Werner Herzog

(Face), Clara Thomas (Little Girl at Lake), Benjamin Brock (Little Boy at Lake).

Writer: Ron Bass, based on the novel by Richard Matheson

Music: Michael Kamen

Rated PG-13

113 minutes

PATCH ADAMS (1998)

Director: Tom Shadyac

Cast: Robin Williams (Patch Adams), Daniel London (Truman), Monica Potter (Carin), Philip Seymour Hoffman (Mitch), Bob Gunton (Dean Walcott), Josef Sommer (Dr. Eaton), Irma P. Hall (Joletta), Frances Lee McCain (Judy), Harve Presnell (Dean Anderson), Daniella Kuhn (Adelane), Peter Coyote (Bill Davis), James Greene (Bile), Michael Jeter (Rudy), Harold Gould (Arthur Mendelson), Bruce Bohne (Trevor Beene), Harry Groener (Dr. Prack), Barry Shabaka Henley (Emmet), Steven Anthony Jones (Charlie), Richard Kiley (Dr. Titan), Douglas Roberts (Larry), Ellen Albertini Dow (Aggie), Alan Tudyk (Everton), Ryan Hurst (Neil), Peter Siiteri (Chess Man), Don West (Instructor).

Writer: Steve Oedekerk, based on the book by Hunter Doherty Adams and Maureen Mylander

Music: Marc Shaiman

Rated PG-13

115 minutes

JAKOB THE LIAR (1999)

Director: Peter Kassovitz

Cast: Robin Williams (Jakob Heym), Hannah Taylor Gordon (Lina), Eva Igo (Lina's Mother), Istvan Balint (Lina's Father),

Justus von Dohnányi (Preuss), Kathleen Gati (Hooker), Bob Balaban (Kowalsky), Alan Arkin (Frankfurter), Michael Jeter (Avron), Mark Margolis (Fajngold), Janos Gosztonyi (Samuel), Liev Schreiber (Mischa), Armin Mueller-Stahl (Kirschbaum), Adam Rajhona (The Whistler), Antal Leisen (Peg-Leg), Mathieu Kassovitz (Herschel), Peter Rudolf (Roman), Jan Becker (Young German), Janos Kulka (Nathan), Gregg Bello (Blumenthal), Nina Siemaszko (Rosa), Grazyna Barszczewska (Mrs. Frankfurter), Judit Sagi (Mrs. Avron), Ilona Psota (Grandmother), Agi Margitai (Miss Esther), Ivan Darvas (Hardtloff), Laszlo Borbely (Doctor), Zoli Anders (Meyer), Miroslaw Zbrojewicz (SS Officer 1), Jozef Mika (Soldier), György Szkladányi (SS Officer 2), Zofia Saretok (Neighbor), Michael Mehlmann (Escaping Man), Micheller Myrtill (Lady Singer), Orsolya Pflum (Lady Singer), Beatrix Bisztricsan (Lady Singer).

Writers: Peter Kassovitz, Didier Decoin, based on the book by Jurek Becker

Music: Edward Shearmur

Rated PG-13

120 minutes

BICENTENNIAL MAN (1999)

Director: Chris Columbus

Cast: Robin Williams (Andrew Martin), Embeth Davidtz (Little Miss Amanda Martin/Portia Charney), Sam Neill ('Sir' Richard Martin), Oliver Platt (Rupert Burns), Kiersten Warren (Galatea), Wendy Crewson ('Ma'am' Martin), Hallie Kate Eisenberg (Little Miss Amanda Martin - Age 7), Lindze Letherman ('Miss' Grace Martin - Age 9), Angela Landis ('Miss' Grace Martin), John Michael Higgins (Bill Feingold - Martin's Lawyer), Bradley Whitford (Lloyd Charney), Igor

Hiller (Lloyd Charney - Age 10), Joe Bellan (Robot Delivery Man #1), Brett Wagner (Robot Delivery Man #2), Stephen Root (Dennis Mansky - Head of NorthAm Robotics), Scott Waugh (Motorcycle Punk), Quinn Smith (Frank Charney), Kristy Connelly (Monica), Jay Johnston (Charles), George D. Wallace (Male President), Lynne Thigpen (President Marjorie Bota), Ples Griffin (Zimbabwe Representative), Marcia Pizzo (Lloyd Charney's Wife), Paula Dupre Pesmen (Bill Feingold's Assistant), Clarke Devereux (Priest), Bruce Kenneth Wagner (Engagement Party Guest), Paula West (Singer), Kevin 'Tiny' Ancell (Restoration Worker #1), Richard Cross (Restoration Worker #2), Adam Bryant (Humanoid Head).

Puppeteers: Eric Fiedler, Billy Bryan, Christopher Nelson, Jim Kundig, Terry Sandin, Mike Elizalde, Mark Garbarino, Christian Ristow, Lennie MacDonald, Dan Rebett, Bernhard Eicholz, Evan Brainard, Benny Buettner, Kamela Portuges, Michael F. Steffe, Mark J. Walas.

Writer: Nicholas Kazan, based on the novella "The Bicentennial Man" by Isaac Asimov and the novel *The Positronic Man* by Isaac Asimov and Robert Silverberg

Music: James Horner

Rated PG

132 minutes

A. I. ARTIFICIAL INTELLIGENCE (2001)

Director: Steven Spielberg

Cast: Robin Williams (Dr. Know (voice)), Haley Joel Osment (David), Frances O'Connor (Monica Swinton), Sam Robards (Henry Swinton), Jake Thomas (Martin Swinton), Jude Law (Gigolo Joe), William Hurt (Prof. Hobby), Ken Leung (Syatyoo-Sama), Ben Kingsley (Specialist (voice)), Meryl Streep (Blue Mecha (voice)), Chris Rock (Comedian (voice)), Clark Gregg (Supernerd), Kevin Sussman (Supernerd), Tom Gallop (Supernerd), Eugene Osment (Supernerd), April Grace (Female Colleague), Matt Winston (Executive), Sabrina Grdevich (Sheila), Theo Greenly (Todd), Jeremy James Kissner (Kid), Dillon McEwin (Kid), Andy Morrow (Kid), Curt Youngberg (Kid), Ashley Scott (Gigolo Jane), John Prosky (Mr. Williamson, the Bellman), Enrico Colantoni (The Murderer), Paula Malcolmson (Patricia in Mirrored Room), Brendan Gleeson (Lord Johnson-Johnson), Michael Berresse (Stage Manager), Haley King (Amanda), Kathryn Morris (Teenage Honey), Daveigh Chase (Child Singer (scenes deleted)), Brian Turk (Backstage Bull), Justina Machado (Assistant), Tim Rigby (Yeoman), Lily Knight (Voice in the Crowd (voice)), Vito Carenzo (Big Man), Rena Owen (Ticket Taker), J. Alan Scott (Worker), Adam Alexi-Malle (Crowd Member), Laurence Mason (Tech Director), Brent Sexton (Russell), Ken Palmer (Percussionist), Jason Sutter (Percussionist), Michael Shamus Wiles (Cop), Kelly McCool (Kate the Holographic Girl), Clara Bellar (FemMecha Nanny), Keith Campbell (Roadworker), Tim Rhoze (Laboratory Technician), Jim Jansen (Chef), Eliza Coleman (General Circuita), R. David Smith (Welder), Wayne Wilderson (Comedian), Bobby Harwell (TV Face), Billy Scudder (Mechanic), Jack Angel (Teddy (voice)), Erik Bauersfeld (Gardener (voice)), Michael Mantell (Dr. Frazier at Cryogenic Institute), Miguel Perez (Robot Repairman), Matt Malloy (Robot Repairman), Adrian Grenier (Teen in Van), Mark Staubach (Teen in Van), Michael Fishman (Teen in Van), Jeanine Salla (Sentient Machine Therapist), Laia Salla (Mr. Chan's Assistant), Diane Fletcher (Sentient Machine Security), Kate Nei (Toe Bell Ringing), Claude Gilbert (Cybertronics - Room 93056), Red King (Covert Information Retrieval).

Writers: Steven Spielberg, screenplay; Ian Watson, screen story; based on the short story "Supertoys Last All Summer Long" by Brian Aldiss
Music: John Williams
Rated PG-13
146 minutes

DEATH TO SMOOCHY (2002)

Director: Danny DeVito
Cast: Robin Williams (Rainbow Randolph), Edward Norton (Sheldon Mopes/Smoochy the Rhino), Catherine Keener (Nora Wells), Danny DeVito (Burke Bennett), Jon Stewart (Marion Frank Stokes), Pam Ferris (Tommy Cotter), Danny Woodburn (Angelo Pike), Michael Rispoli (Spinner Dunn), Harvey Fierstein (Merv Green), Vincent Schiavelli (Buggy Ding Dong), Craig Eldridge (Husband), Judy White (Wife), Tim MacMenamin (Danny), Bruce McFee (Roy), Glen Cross (Jimmy), Bill Lake (Bartender), Nick Taylor (Henry the Thug), Richard A. Cocchiaro Jr. (Mitch the Thug), Tracey Walter (Ben Franks), Louis Giambalvo (Sonny Gordon), Colin Moult (Rhinette/Krinkle Kid #1), Nikolai Tichtchenko (Rhinette/Krinkle Kid #2), Martin Klebba (Rhinette/Krinkle Kid #3), Tonya Reneé Banks (Rhinette/Krinkle Kid #4), Christy Artran (Rhinette/Krinkle Kid #5), Philip Craig (Senator), Natasha Kinne (Smoochy's Secretary), Richard Hamilton (Old Vagrant), Shawn Byfield (Rickets), Todd Graff (Skip Kleinman), Melissa DiMarco (Tara), Dan Duran (Hunter).
Writer: Adam Resnick
Music: David Newman
Rated R
109 minutes

INSOMNIA (2002)

Director: Christopher Nolan

Cast: Robin Williams (Walter Finch), Al Pacino (Will Dormer), Martin Donovan (Hap Eckhart), Oliver 'Ole' Zemen (Pilot), Hilary Swank (Ellie Burr), Paul Dooley (Chief Nyback), Nicky Katt (Fred Duggar), Larry Holden (Farrell), Jay Brazeau (Francis), Lorne Cardinal (Rich), James Hutson (Officer #1), Andrew Campbell (Officer #2), Paula Shaw (Coroner), Crystal Lowe (Kay Connell), Tasha Simms (Mrs. Connell), Maura Tierney (Rachel Clement), Jonathan Jackson (Randy Stetz), Malcolm Boddington (Principal), Katharine Isabelle (Tanya Francke), Kerry Sandomirsky (Trish Eckhart), Chris Guthior (Uniformed Officer), Ian Tracey (Warfield (voice)), Kate Robbins (Woman on the Road), Emily Jane Perkins (Girl at Funeral), Dean Wray (Ticket Taker).

Writer: Hillary Seitz

Music: David Julyan

Rated R

118 minutes

ONE HOUR PHOTO (2002)

Director: Mark Romanek

Cast: Robin Williams (Seymour Parrish), Connie Nielsen (Nina Yorkin), Michael Vartan (Will Yorkin), Dylan Smith (Jakob Yorkin), Erin Daniels (Maya Burson), Paul Hansen Kim (Yoshi Araki), Lee Garlington (Waitress), Gary Cole (Bill Owens), Marion Calvert (Mrs. Von Unwerth), David Moreland (Mr. Siskind), Shaun P. O'Hagan (Young Father), Jim Rash (Amateur Porn Guy), Nick Searcy (Repairman), Dave Engfer (Sav-Mart Clerk), Jimmy Shubert (Soccer Coach), Eriq La Salle (Det. James Van Der Zee), Clark Gregg (Det. Paul Outerbridge), Andrew A. Rolfes (Officer Lyon), Carmen

Mormino (Officer Bravo), Izrel Katz (Superintendent), Peter Mackenzie (Hotel Desk Manager), Andy Comeau (Duane), Robert Clotworthy (Eye Surgeon), Jesse Borja (Cook), Jeana Wilson (Nurse), Megan Corletto (Risa Owens).
Writer: Mark Romanek
Music: Reinhold Heil, Johnny Klimek
Rated R
96 minutes

THE RUTLES 2: CAN'T BUY ME LUNCH (2004)

Director: Eric Idle
Cast: Robin Williams (Hans Hänkie), Eric Idle (Narrator/Dirk McQuickly/Lady Beth Mouse-Peddler), Neil Innes (Ron Nasty (archive footage)), Ricky Fataar (Stig O'Hara (archive footage)), John Halsey (Barry Wom (archive footage)), Terence Bayler (Leggy Mountintaback (archive footage)), Mariela Comitini (Jennifer Lopez), Peter Crabbe (Police Officer), Jimmy Fallon (Melvin's Son), Tasha Goldthwaite (Rutles Fan), Samantha Harris (The Jogger), Lily Idle (Rutles Fan), Bianca Jagger (Martini (archive footage)), Bill Murray (Bill Murray the K (archive footage)), Kevin Nealon (Kevin Wongle), Catherine O'Hara (Astro Glide), Jim Piddock (Troy Nixon), Gwen Taylor (Chastity (archive footage)), Carinthia West (Carintha (archive footage)), Henry Woolf (Arthur Sultan (archive footage)), Peter Asher (Peter Asher - Interviewee), Clint Black (Clint Black - Interviewee), David Bowie (David Bowie - Interviewee), Billy Connolly (Billy Connolly - Interviewee), Tom Hank (s (Tom Hanks - Interviewee), Carrie Fisher (Carrie Fisher - Interviewee), Mick Jagger (Mick Jagger - Interviewee (archive footage)), Jewel (Jewel - Interviewee), Steve Martin (Steve Martin - Interviewee), Graham Nash (Graham Nash - Interviewee), Mike Nichols (Mike Nich-

ols - Interviewee), Conan O'Brien (Conan O'Brien - Interviewee), Bonnie Raitt (Bonnie Raitt - Interviewee), Salman Rushdie (Salman Rushdie - Interviewee), Garry Shandling (Garry Shandling - Interviewee), Dave Stewart (Dave Stewart – Interviewee), James Taylor (James Taylor - Interviewee), Jann Wenner (Jann Wenner - Interviewee).

Writer: Eric Idle
Music: Neil Innes
Rated PG-13
84 minutes

HOUSE OF D (2004)

Director: David Duchovny
Cast: Robin Williams (Pappass), Anton Yelchin (Tommy Washaw), Téa Leoni (Mrs. Warshaw), Erykah Badu (Lady/Bernadette), David Duchovny (Tom Warshaw), Frank Langella (Reverend Duncan), Zelda Williams (Melissa Loggia), Magali Amadei (Coralie Warshaw), Olga Sosnovska (Simone), Orlando Jones (Superfly), Bernard Sheredy (Sasha), Stephen Spinella (Ticket Seller), Alice Drummond (Mrs. Brevoort), Harold Cartier (Odell Warshaw), Mark Margolis (Mr. Pappass), Claire Lautier (Madam Chatquipet), Willie Garson (Ticket Agent), Gideon Jacobs (Gerard), Adam LeFevre (Monty), Leslie Lyles (Sondra), Mark Richard Keith (Pitcher), James Ockimey (Another Kid), Jonah Meyerson (Kid #2), Jill Shackner (Lead Girl in Gym), Lisby Larson (Mrs. Loggia), Michael Chapman (Doorman), Henry Strozier (Civil Servant), Andree Damant (French Woman in Window), Etienne Drabier (French Man in Window), Chantal Guarrigues (French Wife in Window), Mary A. Fortune (Nurse #1), Lester Cohen (Irate Trotskyite), Roxy Toporowych (Miss Johnson), Francesca Buccellato (Mrs. Robinson), Erica N. Tazel (Reader).

Writer: David Duchovny
Music: Geoff Zanelli
Rated PG-13
96 minutes

THE FINAL CUT (2004)

Director: Omar Naïm
Cast: Robin Williams (Alan Hakman), Mira Sorvino (Delila), Jim Caviezel (Fletcher), Mimi Kuzyk (Thelma), Stephanie Romanov (Jennifer Bannister), Thom Bishops (Hasan), Genevieve Buechner (Isabel Bannister), Brendan Fletcher (Michael), Vincent Gale (Simon).
Writer: Omar Naïm
Music: Brian Tyler
Rated PG-13
95 minutes

NOEL (2004)

Director: Chazz Palminteri
Cast: Robin Williams (Charlie Boyd/The Priest (uncredited)), Susan Sarandon (Rose Collins), Paul Walker (Mike Riley), Penelope Cruz (Nina Vasquez), Alan Arkin (Artie), Marcus Thomas (Jules Calvert), Sonny Marinelli (Dennis), Daniel Sunjata (Marco), Chazz Palminteri (Arizona), Rob Daly (Paul), John Doman (Dr. Baron), Billy Porter (Randy), Carmen Ejogo (Dr. Batiste), Donna Hanover (Debbie Carmichael), Merwin Mondesir (Glenn), Una Kay (Helen), Sonia Benezra (Aunt Sonya), Marcia Bennett (Nurse Stein), Howard Rosenstein (ER Doctor), Jane Wheeler (Karen), David Hirsh (Barton), Marguerite Kinh (Mrs. Lee), Arthur

Holden (Piano Player), Maurizio Terrazzano (Tom), Rachelle Lefevre (Holly), Erika Rosenbaum (Merry).

Writer: David Hubbard
Music: Alan Menken
Rated PG
96 minutes

ROBOTS (2005)

Directors: Chris Wedge, Carlos Saldanha
Voices: Robin Williams (Fender), Paula Abdul (Watch), Halle Berry (Cappy), Lucille Bliss (Pigeon Lady), Terry Bradshaw (Broken Arm Bot), Jim Broadbent (Madame Gasket), Mel Brooks (Bigweld), Amanda Bynes (Piper), Drew Carey (Crank), Jennifer Coolidge (Aunt Fanny), Dylan Denton (Youngest Rodney), Will Denton (Young Rodney), Marshall Efron (Lamppost/Toilet Bot/Bass Drum/Microphone), Damien Fahey (Stage Announcer), Lowell Ganz (Mr. Gasket), Paul Giamatti (Tim the Gate Guard), Dan Hedaya (Mr. Gunk), Jackie Hoffman (Water Cooler), James Earl Jones (Voice Box at Hardware Store), Greg Kinnear (Ratchet), Jay Leno (Fire Hydrant), Natasha Lyonne (Loretta Geargrinder), Brian McFadden (Trashcan Bot), Ewan McGregor (Rodney Copperbottom), Tim Nordquist (Tin Man), Jansen Panettiere (Younger Rodney), Al Roker (Mailbox), Alan Rosenberg (Jack Hammer), Stephen Tobolowsky (Bigmouth Executive/Forge), Stanley Tucci (Herb Copperbottom), Chris Wedge (Wonderbot/Phone Booth), Dianne Wiest (Mrs. Copperbottom), Harland Williams (Lug), Crawford Wilson (Young Rodney).
Writers: David Lindsay-Abaire, Lowell Ganz, Babaloo Mandel
Music: John Powell

Rated PG
91 minutes

THE BIG WHITE (2005)

Director: Mark Mylod
Cast: Robin Williams (Paul Barnell), Holly Hunter (Margaret Barnell), Giovanni Ribisi (Ted Waters), Tim Blake Nelson (Gary), W. Earl Brown (Jimbo), Woody Harrelson (Raymond Barnell), Alison Lohman (Tiffany), William Merasty (Cam), Marina Stephenson Kerr (Avis), Ralph Alderman (Mr. Branch), Frank Adamson (Detective), Andrea Shawcross (Hair Stylist), Ryan Miranda (Korean-am teenager), Craig March (Howard), Ty Wood (Paperboy), Frank C. Turner (Dave), Brenda Mcdonald (Mrs. Wherry), Deena Fontaine (Female Cop), Joanne Rodriguez (TV Reporter), Eric Epstein (Minister), Harry Nelken (Warehouse Owner Spellman), Jeff Skinner (Arnith), Stephen Eric Mcintyre (City Worker #2 - Bill).
Writer: Collin Friesen
Music: Mark Mothersbaugh
Rated R
100 minutes

RV (2006)

Director: Barry Sonnenfeld
Cast: Robin Williams (Bob Munro), Cheryl Hines (Jamie Munro), Joanna "JoJo" Levesque (Cassie Munro), Josh Hutcherson (Carl Munro), Jeff Daniels (Travis Gornicke), Kristin Chenoweth (Mary Jo Gornicke), Hunter Parrish (Earl Gornicke), Chloe Sonnenfeld (Moon Gornicke), Alex Ferris (Billy Gornicke), Will Arnett (Todd Mallory), Tony

Hale (Frank), Brian Howe (Marty), Richard Cox (Laird), Erika-Shayne Gair (Cassie (age 5)), Veronika Sztopa (Gretchen), Rob LaBelle (Larry Moiphine), Brian Markinson (Garry Moiphine), Kirsten Williamson (Tammy), Brendan Fletcher (Howie), Matthew Gray Gubler (Joe Joe), Stephen E. Miller (Organ Stew Guy), Malcolm Scott (Kenny), Deborah DeMille (Dump Lady), Chad Krowchuk (Scruffy Teenager), Ty Olsson (Diablo Pass Officer), Bruce McFee (Independence Pass Officer), Rebecca Erwin Spencer (Waitress), Giacomo Baessato (Hip Hop Wannabe), Justin Chartier (Hip Hop Wannabe), Andrew Botz (Hip Hop Wannabe), Barry Sonnenfeld (Irv).

Writer: Geoff Rodkey
Music: James Newton Howard
Rated PG
99 minutes

THE NIGHT LISTENER (2006)

Director: Patrick Stettner
Cast: Robin Williams (Gabriel Noone), Toni Collette (Donna D. Logand), Joe Morton (Ashe), Bobby Cannavale (Jess), Rory Culkin (Pete D. Logand), Sandra Oh (Anna), Rodrigo Lopresti (Young Man at Party), John Cullum (Pap Noone), Lisa Emery (Darlie Noone), Guenia Lemos (Female Neighbor), Marcia Halfrecht (Pant Suited Woman), Nick Gregory (Flight Attendant), Ed Jewett (Mail Clerk), Becky Ann Baker (Waitress), Billy Van (Taxi Driver), E.J. Carroll (Hospital Security Guard), James Stankunas (Boy in Hospital), Marceline Hugot (Nurse), Joel Marsh Garland (Officer), Hal Robinson (Male Friend #1), Keith Reddin (Male Friend #2), Meg Gibson (Female Friend), Maryann Plunkett (Alice - Female

Realtor), Mark Jacoby (Male Realtor (credit only)), Kelly (German Shepherd Dog), Riley (Hugo).

Writers: Armistead Maupin, Terry Anderson, Patrick Stettner, based on a novel by Armistead Maupin

Music: Peter Nashel

Rated R

91 minutes

EVERYONE'S HERO (2006)

Directors: Christopher Reeve, Colin Brady, Daniel St. Pierre

Voices: Robin Williams (Napoleon Cross (uncredited)), Ritchie Allen (Officer Bryant/Additional Voices), Jake T. Austin (Yankee Irving), Cherise Boothe (Rosetta Brewster), Jesse Bronstein (Sandlot Kid #1), Ralph Coppola (Sandlot Kid #2), Brian Dennehy (Babe Ruth), Whoopi Goldberg (Darlin'), Jason Harris (Announcer), Ed Helms (Hobo Louie), Ray Iannicelli (Conductors/Umpire), Gideon Jacobs (Bully Kid Tubby), Richard Kind (Hobo Andy/Maître D'), William H. Macy (Lefty Maginnis), Marcus Maurice (Willie), Amanda Parsons (Emily Irving), Mandy Patinkin (Stanley Irving), Dana Reeve (Emily Irving), Will Reeve (Big Kid), Rob Reiner (Screwie), Raven-Symoné (Marti Brewster), Ron Tippe (Hobo Jack), Joe Torre (Yankees' Manager), Robert Wagner (Mr. Robinson), Forest Whitaker (Lonnie Brewster), Conor White (Bully Kid Arnold).

Writers: Robert Kurtz, Jeff Hand, story by Howard Jonas

Music: John Debney

Rated G

87 minutes

MAN OF THE YEAR (2006)

Director: Barry Levinson

Cast: Robin Williams (Tom Dobbs), Christopher Walken (Jack Menken), Laura Linney (Eleanor Green), Lewis Black (Eddie Langston), Jeff Goldblum (Stewart), David Alpay (Danny), Faith Daniels (Moderator), Tina Fey (Tina Fey), Amy Poehler (Amy Poehler), Doug Murray (Mathias), Chris Matthews (News Anchor #1), James Carville (Political Commentator #1), Catherine Crier (Political Commentator #2), Rick Roberts (Hemmings), Karen Hines (Alison McAndrews), Linda Kash (Jenny Adams), Dave Nichols (President Kellogg), David Ferry (Senator Mills), Dmitry Chepovetsky (Eckhart), Brandon Firla (Grimaldi), Sasha Roiz (Donald Tilson), J.C. Kenny (News Anchor #2), Jef Mallory (Angus), Mark Andrada (Young Guy), Marcia Laskowski (Marjorie), Kim Roberts (Make-Up Artist), George King (Motel Manager), Sabrina Sanchez (Sales Girl), Jacqueline Pillon (Security Tech).

Writer: Barry Levinson
Music: Graeme Revell
Rated PG-13
115 minutes

HAPPY FEET (2006)

Directors: George Miller, Warren Coleman, Judy Morris
Voices: Robin Williams (Ramon/Lovelace), Carlos Alazraqui (Nestor), Lombardo Boyar (Raul), Jeff Garcia (Rinaldo), Johnny Sanchez III (Lombardo), Elijah Wood (Mumble), Brittany Murphy (Gloria), Hugh Jackman (Memphis), Nicole Kidman (Norma Jean), Hugo Weaving (Noah the Elder), E.G. Daily (Baby Mumble), Magda Szubanski (Miss Viola), Miriam Margolyes (Mrs. Astrakhan), Fat Joe (Seymour), Alyssa Shafer (Baby Gloria), Cesar Flores (Baby Seymour), Anthony LaPaglia (Boss Skua), Danny Mann (Dino/

Zoo Penguin), Mark Klastorin (Vinnie), Michael Cornacchia (Frankie), Steve Irwin (Trev), Nicholas McKay (Nev), Tiriel Mora (Kev), Richard Carter (Barry/Live Action Cast), Lee Perry (Elder/Zoo Penguin), Alan Shearman (Elder), Larry Moss (Elder), Peter Carroll (Elder), Giselle Loren (Adélie Chica), Michelle Arthur (Adélie Chica), Denise Blasor (Adélie Chica), Dee Bradley Baker (Maurice), Roger Rose (Leopard Seal), Chrissie Hynde (Michelle).

Writers: George Miller, John Collee, Judy Morris, Warren Coleman

Music: John Powell

Rated PG

108 minutes

HAPPY FEET TWO (2011)

Directors: George Miller, Gary Eck, David Peers

Cast: Robin Williams (Ramon/Lovelace), Carlos Alazraqui (Nestor), Lombardo Boyar (Raul), Jeff Garcia (Rinaldo), Johnny Sanchez III (Lombardo), Sofía Vergara (Carmen), Elijah Wood (Mumble), Alicia Moore "P!nk" (Gloria), Ava Acres (Erik), Benjamin "Lil P-Nut" Flores Jr. (Atticus), Meibh Campbell (Bo), Common (Seymour), Magda Szubanski (Miss Viola), Hugo Weaving (Noah the Elder), Brad Pitt (Will the Krill), Matt Damon (Bill the Krill), Hank Azaria (The Mighty Sven), Richard Carter (Bryan the Beachmaster), Lee Perry (Wayne the Challenger/Francesco/Eggbert/Leopard Seal), Jai Sloper (Weaner Pup), Oscar Beard (Weaner Pup), Anthony LaPaglia (The Alpha Skua), Danny Mann (Brokebeak), Denise Blasor (Adélie Chica), Roger Narayan (Bollywood Indian Penguin), Septimus Caton (Guitarist), Ivan Vunich (Beanie Man).

Writers: George Miller, Gary Eck, Warren Coleman, Paul Livingston
Music: John Powell
Rated PG
100 minutes

NIGHT AT THE MUSEUM (2006)

Director: Shawn Levy
Cast: Robin Williams (Teddy Roosevelt), Ben Stiller (Larry Daley), Carla Gugino (Rebecca), Dick Van Dyke (Cecil), Mickey Rooney (Gus), Bill Cobbs (Reginald), Jake Cherry (Nick Daley), Ricky Gervais (Dr. McPhee), Kim Raver (Erica Daley), Patrick Gallagher (Attila the Hun), Rami Malek (Ahkmenrah), Pierfrancesco Favino (Christopher Columbus), Charlie Murphy (Taxi Driver), Steve Coogan (Octavius), Mizuo Peck (Sacajawea), Kerry Van Der Griend (Neanderthal #1), Dan Rizzuto (Neanderthal #2), Matthew Harrison (Neanderthal #3), Jody Racicot (Neanderthal #4), Paul Rudd (Don), Anne Meara (Debbie), Martin Christopher (Merriweather Lewis), Martin Sims (William Clark), Randy Lee (Hun #1), Darryl Quon (Hun #2), Gerald Wong (Hun #3), Paul Chic-Ping Cheng (Hun #4), Teagle F. Bougere (Teacher - Mike), Pat Kiernan (TV News Anchor), Nico McEown (Friend #1), Meshach Peters (Friend #2), Matthew Walker (Politician), Jason McKinnon (Irish Worker), Jonathan Lee (Chinese Rail Worker), Jason Vaisvila (Viking), Cade Wagar (Viking), Cory Martin (Chinese Terra Cota Soldier), Brad Garrett (Easter Island Head (voice)), Crystal the Monkey (Dexter), Owen Wilson (Jedediah (uncredited)).
Writers: Robert Ben Garant, Thomas Lennon, based on the book by Milan Trenc
Music: Alan Silvestri

Rated PG

108 minutes

NIGHT AT THE MUSEUM: BATTLE OF THE SMITHSONIAN (2009)

Director: Shawn Levy

Cast: Robin Williams (Teddy Roosevelt), Ben Stiller (Larry Daley), Amy Adams (Amelia Earhart), Owen Wilson (Jedediah), Hank Azaria (Kahmunrah/The Thinker (voice)/Abe Lincoln (voice)), Christopher Guest (Ivan the Terrible), Alain Chabat (Napoleon Bonaparte), Steve Coogan (Octavius), Ricky Gervais (Dr. McPhee), Bill Hader (George Armstrong Custer), Jon Bernthal (Al Capone), Patrick Gallagher (Attila the Hun), Jake Cherry (Nicky), Rami Malek (Ahkmenrah), Mizuo Peck (Sacajawea), Kerry Van Der Griend (Neanderthal #1), Matthew Harrison (Neanderthal #2), Riccardo Dobran (Neanderthal #3), Randy Lee (Hun #1), Darryl Quon (Hun #2), Gerald Wong (Hun #3), Paul Chih-Ping Cheng (Hun #4), Jay Baruchel (Sailor Joey Motorola), Mindy Kaling (Docent), Keith Powell (Tuskegee Airman #1), Craig Robinson (Tuskegee Airman #2), Samuel Chu (Teenage Boy #1), Augustus Oicle (Teenage Boy #2), Kai James (Teenage Boy #3), Clint Howard (Air and Space Mission Control Tech #1), Matty Finochio (Air and Space Mission Control Tech #2), George Foreman Sr. (Himself), Josh Byer (Capone Gangster #1), Sophie Levy (Young Girl #1), Tess Levy (Young Girl #2), Christina Schild ("American Gothic" Woman), Robert Thurston ("American Gothic" Farmer), Alberta Mayne (Kissing Nurse), Clifton Murray (Kissing Sailor), Caroll Spinney (Oscar the Grouch (voice)), Thomas Morley (Darth Vader), Dan Joffre (Town Car Driver), Dave Hospes (Astronaut),

Regina Taufen (New York Reporter), Shawn Levy (Infomercial Father), Kevin Jonas (Cherub (voice)), Joe Jonas (Cherub (voice)), Nick Jonas (Cherub (voice)), Eugene Levy (Albert Einstein (voice)), Brad Garrett (Easter Island Head (voice)). Jonah Hill (Brandon/Brundon the Security Guard (uncredited)).

Writers: Robert Ben Garant, Thomas Lennon
Music: Alan Silvestri
Rated PG
105 minutes

NIGHT AT THE MUSEUM: SECRET OF THE TOMB (2014)

Director: Shawn Levy
Cast: Robin Williams (Teddy Roosevelt/Voice of Garuda), Ben Stiller (Larry Daley/Laaa), Owen Wilson (Jedediah), Steve Coogan (Octavius), Ricky Gervais (Dr. McPhee), Dan Stevens (Sir Lancelot), Rebel Wilson (Tilly), Skyler Gisondo (Nick Daley), Rami Malek (Ahkmenrah), Patrick Gallagher (Attila), Mizuo Peck (Sacajawea), Ben Kingsley (Merenkahre (Ahk's Father)), Crystal the Monkey (Dexter), Dick Van Dyke (Cecil), Mickey Rooney (Gus), Bill Cobbs (Reginald), Andrea Martin (Rose (Archivist)), Rachael Harris (Madeline Phelps), Matt Frewer (Archibald Stanley), Brad Garrett (Easter Island Head (voice)), Regina Taufen (NY Reporter (voice)), Percy Hynes-White (C. J. Fredericks), Brennan Elliott (Robert Fredericks), Kerry van der Griend (Neanderthal #1), Matthew Harrison (Neanderthal #2), Jody Racicot (Neanderthal #3), Randy Lee (Hun #1), Darryl Quon (Hun #2), Paul Cheng (Hun #3), Gerald Wong (Hun #4), Anjali Jay (Shepseheret (Ahk's Mother)), Matty Finochio (Roman

Sentry), Patrick Sabongui (Amir), Amir Korangy (1938
Egyptian Worker), Louriza Tronco (Andrea (Nick's Party)),
Sophie Levy (Sophie (Nick's Party)), Jin Sangha (Egyptian
High Priest), James Neate (Augustus Statue), Hugh Jackman
(Hugh Jackman (uncredited)), Alice Eve (Alice Eve (uncred-
ited)).

Writers: David Guion, Michael Handelman
Music: Alan Silvestri
Rated PG
98 minutes

LICENSE TO WED (2007)

Director: Ken Kwapis
Cast: Robin Williams (Reverend Frank), Mandy Moore (Sadie
Jones), John Krasinski (Ben Murphy), Eric Christian Olsen
(Carlisle), Christine Taylor (Lindsey Jones), Josh Flitter
(Choir Boy), DeRay Davis (Joel), Peter Strauss (Mr. Jones),
Grace Zabriskie (Grandma Jones), Roxanne Hart (Mrs.
Jones), Mindy Kaling (Shelly), Angela Kinsey (Judith the
Jewelry Clerk), Rachael Harris (Janine), Brian Baumgart-
ner (Jim), Jess Rosenthal (Jewelry Clerk), Val Almendarez
(Jewelry Store Customer), Nicole Randall Johnson (Louise),
Tashana Haye (Church Kid Sarah), Sarah Kate Johnson
(Church Kid Laurie), Travis Flory (Church Kid Manny),
Dominic Swingler (Joel & Shelly's Kid), Devin Swingler (Joel
& Shelly's Kid), Diego Swingler (Joel & Shelly's Kid), Cyn-
thia Ettinger (Macy's Clerk), Gillian Skupa (Macy's Chang-
ing Room Lady), Poncho Hodges (Macy's Security Guard),
Ruben Garfias (Coach), Kelsey Harper (Carlisle's Girlfriend),
David Quinlan (Expectant Father), Irene Karas (Birthing
Mom), Derek Green (Doctor), Christine Cannon (Delivery

Doctor), Anelia Dyoulgerova (Belly Dancer), Wanda Sykes (Doctor (uncredited)).

Writers: Kim Barker, Tim Rasmussen, Vince Di Meglio
Music: Christophe Beck
Rated PG-13
91 minutes

AUGUST RUSH (2007)

Director: Kirsten Sheridan
Cast: Robin Williams (Maxwell "Wizard" Wallace), Freddie Highmore (August Rush), Keri Russell (Lyla Novacek), Jonathan Rhys Meyers (Louis Connelly), Terrence Howard (Richard Jeffries), William Sadler (Thomas Novacek), Marian Seldes (The Dean), Mykelti Williamson (Reverend James), Leon Thomas III (Arthur), Aaron Staton (Nick), Alex O'Loughlin (Marshall), Jamia Simone Nash (Hope), Ronald Guttman (Professor), Bonnie McKee (Lizzy), Michael Drayer (Mannix), Jamie O'Keefe (Steve), Becki Newton (Jennifer), Tyler McGuckin (Peter), Megan Gallagher (Megan), Anais Martinez (Backbeat), Bilal Bishop (Roller Bull), Michael Roderick Hammonds III (Feedback), Timothy T. Mitchum (Joey), Henry Caplan (Bill), John Knox (Club Manager), Amy V. Dewhurst (Receptionist), Victor Verhaeghe (Cop), Darrie Lawrence (Old Neighbor), Sean Haberle (Frank), Jamal Joseph (Driver), Robert Aberdeen (Record Executive), Georgia Creighton (Apartment Owner), Joshua Jaymz Doss (Orphanage Kid), Craig Johnson (Orphanage Boy), Dominic Colón (Policeman), Zach Page (Child Guitar Player).

Writers: Nick Castle, James V. Hart
Music: Mark Mancina
Rated PG
114 minutes

SHRINK (2009)

Director: Jonas Pate

Cast: Robin Williams (Jack Holden (uncredited)), Kevin Spacey (Henry Carter), Joseph A. Nuñez (Recording Supervisor), Mark Webber (Jeremy), Keke Palmer (Jemma), Sierra Aylina McClain (Carina), Ada Luz Pla (Teacher), Saffron Burrows (Kate), Jack Huston (Shamus), Pell James (Daisy), Mei Melançon (Miyu), Dallas Roberts (Patrick), Andrew Sibner (Richie), Troy Metcalf (O.T.), Kendall Clement (Uncle Jim), Jesse Plemons (Jesus), Braxton Pope (Braxton), Robert Loggia (Dr. Robert Carter), Clayton Rohner (Dr. McBurney), Ken Weiler (Jason), Joel Gretsch (Evan), Aimee Garcia (Check-out Girl), Tiernan Burns (Tiernan), Mystro Clark (Dr. Morton), Justin Alston (Rio), Brian Palermo (Mitch), Philip Pavel (Neil), Michelle Columbia (Geisha Hostess), Laura Ramsey (Keira), Ashley Michele Greene (Missy), Robert Farrior (Bryce), Branden Morgan (Eric), Brian Huskey (Film Executive #1), Jillian Armenante (Karen), Jennifer Rade (Fan (Woman)), Derek Alvarado (Ramirez), Thomas Moffett (Director), Joe Nieves (Lil King), Bobby Arnot (Intern), Weston Middleton (P.A.), Mina Olivera (Make-up Girl), Gore Vidal (George Charles).

Writer: Thomas Moffat

Music: Ken Andrews, Brian Reitzell

Rated R

104 minutes

WORLD'S GREATEST DAD (2009)

Director: Bobcat Goldthwait

Cast: Robin Williams (Lance), Daryl Sabara (Kyle Clayton), Morgan Murphy (Morgan), Naomi Glick (Ginger), Dan Spencer (Dan Spencer), Geoff Pierson (Principal Anderson),

Henry Simmons (Mike Lane), Zach Sanchez (Peter), Alexie Gilmore (Claire Reed), Evan Martin (Andrew), Ellie Jameson (Jennifer), Michael Moore (Chris), Alles Mist (Metal Kid), Jermaine Williams (Jason), Lorraine Nicholson [Jack Nicholson's daughter] (Heather), Mitzi McCall (Bonnie), Rebecca Erwin Spencer (Nosy Neighbor), Cheri Minns (Nosy Neighbor), Zazu (Nosy Neighbor), Tony V. (Dr. Pentola), Krist Novoselic [Nirvana bassist] (Newsstand Vendor), Mable Mae (Mabel), Zoe (The Fighting Pug), Tom Kenny (Jerry Klein), Jill Talley (Make-Up Woman), Toby Huss (Bert Green), Deborah Horne (Dr. Dana), Bruce Hornsby (Bruce Hornsby), Riley Dean Stone (Bruce Hornsby's Mic Stand), Bobcat Goldthwait (Chauffeur (uncredited)).

Writer: Bobcat Goldthwait

Music: Gerald Brunskill; "Mandolin Wind" performed by Bruce Hornsby

Rated R

99 minutes

OLD DOGS (2009)

Director: Walt Becker

Cast: Robin Williams (Dan), John Travolta (Charlie), Kelly Preston (Vicki), Conner Rayburn (Zach), Ella Bleu Travolta (Emily), Lori Loughlin (Amanda), Seth Green (Craig), Bernie Mac (Jimmy Lunchbox), Matt Dillon (Barry), Ann-Margret (Martha), Rita Wilson (Jenna), Amy Sedaris (Condo Woman), Residente (Tattoo Artist), Saburo Shimono (Yoshiro Nishamura), Kevin W. Yamada (Riku), Kevin Dean-Hackett (Tijuana Priest), Laura Allen (Kelly), Sam Travolta (Singing Waiter), Margaret Travolta (Singing Hostess), Nick Loren (Singing Waiter 2), Kenneth Maharaj (Indian Guy), Nova Mejia (Hot Waitress), Margaret Goodman

(Grandma), Jerome Weinstein (Grandpa), Allie Woods (Old Guy), Michael Enright (Singing Waiter 3), Alexa Havins (Hot Waitress 2), Keenan Shimizu (Japanese Executive), Akira Takayama (Japanese Executive), Shirô Oishi (Japanese Executive), Yoshio Mita (Japanese Executive), Seiji Kakizaki (Japanese Executive), Keisuke Jim Nagahama (Japanese Executive), Dominick Riccardi (Driver), Costas Panay (Little Kid), Kate Lacey (Rayburn & Reed Employee), Denise Violante (Spanish Lady), Tonia-Marie Gallo (Lazy Pooch Employee), Jin Hwa Hwang (Japanese Flight Attendant), Marcel Becker (Waiter), Alison Pelletier (Hot Waitress 3), Dylan Sprayberry (Cute Soccer Kid), Bradley Steven Perry (Soccer Kid), Joey Pordan (Soccer Kid).

Writers: David Diamond, David Weissman
Music: John Debney
Rated PG
88 minutes

THE BIG WEDDING (2013)

Director: Justin Zackham
Cast: Robin Williams (Father Moinighan), Robert De Niro (Don), Katherine Heigl (Lyla), Diane Keaton (Ellie), Amanda Seyfried (Missy), Topher Grace (Jared), Susan Sarandon (Bebe), Ben Barnes (Alejandro), Christine Ebersole (Muffin), David Rasche (Barry), Patricia Rae (Madonna), Ana Ayora (Nuria), Kyle Bornheimer (Andrew), Megan Ketch (Jane), Christa Campbell (Kim), Ian Blackman (Maître D'), Shana Dowdeswell (Waitress), Doug Torres (Waiting Father), Marvina Vinique (Mother), Joshua Nelson (Worker #1), Quincy Dunn-Baker (Kevin), Sylvia Kauders (Elderly Wife), Edmund Lyndeck (Elderly Husband).

Writer: Justin Zackham, based on the movie *Mon Frère se Marie*, by Jean-Stéphane Bron and Karine Sudan
Music: Nathan Barr
Rated R
89 minutes

LEE DANIELS' THE BUTLER (2013)

Director: Lee Daniels
Cast: Robin Williams (Dwight D. Eisenhower), Forest Whitaker (Cecil Gaines), David Banner (Earl Gaines), Michael Rainey Jr. (Cecil Gaines (8)), LaJessie Smith (Abraham), Mariah Carey (Hattie Pearl), Alex Pettyfer (Thomas Westfall), Vanessa Redgrave (Annabeth Westfall), Aml Ameen (Cecil Gaines (15)), Clarence Williams III (Maynard), John Fertitta (Mr. Jenkins), Jim Gleason (R.D. Warner), Oprah Winfrey (Gloria Gaines), Isaac White (Charlie Gaines (10)), David Oyelowo (Louis Gaines), Joe Chrest (White Usher), Colman Domingo (Freddie Fallows), Adriane Lenox (Gina), Terrence Howard (Howard), Tyson Ford (Elroy), Cuba Gooding Jr. (Carter Wilson), Lenny Kravitz (James Holloway), Pernell Walker (Lorraine), James DuMont (Sherman Adams), Robert Aberdeen (Herbert Brownell), John Cusack (Richard Nixon), Olivia Washington (Olivia), Yaya Alafia (Carol Hammie), Jesse Williams (James Lawson), Margaret M. Owens (Woolworth Diner Patron #1), Eric Ducote (Woolworth Diner Patron #2), James Marsden (John F. Kennedy), Minka Kelly (Jacqueline Kennedy), Chloe Barach (Caroline Kennedy), Danny Strong (Freedom Bus Journalist), Clara Hopkins Daniels (Freedom Bus Rider), Elijah Kelley (Charlie Gaines (15-18)), Liev Schreiber (Lyndon B. Johnson), Dana Gourrier (Helen Holloway), Shirley Pugh (Malcolm X Goer), Bill Newman (Pastor), Nelsan Ellis (Martin Luther King

Jr.), Colin Walker (John Ehrlichman), Alex Manette (Bob Haldeman), Mo McRae (Eldridge Huggins), Alan Rickman (Ronald Reagan), Jane Fonda (Nancy Reagan), Rusty Robertson (Senator Robertson), Nealla Gordon (Senator Kassebaum), Stephen Rider (Admiral Rochon).

Writer: Danny Strong, based on an article by Wil Haygood
Music: Rodrigo Leão
Rated PG-13
132 minutes

THE FACE OF LOVE (2013)

Director: Arie Posin
Cast: Robin Williams (Roger Stillman), Annette Bening (Nikki Lostrom), Ed Harris (Garret Mathis/Tom Young), Jess Weixler (Summer), Linda Park (Jan), Jeffrey Vincent Parise (Nicholas), Horacio Cerutti (Gardener), Amy Brenneman (Ann), Clyde Kusatsu (Sushi Chef), Eli Vargas (Bell Boy), Miguel Pérez (Bartender).
Writers: Matthew McDuffie, Arie Posin
Music: Marcelo Zarvos
Rated PG-13
92 minutes

THE ANGRIEST MAN IN BROOKLYN (2014)

Director: Phil Alden Robinson
Cast: Robin Williams (Henry Altmann), Mila Kunis (Dr. Sharon Gill), Peter Dinklage (Aaron Altmann), Melissa Leo (Bette Altmann), Hamish Linklater (Tommy Altmann), Sutton Foster (Adela), James Earl Jones (Ruben), Richard Kind (Bix Field), Daniel Raymont (Ulugbek), Chris Gethard (Dr. Jordan Reed), Jerry Adler (Cooper), Isiah Whitlock

Jr. (Yates), Da'Vine Joy Randolph (Nurse Rowan), Jeremie Harris (Leon), Lee Garlington (Gummy), Roy Milton Davis (Buster), Olga Merediz (Jane), Hank Chen (Damien), Rock Kohli (Gurjot), Kirk Taylor (Cop), Sunah Bilsted (Elevator Mother), Tucker Brown (Paul (Elevator Kid)), Len Murach (Boat Captain), Noah Radcliffe (Tommy (10 Years Old)), Sawyer Ever (Tommy (5 Years Old)), Adam Chernick (Peter (7 Years Old)).

Writer: Daniel Taplitz, based on the film *The 92 Minutes of Mr. Baum* by Assi Dayan

Music: Mateo Messina

Rated R

83 minutes

BOULEVARD (2014)

Director: Dito Montiel

Cast: Robin Williams (Nolan Mack), Kathy Baker (Joy), Roberto Aguire (Leo), Giles Matthey (Eddie), Eleonore Hendricks (Patty), Bob Odenkirk (Winston), Henry Haggard (Beaumont), Gary Gardner (Lionel Mack (Father)), Crystal Gray (Nurse), Joshua Decker (ER Doctor), Sondra Morton (Gloria Beaumont), Jerry Chipman (Blyden), Steven Randazzo (Guard Walt), J. Karen Thomas (Cat), Becky Fly (Night Nurse), Brandon Hirsch (Brad), Landon Marshall (Mark), David Ditmore (Middle-Aged Man), Billy Lewis (Mini-Mart Clerk), Reegus Flenory (Cop #1), Gary Willis (Cop #2).

Writer: Douglas Soesbe

Music: Jimmy Haun, David Wittman

Rated R

88 minutes

A MERRY FRIGGIN' CHRISTMAS (2014)

Director: Tristram Shapeero

Cast: Robin Williams (Virgil Mitchler), Joel McHale (Boyd Mitchler), Lauren Graham (Luann Mitchler), Clark Duke (Nelson Mitchler), Oliver Platt (Hobo Santa), Wendi McLendon-Covey (Shauna Weinke), Tim Heidecker (Dave Weinke), Candice Bergen (Donna Mitchler), Pierce Gagnon (Douglas Mitchler), Bebe Wood (Vera Mitchler), Ryan Lee (Rance Weinke), Amara Miller (Pam Weinke), Mark Proksch (Trooper Zblocki), Jeffrey Tambor (Snow Globe Snowman (voice)), Amir Arison (Farhad), Steele Gagnon (Cale Weinke), JJ Jones (Young Boyd), Gene Jones (Glen), Matt Jones (Cowboy Dick), Barak Hardley (Cowboy Bob), William Sanderson (Father Jugo), Karan Kendrick (Mom at Santa's Village), Parisa Johnston (Farhad's Mom), Michael Shikany (Farhad's Uncle), Janet Meshad (Farhad's Grandmother).

Writer: Phil Johnson writing as "Michael Brown"

Music: Ludwig Göransson

Rated PG-13

88 minutes

ABSOLUTELY ANYTHING (2015)

Director: Terry Jones

Cast: Robin Williams (Dennis the Dog (voice)), Simon Pegg (Neil), Kate Beckinsale (Catherine), Sanjeev Bhaskar (Ray), Rob Riggle (Grant), Robert Bathurst (James Cleverill), Eddie Izzard (Headmaster), Joanna Lumley (Fenella), Marianne Oldham (Rosie), Emma Pierson (Miss Pringle), Meera Syal (Fiona), John Cleese (Chief Alien (voice)), Terry Gilliam (Nasty Alien (voice)), Eric Idle (Salubrious Gat (voice)).

Writers: Terry Jones, Gavin Scott, based on a short story by Douglas Adams

Music: George Fenton

Rated R

85 minutes

ACKNOWLEDGMENTS

I'd like to offer as much thanks and love as I can muster to **VALERIE BARNES** for her invaluable help with this book, I couldn't have done it without you, sweetie.

Also, boatloads of thanks to my agent **JOHN WHITE** and my friend and often literary co-conspirator **MICHAEL LEWIS** for their ongoing love and support.

I'd like to also thank the magnificent folks at Post Hill Press, especially **MICHAEL WILSON**, my editor **MADDIE STURGEON**, my publicist **DEVON BROWN,** and my editor **HEATHER STEADHAM.** These folks not only know what they're doing to the nth degree, but they and everyone I've met at Post Hill share a love of books and the written word. It's a nice place to work.

Also, special thanks must be extended to my family and closest friends, especially my sister **JANET DANIW**, who kept me mobile; and my friends **JIM COLE, ANDY RAUSCH, TONY NORTHRUP, GENA NORTHRUP,** and **DAVE HINCHBERGER**, all of whom are Robin Williams fans and all of whom were incredibly supportive as I put this tome together.

And lastly, I'd like to express my deepest, most heartfelt thanks to two women who have made my life easier in the past several months—**CHERYL MASELLI** and **CHRISTINA VOONASIS**—and who both know why they have my gratitude.

STEPHEN SPIGNESI
BIBLIOGRAPHY

ABOUT STEPHEN KING

- *The Complete Stephen King Encyclopedia*
- *The Stephen King Quiz Book, Vols. 1 & 2*
- *The Lost Work of Stephen King*
- *The Essential Stephen King*
- *Stephen King, American Master*

ABOUT THE BEATLES & MUSIC

- *The Beatles Book of Lists*
- *She Came In Through the Kitchen Window*
- *The 100 Best Beatles Songs*
- *Elton John: Fifty Years On*

THE "FOR DUMMIES" BOOKS

- *Second Homes for Dummies (with Bridget McRae)*
- *Native American History for Dummies*
- *Lost Books of the Bible for Dummies*
- *The Titanic for Dummies*

THE WEIRD & THE PARANORMAL

- *The Odd Index*
- *Crop Circles: Signs of Contact (with Colin Andrews)*
- *The UFO Book of Lists*
- *The Weird 100*
- *The Big Book of UFO Facts. Figures & Truth*
- *Dr. Bizarro's Eclectic Collection of Strange & Obscure Facts*

AMERICAN & WORLD HISTORY

- *J.F.K. Jr.*
- *The Italian 100*
- *Young Kennedys: The New Generation*
- *The Complete Titanic*
- *The USA Book of Lists*
- *American Firsts*
- *What's Your Red, White & Blue IQ?*
- *George Washington's Leadership Lessons (with James Rees)*
- *From Michelangelo to Mozzarella: The Italian IQ Test*
- *Grover Cleveland's Rubber Jaw*
- *499 Facts About Hip-Hop Hamilton and the Rest of America's Founding Fathers*
- *Catastrophe! The World's Greatest Disasters*
- *In the Crosshairs*

TV

- *Mayberry, My Hometown*
- *What's Your "Mad About You" IQ?*
- *The "ER" Companion*

❑ *What's Your "Friends" IQ?*

❑ *635 Things I Learned from The Sopranos*

MOVIES

❑ *The Woody Allen Companion*

❑ *The Official "Gone With the Wind" Companion*

❑ *The Gore Galore Video Quiz Book*

❑ *The Celebrity Baby Name Book*

❑ *The Robin Williams Scrapbook*

❑ *The Hollywood Book of Lists*

TRIVIA & MISCELLANEOUS

❑ *The V. C. Andrews Trivia and Quiz Book*

❑ *The Cat Book of Lists*

❑ *Gems, Jewels, & Treasures*

❑ *How To Be An Instant Expert*

❑ *The Third Act of Life (with Jerome Ellison)*

FICTION

❑ *Dialogues: A Novel of Suspense*